Readings in Kinship
in Urban Society

Edited by

C. C. HARRIS

PERGAMON PRESS

Oxford · New York · Toronto
Sydney · Braunschweig

Pergamon Press Ltd., Headington Hill Hall, Oxford

Pergamon Press Inc., Maxwell House, Fairview Park, Elmsford,
New York 10523

Pergamon of Canada Ltd., 207 Queen's Quay West, Toronto 1

Pergamon Press (Aust.) Pty. Ltd., 19a Boundary Street,
Rushcutters Bay, N.S.W. 2011, Australia

Vieweg & Sohn GmbH, Burgplatz 1, Braunschweig

First edition 1970

Library of Congress Catalog Card No. 78–120133

Printed in Great Britain by A. Wheaton & Co., Exeter

08 016038 7 (flexicover)
08 016039 5 (hard cover)

READINGS ʳ

'ı

Itly

Contents

Urbanization and the Family

Old Age

Preface

THIS is one of a series of volumes published by Pergamon Press. Each consists of a collection of articles on a specialized aspect of Sociology and Social Psychology, together with an introduction designed to relate the Selected Readings to the state of knowledge and research in the field in question. Each volume of Readings has been prepared by a distinguished scholar who has specialized in the area.

A characteristic feature of the series is the inclusion in each volume of a number of articles translated into English from European and other sources. English-speaking scholars and students will have an opportunity of reading articles which would not otherwise be readily available to them. Many important contributions made by European and other writers will be given a wider circulation in this way. It is hoped that the series will contribute to an international cross-fertilization of theory and research.

York University   ANTHONY H. RICHMOND
Toronto   *General Editor*

vii

Acknowledgements

ACKNOWLEDGEMENT is due to the publishers, editors, and authors whose material has been reprinted in this volume.

"The Kindred in a Greek Mountain Community" by J. K. Campbell is reprinted from *Mediterranean Countrymen* edited by J. Pitt-Rivers, with permission from Messrs Mouton & Co., n.v. Messrs E. J. Brill, Leiden, gave their permission for us to reproduce "A Study of French Canadian Kinship" by Ralph Piddington from the *International Journal of Comparative Sociology* (vol. 12, no. 1, March 1965). "Relations with Neighbours and Relatives in Working Class Families of the Département de la Seine" by Andrée Vieille is reproduced from *Cahiers Internationaux de Sociologie*, 1954, by permission of Presses Universitaires de France. "The Family in a Greek Village; Dowry and Inheritance; Formal Structure" is from *Vasilika: A Village in Modern Greece*, by Ernestine Friedl. Copyright 1952 by Holt, Rinehart & Winston, Inc. Reprinted by permission of Holt, Rinehart & Winston, Inc., Publishers, New York. "The Family in a Spanish Town" is an extract from chapter 7 of *Belmonte de los Caballeros* by C. Lison-Tolosana, and is reproduced by permission of the Clarendon Press. "Composite Descent Groups in Canada" by E. Leyton is reproduced from *Man*, 1965, 98, by permission of the Royal Anthropological Institute of Great Britain and Ireland. "Kinship and Crisis in South Wales" by J. B. Loudon is reprinted from the *British Journal of Sociology* (vol. 4, no. 12, 1961) by permission of Routledge & Kegan Paul Ltd. The Clarendon Press gave their permission for us to reproduce "Mobility and the Middle Class Extended Family" by Colin Bell from *Sociology*, vol. 2, no. 2 (May 1968). The University of Helsinki gave permission for us to reproduce "Mate Selection in Various Ethnic Groups in France" by Andrée Michel (née Vieille) from *Acta*

Sociologica, vol. 8, 1965. "Conjugal Roles and Social Networks" by Christopher Turner is reproduced from *Human Relations*, vol. 20, no. 2, May 1967, by permission of the Plenum Publishing Co. Ltd. "Traditional Household and Neighbourhood Group" by E. W. Hofstee and G. A. Kooy and "Qualitative Changes in Family Life in the Netherlands" by J. Ponsioen, both from *Transactions of the Third World Congress of Sociology*, appear by permission of the International Sociological Association. "New Aspects of Rural-Urban Differentials in Family Values and Family Structure" by G. Baumert and E. Lupri and "Urbanization and Nuclear Family Individualization" by G. A. Kooy are reproduced from *Current Sociology*, vol. 12 (1), 1963–4. "The Extended Family on Transition" by P. Taietz is reproduced from *Sociologia Ruralis*, no. 1, 1964, by permission of the European Society for Rural Sociology. Jan Stehouwer "Relations between Generations and the Three-generation Household in Denmark" in *Social Structure and the Family: Generational Relations*, Ethel Shanas and Gordon F. Streib (Eds.), 1965, is reprinted by permission of Prentice-Hall, Inc., Englewood Cliffs, N. J., U.S.A. "Family Relations of the Elderly" by Leopold Rosenmayr is reproduced from *Journal of Marriage and the Family* (November 1968) by permission of the National Council of Family Relations.

Every effort has been made to trace and acknowledge ownership of copyright. The publishers will be glad to make suitable arrangements with any copyright holders whom it has not been possible to contact.

Introduction

C. C. HARRIS

THE compilation of any "reader" is no easy task. This is so not merely because of the size of the mass of material from which selection has to be made but also because there are many principles of selection which are not entirely consistent. First, it is desirable to include as wide a range of readings as possible. Secondly, it is necessary that readings should be *readings* and not mere snippets or fragments. They should be long enough either to present a coherent argument or to provide the reader with a substantial body of ethnographic data. Thirdly, it is desirable that the selection should provide the reader with a range of materials which enables him to get "the feel" of the area concerned. Fourthly, it is fairly pointless to publish seminal articles and extracts which are well known and easily available elsewhere. Hence one of the purposes of a reader is to make available lesser known materials. This end is by no means always consistent with a desire to include only materials of high quality.

Any reader is largely the outcome of a series of compromises between all these conflicting criteria, and the result is usually highly unsatisfactory. In the case of the present compilation, however, further peculiar difficulties arise. The range of materials on family and kinship is enormous, but the quality of a great deal of it very poor. The volume of the American material is very substantial, and it is doubtful if it would be possible to do it justice even within the scope of a publication devoted entirely to the United States. For this reason, and to redress the bias towards United States material, this book focuses primarily on contributions drawn from the old world rather than the new.

A more difficult problem is posed by the range of orientations exhibited by the authors of the available material. Three broad types of orientation may be distinguished. First that of British structural anthropology; secondly that whose origins are to be found in the tradition of the empirical investigation of social problems; and thirdly that of continental scholars heavily influenced by work in the United States, of those who describe themselves as "students of the family" rather than "students of the sociology of the family".

Perhaps the most difficult problems involved in the compilation of this selection were theoretical ones. Before setting out to compile a reader in kinship in urban society one needs to be fairly clear about what is meant by the terms "kinship" and "urban".

Now British sociologists have, on the whole, tended to think of kinship as referring to extra-familial kin relationships. Hence they speak of "family *and* kinship". Anthropologists on the other hand speak merely of kinship, regarding the family as a type of kin group. A reader in "kinship" would, according to the first definition, focus on studies concerned with relationships between members of different familial groups rather than within them. If the second definition is preferred, then materials should be included ranging from the analysis of marital roles to the analysis of extended kinship networks.

Equally difficult problems are raised by any definition of "urban". Not only are urban sociologists as unclear as ever about what the term may most usefully be made to mean, but simply to speak of "urban kinship" does not make it clear whether one is concerned with kinship in urban settlements or within urban societies. Even if a theoretically adequate definition of "urban settlement" were forthcoming, the problem of the relationship between the terms "urban settlement" and "urban society" would still have to be solved.

Used loosely, the term "urban society" refers to a category of actually existing societies, rather than to a theoretical type. Even at this level it is not clear whether the societies pointed out by the term ought not more properly to be regarded as "industrial" societies. Such problems cannot be avoided by the students of kinship unless they wish to eschew entirely any attempt to understand kinship institutions in their structural context, and prefer to remain forever at the level of the analysis of interpersonal relationships.

For the purposes of this reader, as for any comparative study, it has been necessary to regard the family as a variable kin grouping within a variable universe of recognized kin, rather than as a fixed reference point which determines which kin relationships lie within the family and which outside it. In consequence primacy has been given to studies concerned with variations in familial grouping and the relation of kinship to other systems in the society, rather than to the discussion of the internal structure of a given familial type.

The term "urban" has been interpreted extremely loosely to include studies of kinship in urban settlements, studies of kinship in rural settlements in societies which are dominated by urban settlements, and also articles concerning systems of kinship in primarily rural societies which are of interest because of the light which they shed on bilateral systems which are characteristic of urban societies, though not of course confined to them.

It cannot be pretended that the result is particularly satisfactory. Nevertheless it is hoped that the present selection will provide the reader with easily available comparative ethnographic data, and constitute an introduction to the very different types of study and approach which are currently beginning to be found outside the narrow world of British social inquiry.

KINSHIP IN URBAN SOCIETY

This reader is concerned with kinship in a category of societies which is defined empirically rather than theoretically. The societies of Western Europe and the Mediterranean share a common history, urban patterns of settlement, varying degrees of industrialization, and systems of bilateral kinship. The first reading has been chosen because it is an exceptionally clear description of a bilateral kinship system and an understanding of such a system is a necessary prerequisite to the understanding of urban kinship.

Systems of Kinship and the Recognition of Relationships

Many societies with whom anthropologists concern themselves are not bilateral but unilineal societies characterized by the formation of descent groups. To speak of descent is to speak of the notion of a category of individuals recognizing their "descent" from a common ancestor or ancestors. Since the number of an individual's ancestors increases geometrically with each generation, it follows that any individual is simultaneously the member of a large number of "descent" categories and shares the same descent only with his sibs. The tracing of descent along all the lines extending upward from a single individual or ego cannot therefore lead to the formation of exclusive categories of kindred. A unilineal principle of tracing descent utilizes either links through males or through females, and ignores ties through the other sex. Such a system makes possible the transmission of the membership of exclusive categories between the generations. These categories can then be used for the formation of exclusive groups of which the society is made up. Rights and duties of a political economic or religious nature associated with the membership of the group may then be said to descend through the male or the female line. When we find a group whose members inherit such rights and duties in this way, we may be said to be dealing with a system of descent. It is not possible to have an "omnilineal" *descent* system.

Although many societies are characterized by unilineal descent systems, it is generally accepted that by contrast the recognition of kinship is universally bilateral. That is to say relationships through *both parents* are recognized, or relationships with cognates on *both sides* are deemed to exist. A bilateral system is therefore "omnilineal" in the sense that relationships through all the lines are recognized. However, this principle is not taken very far in the case of the people whom Campbell describes. A man's kindred, that is to say the category of people in whom he recognizes a relationship by virtue of a cognatic tie, consists of all those persons descended of the four sibling groups of a man's two grandfathers and grandmothers (with certain exceptions). This is not surprising. Taken to its logical conclusion a principle of "omnilineality" would involve each individual recognizing relationships to virtually everyone. But, says Campbell, the representation of a man's kindred as four interlocking pyramids of cognatic descent, bears no relation to the mental image which a Sarakatsanos forms of his kindred, in which relations are conceived in terms of extension from the family of origin, not descent from a common ancestor.

In other words the individual traces "ascent" rather than "descent", beginning with himself and working upwards, rather than beginning with a set of ancestors and working downwards. It is therefore most misleading to think in terms of "bilateral descent" or an "omnilineal" descent system.[1] Campbell's term for the principle involved, and it is a most useful one, is "equivalent bilateral extension". Equivalence is intended to imply both equality in the range of recognition of relationships (collaterals on both sides are recognized), and also equality in the nature of the relationships.

A further restriction on the number of kin recognized is also found among the Sarakatsani, however. The kindred of any one ego does not include all the descendants of the sibling groups of his grandparents. All their descendants in the generations ascendant to ego are included except the grandchildren of his grandparents' sibs, but the great grandchildren of his parents' sibs, and the great grandchildren of his own sibs are excluded. That is, the degree of collateral recognition becomes relatively less wide in each descendant generation.

We are dealing here with two interrelated processes, both of which tend to increase the size of the kindred. The first is the

[1] On this point see Firth, R., *Two Studies of Kinship in London*, Athlone Press, 1956, p. 17.

succession of the generations. Among the Sarakatsani each successive generation does not inherit all the kin of the previous generation, and thus the "accumulation" of kin is prevented. However, we are also dealing with the progression of an individual through a life cycle. At birth he has no kin in the descendant generations, only in the ascendant. At death he has no kin in the ascendant generations, only in the descendant. However, the number of kin at the end of the life cycle will be larger than at the beginning if all the descendants of the sibling groups of his four grandparents are recognized. In this particular case the latter difficulty is overcome by restricting the recognition of collaterals.

The important point to note here is not that this is the case, nor that it has the effect of keeping the number of kin to whom ego has obligations at any given time reasonably small, though both of these facts are of importance for understanding this particular system. What is important is Campbell's explanation. "With the passage of time" he writes, "parents turn their loyalty and interest from the collateral kinsmen of their own generation to their direct descendants and to only those collateral descendants who remain relevant for their own descendants."

In other words the system of recognition is to be understood in relation primarily to the activities central to any kinship system: marriage, procreation, and the rearing of children, and the groups within which they are carried out. Campbell is at pains to point out that among the Sarakatsani, the biological group of parents and offspring which performs these activities (or elementary family) is also a property holding, political, and religious group. However, it is not economic, political, or religious considerations which determine its membership. Its membership is defined in terms of its biological activities, which constitute the only universal principle of kin grouping within the society. Within this basic unit are found two types of relationship (parent–child and sib) which are utilized in the formation of kindreds. Each family lies at the centre of as many overlapping kindreds as it has members, and each kindred may be seen to be constructed out of the overlapping elementary families linked by ties of filiation and sibship, which are or were at one time domestic groups.[2]

Such groups are not only linked by ties of filiation and sibship, however, but by ties of marriage. Though affines are not counted as kin, ego's affines are, of course, the kin of his children. To the ties of filiation and sibship which constitute the links whereby an individual's different elementary families overlap, must be added ties of marriage whereby, within a generation, they are conjoined. As in any kinship system these three basic types of relationship constitute the building blocks of the system, but just as within the class of unilineal systems one finds many different variants, so within bilateral systems one may find many different types of system of recognition, according to the relative weight that is attached to the different types of tie.

In the case of the Sarakatsani, Campbell makes it clear that, since affines are not members of the kindred, marriage to non-related persons (a Sarakatsanos must marry outside his kindred) weakens the ties between ego and his collaterals in descending generations. The solidarity of the sibling group diminishes as its members become differentiated by their marriages and young families. There is, as a result, a growing tendency to the "isolation" of the elementary family from all collateral lines, and affines, though not members of a man's kindred, grow in importance with the life cycle since they are the kin of his children. Hence, given the cultural "decision" to stress ties of filiation over and against ties of sibship, the importance of affinal relatives follows automatically. Such a decision can only be understood in relation to the predominance of the *elementary* family.

To speak of the *nuclear* family is to refer to a group whose solidarity derives from the performance of the basic biological activities of procreation and rearing of children. To speak of the elementary family is to refer to a group whose solidarity is the resultant of the members of the nuclear family having interacted as a group over a

---

[2] For a more detailed discussion of this point see Harris, C. C., *The Family*, Allen & Unwin, 1969, ch. 3.

prolonged period of time. The *nuclear* family disappears as its distinctive activities cease. The existence of the *elementary* family is logically independent of those activities continuing to be performed.

Among the Sarakatsani the formation of the nuclear family is brought about by a marriage which involves the transfer of residence of the wife from her family of origin (in which she played the roles of sister and daughter), either to a new domestic group composed of herself and her husband or to the domestic group of her spouse, in which she plays the roles of wife, mother, and daughter-in-law. The protection of her honour is thenceforth no concern of her brothers, and her working services belong exclusively to the husband's family. It is quite clear that although relationship with her family of origin and kindred are still recognized, her primary duty is to her husband and children. Although the transition is less sharp for the husband, especially as the newly married couple frequently form a joint household with the husband's parents, nevertheless Campbell states that the husband eventually parts from all his remaining obligations as son and brother.

Relationships and obligations within the nuclear family household are dominant and the relationships between members of the elementary families of origin of the spouses become of decreasing importance. The fact that the nuclear family neither gives nor receives unconditional support from the other related elementary families, leads him to speak of the family being "isolated", *even within the kindreds of its members*. In other words, the normative structure of the society is such that the nuclear family is not part of, nor owes any allegiance to, other kinship groups or individuals within the society which conflict with the obligations of its members to one another. Structurally, therefore, it is isolated. This does not imply for one moment that the members of the elementary families from which the spouses are drawn do not see one another, nor does it imply that assistance between related elementary families is not provided, nor that they do not co-operate for certain purposes. What Campbell does state, however, is that the nuclear family neither gives nor receives *unconditional* support. In other words in terms of the *rules* governing kinship relationships, there is no grouping wider than the nuclear family in this system.[3]

In practice, however, related nuclear families do co-operate. The family group is normally unable to manage its flocks without assistance and, *in these circumstances*, two, three, or more families related by kinship or marriage associate to form a "company". However, the relationship between the constituent families is "contractual"; any family may elect to leave the association whenever it wills. In the majority of cases the nucleus of such a group is a number of married brothers with families, but such groups often include persons related in other ways, and it would be possible to produce many examples of different combinations of consanguineal kinsmen and affinal relatives.

We have already noted that, at marriage, the pattern of residence is frequently *viri-local*, that is to say that the wife resides with or near the family of origin of the husband, and also that in many cases the families of origin and procreation of the husband constitute a joint household. Sometimes, however, *uxori-local* residence is found where the wife's family of origin contains no sons. In both of these cases the marriage begins in an extended family *household*; that is to say a domestic group is formed from one elementary family and an extension of it.

The company formed for the purposes of economic co-operation is also a group, formed by the combination of the extensions of an elementary family. In the case of the domestic group, the extension is formed by the utilization of ties of filiation. In the case of the company, the tie more frequently used is that between siblings. In the latter case other relatives may also be included and the marriage tie may also be utilized.

What is being described here is the formation of groups wider than the elementary family, through the utilization of some combination of the interlocking elementary families of which the

---

[3] For a detailed discussion of the confusion that has arisen in the sociological literature over the use of the term "isolation" see Harris, *op. cit.*, pp. 98–116.

kinship system is made up.[4] The formation of such groups is not governed by rules and can only be understood in terms of the *purposes* and *activities* of the set of individuals that constitute them, and the conditions under which they act. Outside such groups are to be found other individuals, not necessarily more distant genealogically from any given member than some of those within it, whom ego recognizes as kin and to whom obligations exist.

Such kin are important to the individual in providing economic assistance; in providing a system of information and intelligence without which he cannot conduct his affairs efficiently or profitably; and in providing hospitality and local information in the course of his movement through a dispersed and scattered community.

We have now referred, through our examination of Campbell's account of the system of kinship of the Sarakatsani transhumant shepherds in rural Greece, to several seminal theoretical issues concerning kinship in urban–industrial societies. The distinctive characteristics of the patterns of kinship found in that class of societies (which we have defined operationally), derive largely from the characteristics of bilateral systems rather than from any mysterious effects that "urbanization" or "industrialization" has upon the family. To say this is not, however, to say that the actual type or species of system, within the class or genus "bilateral", can be understood without reference to the other institutions of the society of which it forms part.

That this is so derives partly from the nature of a bilateral system. Bilaterality entails not that the only groups found are nuclear families but that the only groups *prescribed* are nuclear families. Wider groups may be found and usually are found. If they are found then they will be the result of *ad hoc* arrangements between the parties concerned. This does not mean that there is no pattern or order in the incidence of such grouping, or

[4] The term "extended family" has been used of such groups by sociologists. For a discussion of these usages see: Rosser, C. and Harris, C. C., *The Family and Social Change*, Routledge, 1965, pp. 18–32; Harris, C. C., *The Family*, Allen & Unwin, 1969, pp. 82–7; Stacey, M. (Ed.), *Comparability in Social Research*, Heinemann, B.S.A./S.S.R.C., 1969.

in the types of group so formed. If such order exists it must be explained either in terms of the material or social conditions shared by groups classified as of the same type by virtue of their similarity of purposes, that is, groups classified as the same in terms of the activities which they perform.

The study of familial groupings is therefore distinctively "sociological" within the framework of a bilateral system. When we turn to examine the recognition of relationships, however, it is necessary to note a radical difference between the Sarakatsani and the kinship systems of most urban societies. The people described by Campbell recognize the existence of rules governing the range of recognized kinship. It seems likely that this was once a feature of most European systems of kinship.[5] We do not find, in urban industrial society, that recognition of kinship is governed by precise rules.

This fact creates severe difficulties in the study of kinship in such societies. The seminal studies of both Bott[6] and Firth[7] attempted to deal with this problem. Bott classified the relatives of her respondents as "intimate", "effective", "non-effective" and "unfamiliar".[8] and her classification involves two "dimensions": intimacy and knowledge. By intimacy she means frequent visiting and exchange of services.

Firth and Djamour discuss the problem of differentiation of kin and distinguish between recognized and nominated kin. "The former category is made up of all persons who are recognized by the informant as related to him by consanguinity and affinity whether known by name or not".[9] The latter category includes those known specifically by name. Piddington (pp. 171), in the second contribution to this reader, distinguishes between effective and non-effective kin, subdividing the former category into "priority kin" and "chosen kin".

[5] See Lancaster, L., Kinship in Anglo-Saxon society, I and II, *Brit. J. Sociol.* **9**, 1958.
[6] Bott, E., *Family and Social Network*, Tavistock, 1957.
[7] Firth, *op. cit.*
[8] *op. cit.*, p. 114.
[9] *op. cit.*, p. 42.

Among these three classifications Piddington's alone explicitly includes normative elements. Priority kin are kin with whom there is a "recognized moral obligation to enter into appropriate relationships".

The omission of any normative element in Firth's and Bott's definitions raises questions as to the meaning of the categories thereby defined. Rosser and Harris[10] have argued that it is of vital importance to distinguish between knowledge and recognition and have pointed out that "a man or woman may know the exact genealogical relationships including names, ages, and many further details of the kin of a brother's wife . . . without recognizing any personal relationship to them". In other words, knowledge of biological relations is not to be confused with the recognition of social relationships. Nor is the addition of further criteria (the exchange of services or visits) of any help in determining that a kin relationship exists. After all, neighbours exchange both visits and services and so may friends who are not neighbours, but that does not make them kin. The simple fact that a biological link is known to exist and services, etc., exchanged between the parties, does not by itself entail the relationship is one of kinship.

It is of course true that knowledge of the existence of kin is a necessary condition of their recognition. It is also true that the recognition of kin relationship will involve the acknowledgement or reciprocal rights and duties and hence involve claims for services or assistance being made and fulfilled. It is required to show in each case, however, that the services exchanged are exchanged because of a moral obligation to assist kinsfolk, and not merely because they happen to fall in the category of individuals whom ego knows well enough to ask for assistance.

The great variability in the range of recognition of kin in urban societies which is frequently commented upon, may very well be due to the definitions of "recognition" used. Definitions which depend upon knowledge or the exchange of services are, in fact,

[10] Rosser, C. and Harris, C. C. Relationships through marriage in a Welsh urban area, *Sociol. Rev.* **9** (3), (1961), 303.

measuring the variation in the social conditions under which different populations live. In some cases ego is surrounded by kindred persons. In other cases he is relatively isolated from them. In the former case he will continually be interacting with biologically related persons and in consequence his range of kinship knowledge and the number of active relationships he has with kin will be high. In the latter case both are likely to be low.[11] This has, however, logically nothing to do with the range of recognition of relationships.

This is well brought out by Piddington. One informant and his wife, he tells us, went to Chicago for their honeymoon and stayed in an hotel. On the day of their arrival a murder was committed in the adjoining bedroom. The wife said: "I don't like this place; we have relatives in Milwaukee; let's spend the rest of our honeymoon there"—which they did. Rosser and Harris report a similar incident: a man knocks on the door and says: "I'm Donald from Bolton sent down here for four months by McAlpine's. Can you put me up?" The informant is recorded as continuing: "Good God! I said; come in boy! I hadn't seen him since he was about six, more than thirty years ago . . . but of course he stayed with us."[12]

In both examples the relatives arc accommodated *as a matter of course*, and simply because they are relatives, just as a member of the kindred of a Sarakatsanos would give assistance to his kinsman who was in his locality as a matter of course, because he was a member of his kindred. In all these examples there must be some way of determining whether a particular relative, whether known or not, has a right to certain types of assistance should he turn up and claim it. In the Sarakatsani case the rules determining this are clear. In most urban societies they are not. This does not mean that the normative elements in kinship behaviour can be ignored.

This is not to deny that in urban bilateral societies there is a

[11] See Loudon's comments on this point (p. 192 below).

[12] Rosser, C. and Harris, C. C., *The Family and Social Change*, Routledge, 1965, p. 229. See also Firth, *op. cit.*, p. 39.

considerable range of choice as to the extent to which an individual may honour duties and obligations to priority kin. Such choice arises through the ability of an individual to move out of the range of effective demands upon him.

Equally an individual may choose or select from a reservoir of known kin, wider than the category of priority kin, individuals with whom he establishes relationships of other kinds. Kin relationships, says Piddington, provide bases on which other social relationships may be and often are established, but they do not make mandatory their establishment. Such relationships may, moreover, be maintained over wide distances. Geographical mobility makes possible the sloughing of kin relationship but does not entail it.

Just as the establishment of relationships on a kinship base does not create a specific set of *kinship* duties and obligations, so moving out of effective range of priority kin does not absolve an individual from honouring demands should they be made upon him.

Separation from kin may, however, very well force an individual to utilize other sources of assistance or companionship. Lancaster, stressing the way in which choice is a central element in "systems where there is room to manoeuvre", suggests that specific services, such as child-minding can be studied in terms of available possibilities, and the "weighting" given to different alternatives. Such an approach, she argues, provides a means for studying, in one scheme, neighbours, relatives, and friends as alternative supporters.[13]

To put this a little more sociologically; Lancaster appears to be advocating the study of decision making in the selection of social relationships, explaining variations in patterns of decision in terms of given ends and differing conditions of action whether social or material. The notion of the weighting given to different alternatives presumably refers to the different evaluation placed on the utilization of assistance from different sources.

Looked at in this way, every individual is faced with fields of

[13] Lancaster, L., Some conceptual problems in the study of family and kin ties in the British Isles, *Brit. J. Sociol.* **12**, (1961), 324.

potential social relationships of different kinds; kin, neighbours, workmates, etc. Each field will vary empirically between individuals with respect to its size, the possibility of the establishment of relationships involving different types of activity. Categories of individuals will vary in terms of their needs for relationships of different types (classified in terms of activity), and the values they place on relationships of different kinds (classified in terms of the way the actors categorize them).

The actual pattern of exchange of services found will be a function both of the empirical characteristics of these fields of relationship, and the evaluations placed upon their utilization. Hence changes in or differences between units of study concerning such patterns may be explained in terms of difference in either values or conditions or both. Any account of one such pattern must, however, refer both to conditions and values. Any given pattern cannot be understood either in terms of the norms governing kinship obligation or in terms of the conditions of action *alone*.

Vieille's article (p. 99) provides a vivid illustration of the way in which, because of the dispersal of kin, poor economic circumstances and enforced proximity with neighbours and workmates, relationships in these fields are characterized by the type of activity usually found between relatives in other areas of France. She concludes her fascinating account by a quotation from Marx's *The German Ideology*, in which he says that in the proletariat, "the *idea* of the family does not exist at all, while we observe . . . a propensity to family life based on relationships which are entirely *real*."

Put in less philosophical language, what Marx (and presumably Vieille) are saying, is that relationships which are based on social norms or rules are replaced in this somewhat extreme example by relationships which arise naturally out of the exigencies of daily life: the performance of the activities characteristic of the family and household in conditions of extreme proximity.

The example is somewhat atypical because the situation described is a transitional one. Not only are the inhabitants migrants, but they are also on the lowest rung of a ladder of housing accommodation which will eventually enable them to climb out of the extreme conditions described. In a transitional situation of this kind there is not time, as Vieille makes clear, for normative definitions of the situation ("customs", in her terms) to become established. If the situation of the actors was chronic rather than temporary, there is no reason to suppose that the patterns of behaviour described would not become to be valued as "right" independently of the appropriateness of the situation in which those making such evaluations found themselves.

This observation draws our attention to the fact that, though at any given point in time the norms and conditions which together determine the pattern of relationships and activities which are observed must be regarded as independent, it is nevertheless also true that over time they may be regarded as interacting. Hence an explanation of the differences between units of study may legitimately refer to the differing patterns of interaction between values and conditions of which the observed regularities in contemporary behaviour are the result. Most studies of kinship are content to elaborate the normative structure of a system of kinship or social relations and use it to explain the regularities in behaviour which are observed under certain material and social conditions. Important as this type of work is, it should not prevent us from attempting to explain how the normative structure is related aetiologically to the activities which it governs and the conditions under which they occur.

The Functions of Kinship

Soi-disant functionalist "explanations" cannot, of course, perform this role. In heading the second section, "The Functions of Kinship", the editor had in mind not "social function" in the sense of a "necessary system effect" but rather the uses to which kinship systems are put. To say that a system is "used", need not imply conscious purpose on the part of the actors. It implies merely that, if for some reason the kinship system no longer facilitated the achievement of certain individual ends, then the individuals concerned would have to cast around for some other means for their achievement.

For example, Rosser and Harris[14] in their study of Swansea ascribe two functions to kinship: social identification and social support in need. By so doing they imply that in default of the relevant kinship information, some other means of identifying individuals would be used, or in the absence of kin, support would be sought from other sources in time of need. The identification of such functions by no means explains either the occurrence or persistence of the recognition of extrafamilial kin ties. It does enable us to understand their relation to institutions governing other types of activities and their significance to the actors.

The extracts in this section describe the very various uses which are made, by different groups, of a bilateral system of kinship recognition. The first two extracts refer to villages where the elementary family is an economic unit of production as well as of consumption and ties of filiation are used as the means of transferring property between generations.

Now it does not follow that because the system of recognition of kin relationship is bilateral, that both spouses will inherit property. In fact in both cases cited here they do. Friedl suggests by her account that in Vasilika (p. 121) the dowry brought by the woman is her portion of the inheritance of her sibling group. In the Spanish town studied by Lison–Tolosana (p. 163), although the woman only brings household goods with her at marriage, inheritance by both sexes taking place only at the death of the parents, at their death the property is divided between *all* the children and therefore spouses of both sexes inherit.

Inheritance involves not the transference of rights *in* property but the transference of rights *to* property. That is to say that inheritance, whether at marriage or at the death of the parents, involves the division of the property previously enjoyed by the

---

[14] Rosser and Harris, *op. cit.*, pp. 289–90.

elementary family groups from which the spouses of the new nuclear family come. In bilateral systems marriage actually or potentially involves conflicts which occur at the point of segmentation in descent systems. Ego will not simply acquire rights in a pre-existent property owning group; he forms a new property owning group, using for this purpose, the property of his elementary family together with that portion of the property of his wife's elementary family which she brings as her dowry.

The property which was previously adequate to support the elementary families of origin may no longer be adequate to support all the nuclear families formed by the children. If the system of inheritance is an "equal" system (as in the two cases with which we are concerned), then it will be only possible to maintain the system if the number of children per family is not greater than two, so that the portion received by each child together with that brought by the spouse is equivalent to that previously possessed by the elementary family of origin. In those cases where this condition is not fulfilled, one of the sons (who control the property) will have to "travel", that is renounce claims on the property in order that the portion of the remainder shall be viable. If in the locality as a whole each generation is no greater than its predecessor, the family may be able to provide one of its children with cash rather than land, and the son may be able to buy land locally and set up on his own account. Where this is not possible one or more of the children will have to leave the locality. This implies that there is another locality in which he can obtain a living either by working for money or in which he can purchase land. If there are such other communities, this implies that the families within one locality will eventually become linked to other localities by a network of extended kin ties.[15]

In Redfield's[16] terms, the isolation of the folk community is

[15] For a detailed study of this process in a rural British community see Williams, W. M., *Ashworthy*, Routledge, 1963.
[16] See chap. I of Redfield, R., *The Primitive World and its Transformations*, Cornell Univ. Press, 1953.

thus destroyed. Friedl's account of Vasilika describes how, through education, some of the children are enabled to migrate to the town, and receive only a token portion of the property of their elementary families of origin. In the case of Vasilika we are dealing, therefore, with a property and family system which, while governing agricultural activities taking place within a rural settlement, is nevertheless modified to take account of the existence of the town. We are dealing, in other words, with a peasant society in Redfield's sense.

Friedl makes explicit the incursion of urban values into the rural society of Vasilika; the loss of children to the town is regarded with pride as much as regret. Similarly marriage with a townsman is prized by the women. In consequence, townward migration by children of both sexes has occurred to an extent greater than that necessary to provide for "surplus" children. As a result more property has become available for use in bidding for a town husband for a daughter, and the size of a dowry necessary to attract a town husband has grown. In consequence not only are townsmen and country-men linked by ties of kinship but there is a net export of rural capital to the towns. Ties between urban spouses and their families of origin in the country are maintained because of the part played by those families in making their emigration possible, either by contributing to their education or dowry.

The maintenance of links between related elementary family groups, even though separated by distance and differentiated in terms of occupation, may be understood in terms of an exchange between urban and rural families. The rural family makes possible the migration. The urbanized children bring prestige to the family in the rural locality and at the same time the men, by their departure, increase the supply of land available to those who remain behind. Equally the daughter who marries a townsman may require land for her dowry but this land is usually worked by other villagers, thus increasing the economic resources which are available to the community if not to her family. Hence the transference of wealth to the town may be seen to be conducive to the achievement of the ends of individuals (as culturally defined) that is their rural–urban migration, to the provision by the family for its children, and to the maintenance of a branch at least of the families concerned within their natal community.

In the discussion so far we have omitted to recognize the important fact that all families will not be able equally to endow their children. In consequence even within the farming community itself each marriage will have consequences for the position of the resultant nuclear family in a hierarchy of economic positions. Different marriages contracted by members of the same sibling group will not merely differentiate the sibs by the creation of different affinal ties and distinguish their children in terms of different ties of filiation, but they will also differentiate the group in economic terms. When the system of kinship is used for the transmission of property therefore, Campbell's remark concerning the way in which the importance of the sibling group declines and relationships with affines assume increasing importance over the individual's life cycle, takes on a new significance.

We have seen how in the case of Vasilika activities involving property may constitute a tie between the generations, even where differentiated. Both Friedl and Lison-Tolosana make clear, however, the way in which property and its division is disruptive of the solidarity of the sibling group. It is not by chance that both accounts stress the importance of ties of affinity created by the marriage, for property is acquired from both sides and conflicts ensue over the equity of the division of the property made to establish the new nuclear family by each side. At the same time, as Lison-Tolosana points out, the new spouses' insistence that their rights to inheritance are respected are prompted by consideration for their children's welfare. These children are, of course, equally the kin of the parents of both spouses. Conflict ensues therefore between sibs over the division of the property to which they share a claim, and between affines over the performance of duties in providing for the new nuclear families that link them.

Such conflict arises not merely over the division of land and tools but also over dwellings. Even though the new nuclear family may begin in the household of the parents (or sibs) of one or other of its spouses, it is still an independent unit having control over a distinctive set of properties and being expected to form an independent household eventually. Where the household is both the domestic and economic unit, conflicts between the extensions of the original family cannot be avoided. If the residence is viri-local there are likely to be conflicts between the women over the joint performance of household tasks. If the residence is uxori-local there will be conflict between the men over the performance of economic activities. Where potentially independent units jointly work property in which they all have shares, conflicts will arise over the distribution of the income from the joint resources which will compound conflicts over their eventual distribution, or redistribution.

Such conflicts may be found between affines in most bilateral systems, even where property is not importantly involved. In the case of Vasilika however, because of the importance of property, these conflicts are known and expected, and this is reflected in the fact that there is a kinship terminology for describing affines.

Leyton's account of what he calls a composite descent group in Canada also describes conflict ensuing from the division of property (p. 179). Here the sibling tie was used to create an economic partnership, rather than broken by the need to divide joint property. Segmentation occurred, not because of the conflict between equal partners but because of the dissatisfaction of the junior partners with their promotion prospects. The account illustrates very well the problems involved in trying to use the kinship system as the formal structure of an economic organization in an industrial society. In the first place recruitment is by "ascription" rather than "achievement" and consequently it is impossible to assure that the occupants of kinship statuses will have the characteristics required for the satisfactory performance of economic roles. In this particular case the difficulties were not acute, because, as Leyton explicitly points out, the degree of specialization of skill required was in this case fairly low. Even so, there was still a shortage of males, requiring the utilization of affines. The affines, however, did not possess the loyalty to the cognatic kin group and had to be motivated to retain their statuses within the organization. In a society where "achievement" values are dominant, this meant that they could only be persuaded to stay and perform if the rewards for so doing were high relative to those they could have obtained in other organizations. However the rewards from work are not merely extrinsic but involve the exercise of power and authority in the organization which were, in this case, reserved for male cognates of the founders. The deprivation of the male in-laws resulted in tensions which produced the segmentation of the group.[17]

This account is extremely instructive because it suggests the complexity of the relationship between industrialization and the loss of the co-ordination of co-operative economic activity by family groups which characterizes urban–industrial society. The family can only be used for such purposes where the degree of specialization of skill is fairly low, and where the values of the society do not stress the individual economic mobility of the males. At the same time, however, it draws our attention to the fact that however inadequate kinship relationships are as a basis for the organization of economic activity *throughout* such a society, this does not mean that it may not be economically advantageous to utilize family ties for the creation of co-operative economic groups, *ad hoc*, for specific purposes. Extended kin ties may therefore be used for a wide range of purposes within such a society and because they are not so used throughout society, it does not follow that therefore the incidence of such groupings can be ignored.

We turn now to a very different type of contribution. Loudon (p. 187) identifies three main "functions" of kinship in the area of South Wales which he studied: ceremonial, evaluative, and supportive. In so doing he stresses the way in which the recogni-

---

[17] For an introduction to the literature on the family in industrial society see Harris, C. C., *The Family*, Allen & Unwin, 1969, ch. 4.

tion of kinship depends on the uses to which such recognition is put and the way in which "use" varies with the context of action. In the Vale of Glamorgan we are dealing with a distinctively rural situation in the sense that a large part of the population is relatively stable and this has led not merely to their being members of highly interconnected networks of kin, but also to their playing a large number of roles to each other. The multiplex character of their role relationships, combined with a lack of clear rules determining the range of kinship recognition and the rights and duties involved, provide the individual with a choice in the way relationships are conceptualized which can vary with context. At the same time several types of relationship may all be operative in the same context.

The ethnographic content of the paper is provided by a detailed description of the genealogical connections between those attending the funeral of a well-known local figure. It shows in an extremely vivid way how occasions of this kind mobilize and make visible (for those that have eyes to see) a pattern of relationships of considerable complexity, not easily discernible but of the greatest importance in understanding the actions of those involved in them. The members of such "sections", as Loudon tentatively terms them, are linked to each other not only by ties of kinship but also by ties of other kinds which are built onto and reinforced by ties of kinship. At the same time, persons linked into ego's kinship network by non-kin ties of the same kind that already characterise it constitute a source of potential affines.

Loudon classifies the participants in such ceremonial occasions as funerals into four categories: close relatives, other extrafamilial kin, friends and neighbours (who may also be distant kin) and the remainder. He makes it clear that we are not dealing here with a situation where any clearly defined category of kin has the specific obligation to attend ego's funeral, but that the knowledge of a biological relation may, in certain contexts, evoke a feeling of obligation to lend support to the mourning kin.

The "use" of biological ties to evoke support on ceremonial

occasions Loudon refers to as the ceremonial functions of kinship. He uses the same example to illustrate the way in which individuals evaluate, that is to say categorize and rank, other individuals by means of tracing kin relationships. He asserts that on occasions a placement of an individual in relation to another individual by means of tracing a kin tie may be more important than placement in occupational or wealth categories.

It is relevant for our purposes to make two points about Loudon's article. First, though he does not use the term, what is essentially being described is the importance of kinship *knowledge* in placing individuals in relation to a constellation of other individuals whose positions relative to one another are already known. This is not merely an idle making sense of a social field. On the contrary, the placements made are made along a number of dimensions, whose importance varies with the context in which the individual has to *act*.

To speak of someone acting implies both that he has certain ends-in-view and a certain estimation of the situation in which he has to act. To fully understand the importance of placement in terms of biological relations we need to know both what are the ends in view of those who make that placement and in what way such placement constitutes a significant condition of the action.

This brings us to the second point, which is that we need to know more about the kinship ideologies of the actors which makes their interrelation of significance for action. Loudon asserts that certain pivotal kin remain pivotal after their death and are often used by the living as foci from which genealogical connections stem. But all deceased kin are not pivotal and Loudon makes it clear that prestige or salience in some sphere can determine which individual becomes pivotal. In order to understand the selection of pivots around whom kin are organized we need to know according to what ideas relationship to a salient is significant and what activities determine the criteria of salience used.

We conclude this section with an article which deals with a

very different type of situation. Bell's study of middle class families (p. 209) is an excellent illustration of the way in which differences in the pattern of relationships between kin can be understood in terms of the differing conditions under which they act. Frequent contact between mother and daughter is not possible, nor necessary. On the other hand where the parents are able economically to help their married children, and in the earlier stages of the life cycle their income is relatively small so that they therefore need help, ties of filiation are utilized to channel *financial* aid from the rich oldsters to the poor youngsters. Studies of other areas have shown how relationships between women are significant because they provide the means whereby *domestic* aid is channelled between the generations.[18] The distinction between these two types of activity and the pattern of relationship is quite properly explained in terms of the differing economic conditions of the two categories of families that respectively exhibit them, and the differing degree of geographical dispersion of the members of the elementary family in each category, which is in turn related to the characteristics of the occupations from which they typically derive a living.

This particular study, then, shows how two types of factor are inevitably involved in understanding family behaviour. To speak of the economic and spatial conditions under which families act is to refer to two whole classes of considerations to which the terms "industrial" and "urban" society respectively refer.

Before we turn to a more explicit consideration of the themes of urbanization and industrialization, two brief articles concerning marriage itself are included. Compared with the amount of material on mate selection and marital relationships in the American literature, studies on these topics are relatively sparse. Andrée Michel's article (p. 227) summarizes the findings of French students on patterns of mate selection in her country. Systems of mate selection in Western bilateral kinship systems are "open" systems, that is to say that the selection of a marriage partner is not governed by rules which prescribe either whom one should

[18] The works of the Institute of Community Studies cited by Bell.

marry or which categories of mate are preferred.[19] The actual patterns of mate selection which can be observed are therefore the fortuitous product of a large number of factors: norms governing the choice of mate, norms affecting the choice of mate, parental influence and various types of social and material condition.

Michel is able to show that along a number of dimensions the degree of "homogamy"—that is to say the extent to which like marries like—is still considerable in contemporary France. A substantial proportion of the French marry within their own locality, and persons of similar occupational status. In 1952 only 5 per cent of all marriages were with foreigners.

Michel's discussion of attitudes to intermarriage on the part of different minority ethnic groups in France makes it clear that the high degree of ethnic endogamy must be understood in relation to a large number of different factors: in particular the distinctive kinship systems and religious beliefs of many of these groups would obviously make mates from different cultures difficult to absorb, and the spouses would not share common values in terms of which decisions could be made and legitimated in the course of their married life and would have widely different expectations concerning the performance of their marital roles.

These considerations apply also to the preference for the marriage within one of the sub-groups that compose French society. Different socio-economic groups also have different family systems, differing tastes and values and hence may define a person of another social group as undesirable in terms of the values of their own group without explicitly following a rule which defines out-group marriages as undesirable or illegitimate. At the same time the field of social contacts from which potential mates can be drawn is itself largely determined by considerations of ethnic group and class membership and affected by geographical distance.

[19] For a summary of findings in this area see, Jacobson, P., and Mathery, A., Mate selection in open marriage systems, *Int. J. Comp. Soc.* **3**, (1962), 98. See also Harris, *op. cit.*, p. 152.

Two themes may be drawn out of this brief discussion. First the way kinship behaviour is not governed by clear rules or even norms but nevertheless patterned and intelligible. Secondly the way in which the actions of individuals need to be understood in terms not merely of the membership of the family groups from which they come but in terms also of the wider groups and categories to which they belong.

These two themes underly much of Bott's[20] study of marital role segregation to which Chris Turner's article refers (p. 245).[21] Bott sought to understand the nature of the marital relationship in relation to the type of social network to which the spouses belonged. She was unable to understand the behaviour of her subjects in terms of the rules or norms governing it because her subjects did not seem to take into account any normative considerations in terms of which variations in marital behaviour between families could be understood. She therefore attempted to make sense of differences between families in terms of the differing structures of the networks in which the spouses were encapsulated.

Bott hypothesized that there was a relationship between the degree of connectedness of the network and the degree to which marital roles were segregated. Turner, in his study, found an important relationship between the degree of segregation by sex in the network on the one hand, and the degree of interconnectedness of the network and the degree of marital role segregation on the other. He found, however, that the relation between the degree of network connectedness and marital role segregation was by itself less strong. He examines the importance of other factors—type of occupation, geographic mobility, educational level, stage of the development cycle, and cosmopolitan and local orientations.

Of these factors Turner finds that occupation is of importance in determining role segregation and geographic mobility in determining network connectedness. We are left again with the

[20] Bott, *op. cit.*
[21] For an extended discussion of her work see Harris, *op. cit.*, pp. 169–75.

same two factors salient as those noted at the end of the discussion in Bell's study: economic and spatial factors.

Urbanization and the Family

Urban sociology has been concerned either with describing types of society found to be associated with particular types of settlement or with attempting to derive types of society from the characteristics of the settlement. Any adequate characterization of society must refer to the types of ideas which inform the co-operative activities of its members as well as dealing with the way they are interrelated empirically. This raises the question of the nature of the relationship between settlement characteristics and type of idea and meaning associated with them.

Ponsioen's article (p. 271) raises these problems with reference to the family. He himself does not claim that his elaboration of the six types of family which he describes as existing in Holland is any more than an informed sociological speculation. Nor, I am sure, would he claim that such a typology is in any way exhaustive. His article is included here, however, because it specifically relates family and societal type in a way which is stimulating and has, moreover, had echoes on this side of the channel in recent years.[22]

Its two key ideas are those of the openness of society and of the family. (According to the terminology used in this introduction, "family" should be rendered "nuclear family household".) Basically he describes a situation (with which the opening extracts in this selection will have made us familiar and is further briefly delineated by Hofstee and Kooy's article (p. 263)), where the nuclear family household is part of a wider kin group which is itself an integral part of a wider local community. Small, relatively isolated and agrarian, the local community encompasses

---

[22] The reader may find it interesting to compare his notion of a closed family with John Goldthorpe's notion of a "privatized" worker. See: Goldthorpe, J. H., *et al.*, The affluent worker and the thesis of *embourgeoisement, Sociology*, **1** (1), (1967), 11.

the majority of an individual's kin universe and his network is highly interconnected. "Neighbourhood and family life intermingle freely." The openness of the family is here quite clearly related to the degree of closure of the community—the extent to which it lacks links with the world "outside".

By an "open society", Ponsioen appears to be referring to a society composed of localities which are not isolated from each other, physically, culturally, or socially. But it is quite clear that by an open society Ponsioen means more than this. The open society is quite clearly highly differentiated, but in the sense that it is constituted by a large number of specialized institutions which exercise the co-ordination of co-operative activities once the preserve of the family group, and also in the sense that it is composed of groups with different beliefs, values, and attitudes and possesses a highly differentiated stratification system. Such a society corresponds in many respects to the characterization of those societies which have been described as "urban".

What Ponsioen then does is to describe a series of typical responses of the family to these changed social conditions. It may turn in on itself, attempting to maintain traditional social values and patterns of family behaviour in the face of social change; it may attempt a compromise; it may "degenerate" from a cohesive group into a mere category of people sharing common residence but no common co-operative activities, or it may "adapt" by accepting that the family constitutes only one sphere of social activity among many in the lives of its socially differentiated members.

The "closed family" refers therefore to a maladaptive and "open family" to an adaptive response. The chief deficiency of this treatment is that it does not clearly differentiate the effect of changed empirical conditions in affecting what the family can do, and the role of family ideologies in justifying different responses which different family types make to those changed conditions.

There is a secondary and more general deficiency in this type of approach, however. Categories as broad as "urban" or "open" are too general greatly to aid our understanding of the way in

which societal type and family type are related. If this relationship is to be understood then the relations between the elements
of each type need to be considered, and this requires a far more
detailed analysis of both family and urban structure than is even
hinted at here.

Baumert and Lupri (p. 279) are specifically concerned with
the relation between values and behaviour and seek to relate each
to a simple indicator of urbanization—size of the settlement.
One of the difficulties with this approach is that differences in
family structure and family values are of course part of what is
meant by "urbanization" sociologically defined. Hence it is no
good their saying that by urbanization they refer to the spread of
the urban way of life, thus implying that urbanization is a sociological process of which size of settlement is an indicator. It is
important to be quite clear about this. What they are in fact
attempting is the relation of an element in the sociological
definition of the term "urban" (i.e. certain types of family structure and values) to an ecological variable—not an indicator of a
sociological variable. Their article is an exercise in urban rather
than in family sociology, in the sense that it is concerned with the
relationship of social behaviour and ecological conditions rather
than with the relation between family behaviour and other types
of social behaviour derived from a sociological definition of an
urban society as a distinctive sociological type.

From this it follows that one is not able to infer whether their
data showing differences between settlements of different size are
interpretable in terms of ecological or social factors. Hence it is
not surprising that they conclude that "there is not necessarily a
strong relationship between urbanization as measured by proportions of rural and urban populations on the one hand and the
extension of the urban way of life in the society at large on the
other". It may be doubted whether what is required here is, as
they suggest, an attempt to formulate refined hypotheses on the
basis of further international data. What is required is surely a
few studies which explicitly deal with the relation of the family
to other social institutions in settlements of varying size, showing

the ways in which within different cultures different choices are made between the various structural possibilities opened up by increasing settlement size and showing how such "choices" have consequences for the family both at the level of ideas and at the level of the performance of family activities.

The importance of their work lies primarily in the way in which they are able to show that the changes in family behaviour between generations occur in all types of settlement and that these changes are greater in the larger type of settlement than in the small. If this is not the case in America then this raises a whole set of fascinating questions. Are differences between the two countries to be attributed primarily to their different industrial structure, to the varying degrees of social and geographical mobility, to the different cultures which they possess? In other words any sociological explanation of these differences must depend on placing the family within the structural context of the societies of which it forms part and tracing the way in which each structural feature affects family behaviour.

Kooy's study (p. 297) also focuses on the process of urbanization, but he does not use it as his chief theoretical variable. Rather he hypothesizes that settlement size is related to and therefore an indicator of the four processes which he considers of theoretical importance: mechanization, secularization, socio-cultural differentiation, and individuation. He also uses the term "closed family" but, in contrast to Ponsioen, as a synonym for an independent nuclear family household freed from domination by or incorporation in any wider group. For Kooy the closed family thus defined is an adaptive rather than a maladaptive response to the social changes which he analyses in terms of his four theoretical variables.

His actual indicator of the incidence of closed families is chiefly concerned with the independence of the household. His measure of urbanization involves not merely size, but also the proportion of the population in agricultural as opposed to industrial occupations.

He finds that the individuated nuclear family is emerging in the Dutch countryside as well as in large towns and that its highly uneven distribution is to be understood chiefly in terms of regional cultural patterns and that the degree of urbanization is merely a secondary factor. He concludes that urbanization, far from accounting for everything, may in fact account for little or nothing.

It is hard to disagree with Kooy's conclusion. Either we mean by this term "the concentration of the population into large settlements", in which case it is impossible to show that the large size of settlement determines the nature of the social structure of its inhabitants, or we give the term a sociological definition which involves a description of the very phenomena which we are trying to explain. This does not mean, however, that we cannot use a sociological definition of "urban" which, because it is very general or because it has primary reference to institutional features other than the family, does not beg the very questions we are trying to ask. But both of these ways out of the dilemma involve considering the family in relation to its social environment and tracing the relationship between elements in that environment and the family.

It is to be doubted whether Kooy can have been said to have shown empirically that the incidence of the individuated nuclear family household is related to any of his theoretical variables, one of which is technological and the rest structural. Kooy's study is not as satisfactory as it might be, less because his explanatory categories are too broad than because his methods of research are adequate only to the establishment of descriptive and general propositions rather than to the testing of analytic and explanatory hypotheses.

It may be doubted whether the variable "urbanism" is of much use in studies of the family. Urbanization refers to a whole set of interrelated changes in social structure, at the level of both relationships and ideas, which are historically associated with the growth of industrial towns. These include the effects of the initial rural to urban migration, increased geographical mobility resulting in the dispersal of kin, increased occupational mobility leading to their differentiation, the growth of a more differentiated occupational structure, a shift from agricultural to industrial production, the creation of a highly differentiated social environment, the rise of specialized social agencies, changing beliefs and attitudes towards authority, sexuality, religion, and so on. That this process has had enormous consequences for the family we cannot doubt. If the significance of the process is to be understood in relation to the family the various elements in it must be distinguished and their effects on family structure traced individually.

Studies of the Family and the Aged

Such effects can only be understood if the activities of family members are themselves clearly understood and described, for it is through the changing pattern of family activities that the environment of the family affects its structure. The study of the family life of the elderly may be regarded by some as chiefly an applied field. Indeed care and provision for the old constitutes an enormous social problem, and it is true that the family is of particular importance to those who are concerned with these matters. However, we conclude this selection with three pieces of work which deal with the family life of the old chiefly because of their *theoretical* importance. This lies precisely in the fact that what is crucial both to devising social policy and to furthering our theoretical understanding of the family is an examination of the activities which family members perform.

Philip Taietz's contribution, for example (p. 321), examines the family at the level of values, meanings, and behaviour, and attempts to understand it in terms of clearly specified variables: agricultural occupation, geographical distribution, occupational opportunities, and he is well aware that all these variables are interrelated among themselves. Like Kooy he finds that there is a shift towards the "individuated nuclear family household" pattern but is able to explain this in terms of clearly defined conditions under which family members have to act. He concludes, however, that such "individuation" need not lead to the isolation and alienation of the adult from the aged generation, and this conclusion is in accord with that come to by Professor Rosenmayr.

Rosenmayr (p. 367) explicitly relates the incidence of three-generation households both to the activities of the members and the conditions under which they operate. Hence co-residence comes about for economic reasons or where one family member loses their spouse. Similarly, differences between areas in patterns of residence are related to the differing economic activities performed which render ties through males either of importance (as in rural areas) or irrelevant where the occupations are industrial.

Rosenmayr makes it clear that we must not confuse the household with the family, nor assume that, because the family is isolated in a structural sense—norms and rules do not prescribe its subordination to a wider group, this therefore means that relationships between members of the overlapping nuclear families which make up a bilateral kinship system do not persist even where norms of residence may actually be against joint household formation.

That the old and young retain relationships with each other is amply evidenced by the data provided by Jan Stehouwer's contribution (p. 337). But Stehouwer's account of family relations in Denmark provides us with a salutary warning against explaining family structure solely in terms of activities. He describes a situation where, as he puts it "the generations live in close contact with each other but with a very low degree of mutual functional dependence".

This fact is partly to be explained by the existence of a long tradition of state care for the old. But the provision of such care has not weakened the ties between the generations. To speak of a kin relationship is, as we noted at the beginning of this introduction, to speak of a relationship which is defined in terms of general moral obligation rather than of limited usefulness. Thus while we may explain differences between families in terms of the differing activities they perform and the conditions under which they act, we cannot reduce in a utilitarian fashion the notion of relatedness to the uses to which such relations are put.

We have examined a variety of approaches and a variety of findings relevant to an understanding of the relation of kinship to urban society. Is there any conclusion of a general kind which it is possible to draw from these different studies?

One of the characteristics of urban society is its heterogeneity. That is to say that it is highly differentiated. It comprises a large number of different social worlds. It is not likely, then, that there will be found one distinctive type of urban family, but rather as many different types as there are differing combinations of material and social conditions under which the family has to act. Our job as sociologists is not to seek simple holistic types of family or society but to investigate the detailed ways in which elements in each are interrelated.

*Kinship Systems and the
Recognition of Relationships*

The Kindred in a Greek Mountain Community*

J. K. CAMPBELL

IN THIS essay I discuss certain formal characteristics of the cognatic kinship system of a community of Greek Sarakatsani transhumant shepherds.[1] But although I describe specifically the kinship institutions of a particular shepherd community, the principles and categories which emerge from this discussion are generally valid for rural society in Greece. Indeed, I would claim that if these are not made explicit it will not be possible to understand the structure of any community outside the larger towns; nor, therefore, the moral values and political relations of one half of the Greek nation.

This community of shepherds numbers some 4000 souls. In the summer, from May until October, they graze their sheep and goats in the mountains of Zagori, a district north-east of the town of Jannina on the western flank of the Pindus mountains in the province of Epirus. During these months the shepherds live in small local groups which vary in size from 100 to 300 men, women, and children, each group exploiting the grassland of a single village, high pastures which lie between 3000 and 6000 feet above sea level. By a government decree of 1938 most of these shepherd families now enjoy the same citizenship and graz-

* Dr. J. G. Peristiany, Dr. J. M. Beattie and Dr. Rodney Needham read this essay in manuscript and I am grateful to them for their comments and criticisms.

[1] Communities of Sarakatsani, Σαρακατσαναῖοι or Σαρακατσάνοι, in many areas of continental Greece and in certain districts of Euboea and the northern Peloponnese. Vide 'Αγγελικῆς Χατζημιχάη, Σαρακατσάνοι, Athens, 1957. Vol. I, Part A, the section on "The geographical distribution of the Sarakatsani". This scholarly work contains an excellent bibliography.

ing rights as the sedentary villagers of Zagori, from whom previously they had to rent their pastures.[2] In the winter the community is more widely dispersed. The Sarakatsani move down from the mountains to the coastal plains and valleys over an area which extends from the Albanian frontier as far south as the towns of Arta and Preveza and even beyond. Here many of the shepherds have no grazing rights and they must rent pasture at great cost from village communities or private individuals. Since the First World War the settlement of refugees and the introduction of the tractor and improved farming techniques have progressively reduced the area of grassland in the plains. Each year the search for winter grass by the Sarakatsani becomes wider and more desperate. Quite apart from the greater geographical dispersion of the community in winter, the problems of weather and lambing isolate the shepherds of each flock whose only concern during these months is the care of their animals. In summer, although the Sarakatsani are still dispersed over 390 square miles of mountainous country, there is time to visit kinsmen who live at a distance, weddings and festivals are celebrated, and in general there is a greater sense of the community and its life. Winter in the plains is a kind of exile; the return in spring to the mountains of Zagori is the return home.

The pattern of social groupings in this community is extremely simple. The most restricted unit is the most important. This is the family, whether in its elementary or extended form. To this small group the individual owes almost exclusively his or her time, energy and loyalties. If a man forms an intimate and sympathetic friendship with a person outside his family who is not a kinsman, this represents a kind of treason. However, the family group is normally unable to manage its flocks without some assistance, and in these circumstances, two, three, or more families related by kinship or marriage, associate to form "a company", παρέα, which for functional reasons must include four adult males and generally numbers between 15 and 50 persons of all ages. But the duties

[2] In many areas the declining population of these villages has largely abandoned agriculture for timber felling.

which the individual assumes as a member of the "company" are specific and have an obvious relation to the welfare of his family. The relationship between the constituent families of the group is contractual; any family may elect to leave the association whenever it wills, any family may be expelled by the decision of the other members. Apart from this participation in a group of co-operating and related families, the shepherd normally has no membership in other social groupings which might conflict with his exclusive duties to the family.

It is believed by the Sarakatsani that the interests of unrelated families are opposed and, indeed, mutually destructive. The local gathering of families which in summer happen to graze the pastures and enjoy citizenship rights of the same village, has little cohesion as a group except when, on a rare occasion such as a village festival, it breaks into brief and violent opposition to the villagers; and it has no organization beyond the ephemeral political combinations which appear at the time of local village elections. The idea of the total community is, of course, important: it represents a way of life in opposition to the ways of peasants, merchants, and bureaucrats. But the community, too, lacks any structure of authority or effective organization; and, in part, for the same reasons, that is to say the solidarity, exclusiveness, and mutual opposition of the families which form it.

While it is true that the total community (or the local gathering of families as a segment of it) is not an organized social group, it nevertheless defines a social space within which values are shared and the conduct of men and women is evaluated by other Sarakatsani. These values concern, especially, right ways of acting in family and kinship roles and the sex-linked moral characteristics which a man or woman ought to exhibit when he, or she, stands forward as the protagonist of the family and the guardian of its honour. Such evaluations imply a hierarchy of prestige. And it is precisely through mutual competition in terms of strength, wealth, and a reputation for honourable actions that the opposed families, and groups of related families, are associated with one another in a coherent and regular manner.

With these general features of the community in mind, I turn
now to consider the significance of kinship relations for the Sarakatsani of Zagori.

I

The kindred, τὸ σόϊ, includes only those blood kinsmen of a
man (or woman)[3] who are formally recognized for social purposes. The Sarakatsani recognize as members of the kindred all
cognatic relatives as far as the degree of second cousin, whether
these links are traced through the father's or mother's side of the
family. In this system, all those persons descended from the four
sibling groups of a man's two grandmothers and two grandfathers
are all his kinsmen except the children of his second cousins,
the grandchildren of his first cousins, and the great grandchildren
of his own siblings, who are not members of his kindred. To
express this in more general terms, the recognition for social
purposes of collateral relations is relatively wide in a man's own
generation and subsequently becomes, from his point of view, relatively less wide in each descendant generation. As a man passes
through life, critical events, such as his marriage and the birth
of children, the marriages of these children and the birth of
grandchildren, direct his obligations and interests to his own
immediate descendants to the exclusion of collaterals.

Kindred relationships are considered by the Sarakatsani to be
extensions from the family. Naturally it is always a member of
a man's elementary family who mediates his various relationships
in the kindred, parents providing the links with grandparents,
uncles, aunts, and cousins, siblings those with nephews and
nieces. And although the kindred is a system of personal relations
while the family is a corporate group,[4] the systematic character of

---

[3] Except where there is ambiguity I shall not repeat this cumbersome qualification.

[4] Perpetuity is a quality often premised of corporate kinship groups, whereas
Sarakatsan families are limited to a life of some 40 years, i.e. the period which

the former, and the structure of the latter, are necessarily inter-dependent and consistent.

The Sarakatsan family is not only a domestic association of individuals with mutual affections based on blood relationship, it is a corporate group owning in common all significant property; and of this the leader, whether father or brother, is the trustee not the owner. It strives to become a self-sufficient economic unit with a division of labour organized about the service of its flocks, and its members invariably act together in political activities. The individual in his work and behaviour is entirely committed to his family, whose prestige and reputation for honour are his foremost concern.

The family is also a religious community with its own "sacra", icons and other objects. In the popular mind it is an earthly reflection of the Heavenly Family of God the Father, the Mother of God, and Christ. Relations between members of a family ought to be modelled on the attitudes which, it is imagined inspire the relations of the Heavenly archetype Family and its members. A father ought to have wisdom and foresight, a mother compassion, a son courage and respect, a daughter virginity, and so on.[5] Through grace, which descends in the sacrament of the Eucharist, through the icons, and in other ways, they are helped to achieve these modes of being, and in achieving them they partake, in a sense, of the condition of the Holy Family and are therefore less vulnerable as a group to material disaster or the spiritual attacks of the devil. Through reference to a divine model, a man or woman in family life participates in a reality that transcends

normally elapses between a man's marriage and the division of the joint household by his married sons. Yet so long as it does last, the family group has in other respects a corporate jural existence and personality. Cf. Sir. H. S. Maine, *The Early History of Institutions*, London, 1893, p. 78. The Sarakatsan family is a closed system of relationships and a group with a recognized leader. It holds all property in common and controls the productive powers of all its members and the reproductive capacities of its women. In principle all its members are held to be responsible for the action of any other. It is with regard to these characteristics that I describe this group as "corporate".

[5] In the different aspects of her person, the Mother of God provides a model for both the mother and the daughter in the earthly family.

individuality; the harsh and ceaseless struggle to survive, even items of routine such as carrying water or milking sheep, come to possess a validity which is absolute and intrinsic.

The family is, indeed, the centre of the shepherd's world. Inside its limits he finds support, affection, and a sense of moral obligation. With certain qualifications these attitudes are extended to all the relations of the kindred. But outside the family and the kindred a man meets and expects only hostility and suspicion. There are conventions of conduct, but there is no general conscience of obligation to others. From the viewpoint of each individual the community is divided into those who are kinsmen, a man's own people, δικοί, and those who are not kinsmen, that is strangers, ξένοι. There is a third intermediate category of persons, the affines, συμπέθεροι, strangers with whom a man or his kinsman has become related through a contract of marriage. In this community, confidence, trust, and an altruistic concern about another individual's welfare can only exist between kinsmen, and it is only in a kinship relationship that a man is able to abandon the outlook of self-interest which normally guides him in relations outside the family.

It follows that a man looks towards kinsmen for practical support. As we have seen, unrelated families are mutually opposed. The family, with reference to which the individual must act in almost all contexts of behaviour, faces a hostile community. Therefore this support is peculiarly important. Yet, in relation to the community's population of about 4000 souls, the average size of an individual's kindred is relatively small, seldom exceeding 250 men, women, and children, of whom some 160 will be second cousins, a category of relations who are on the margin of kinship. Kinsmen are rare and therefore correspondingly precious. In summer the kindred is scattered over 390 square miles of tortuous and difficult country, and a man does not, generally, live within an hour's walk of more than one-fifth of his kinsmen. This, in part, is the practical importance of kinship connections; they offer a certain freedom of social manoeuvre. Kinsmen established at strategic points through a community, which is numerically not small and geographically very dispersed, are able to offer hospitality and local information which pride and distrust prevent a man asking of unrelated persons. The network of a man's kinship relations provides him with a system of information and intelligence without which he cannot conduct his affairs efficiently or profitably. The price that he should ask for his milk, his wool, and animals for slaughter, the intrigues of others with merchants and officials, which often vitally affect his own affairs, the ever pressing problem of where winter pasture is to be found, this is the kind of information a man exchanges with his kinsman or, more rarely, with a close and trusted affine.

Kinsmen are indispensable in the delicate negotiations of "match-making", προξενια. Before a girl is sought in marriage, very careful inquiries have to be made concerning her virtue, industry, health, and temperament. A kinsman who lives near the girl's family will be in a position to give accurate details, his information will be trusted, and he will treat the affair with the discretion it demands. For marriage involves a contract between two hostile groups, and offence, given or received by either side, is a question of honour and may lead to violence and killing.

I have introduced the notion that the opposed families of this fragmented community are related through competition for prestige. Certainly, it is impossible to miss the competitive flavour of social life outside the home. Men care passionately about their prestige, the prestige of their families and of their kinsmen. Indeed all these reputations are parts of a single complex. And in a paradoxical fashion they depend upon the opinions of enemies. Whenever there is some incident or affray, the news of it travels with remarkable rapidity to all quarters of the Zagori. Within a matter of 48 hours small groups of Sarakatsani throughout the area will be passing judgement on the behaviour of the people involved, as this is evaluated according to the values of the community. They will analyse minutely what a man is reported to have said and done and they will decide whether he was justified in what he did and whether he displayed manliness, ἀνδρισμός, in defending his honour. In such discussions a man's kinsmen will take his side, acting as advocates and apologists for his behaviour. Furthermore, the mere numerical size of a man's kindred is a matter of prestige, because, other things being equal, it means that he is a man who, wherever he goes, will be taken notice of, assisted and well informed. In discussing kinship the Sarakatsani often say, "Nobody takes account of a man without kinsmen." They use, in this context, a word, λογαριάζω, which expresses both the idea of esteeming another man and of being obliged to take him into consideration before embarking on some course of action.

Consultation between trusted kinsmen about their various affairs is continual. The enterprise itself may be of almost any kind, the marriage of a son or daughter, a decision whether or not to sell sheep to raise money for the payment of a debt, or the acceptance or non-acceptance of an offer of winter pasture. Similarly, when a man is involved in some crisis, a fight with another shepherd, a marriage brawl, or a difficult court case, kinsmen come to him of their own accord with advice and criticism. In this way a man learns which courses of action will enjoy the moral support of his kin and which will not. For a man loses prestige if his kinsman acts wrongly. Therefore, he will always exhort his kinsman to an honourable course of action and dissuade him from any easy road of lesser resistance. Conversely, the principal actor is influenced by the fear of losing the support of his kinsmen, as he may do if he takes decisions which lose him prestige. His kinsmen can then only protect their own prestige by isolating themselves to a greater or lesser degree from social contact with him. Consequently this consultation between kinsmen is not only to a man's advantage in terms of his own prestige, but it is also a subtle sanction for right ways of acting in the community as a whole.

In economic matters, too, a shepherd looks to his kinsmen for help and co-operation. Quite apart from the deep distrust which divides unrelated persons, shame prevents a man from seeking assistance outside the kindred, since this would be a tacit admission that he had been rejected by his own kinsmen. Thus sentiment and convention lead in the same direction. A shepherd lives from one monetary crisis to another. When he needs a small money loan for an operation fee at a Jannina hospital or for the expenses of a wedding, he is often unable to persuade a merchant to grant him an additional advance; but he seldom fails to raise it from his kinsmen if they have the money in hand. Economic co-operation may take other forms. The condition of the family's flocks is not only the basis of its physical existence but the source of pride and prestige. A man fears to meet the appraising eyes of another if his animals are in a meagre and spindle-shanked condition. But grazing, both in the Zagori and in the winter pastures, varies considerably from place to place and from year to year. Therefore, if a kinsman has some grass which is good for fattening lambs or restoring weakened ewes, a man may ask him to take some of his weaker animals which are in difficulties. For this service he will have to pay, but he would not in any circumstances trust his sheep to the care of an unrelated man.

The most intimate form of economic association between kinsmen occurs where a number of autonomous but related families join together for the co-management of their flocks and, in particular, to discover and negotiate for winter pastures, a problem whose solution requires that the group should reach an understanding, whether direct or through an intermediary, with persons of influence in villages and government departments. The leader of such a "company" is known as the Tselingas, ὁ τσέλιγγας. In a majority of cases the nucleus of the group he leads is what may be termed a simple fraternal association, that is a number of married brothers with families, each of whom maintains his own household, his own purse, and has his own animals clearly marked. But such groups often include uncles, nephews, brothers-in-law, paternal and maternal cousins, and it would be possible to produce many examples of different combinations of kinsmen and affinal relatives. At this point, it is sufficient to stress that they are founded upon ties of kinship and marriage, that they are voluntary and often unstable associations in which each family retains its own independent social personality, its own budget, and its own animals.

Thus kinsmen give each other moral and practical support in facing a hostile and competitive world where one man delights openly and with little inhibition in the misfortunes of another. A man co-operates with his kinsmen because he trusts them. There is a sense of security within the kindred which is significantly absent outside its limits. One may not steal from a kinsman's flock, nor cheat him in monetary settlements, nor seduce his sister, nor gossip about his private affairs. But it is necessary to stress that there are definite limits on what may be expected from kinsmen. When honour demands a vengeance killing, kinsmen outside the family will lend moral support but none of them is obliged to pull the trigger or thrust home the knife. Again, money may be loaned between kinsmen but repayment after a reasonable interval is expected, and in almost all cases is met, even where it leads to the sale of sheep. It amounts to this, that a man will help his kinsman and indeed is morally obliged to do so, so long as this assistance does not conflict with the interests of his own family.

II

The kindred of the Sarakatsani has three important formal characteristics. It is bilateral, the limits of its extension are precisely defined, and within these limits a man may not marry.

There is a sense in which almost all kinship systems may be described as bilateral, or to speak more accurately, filiation is normally bilateral and complementary.[6] But in describing the Sarakatsan kindred as bilateral it is my intention also to suggest a certain, though not exact, symmetry in the relations of a man

[6] Meyer Fortes, Structure of unilineal descent groups, *Amer. Anthrop.* **55**, (1953), 33. A much earlier recognition of the same facts is to be found in J R. Swanton, Social organisation of American tribes, *Amer. Anthrop.* **7**, 1905, 663 ff.

to the family of origin[7] of his father on the one hand, and to the family of origin of his mother on the other; and to indicate further that, in principle, a man has equivalent confidence in, and similar rights over and obligations towards, more distant collateral kinsmen such as first or second cousins, whether the relationships with these persons are traced through the father or through the mother.[8] There is always a very strong moral obligation to assist any collateral kinsman. For instance, it often happens at weddings that brawls develop between unrelated guests. Insults and curses are thrown back and forth, blows are exchanged and on occasion knives are drawn. The pattern of these events is always the same. A man is insulted, or imagines that he has been insulted, by another. At once all the relatives of either man range themselves alongside their kinsman; and those who are unrelated to either party, as well as others embarrassed by an equal allegiance to both sides, throw themselves between the two antagonists. But the paternal or maternal origin of the relationship neither increases nor diminishes the obligation to support a kinsman in this or any other situation.

Property and prestige are passed from one generation to the next according to customary rules of inheritance in the one case, and canons of popular judgement in the other, which reflect the symmetry of an individual's relations to the families of origin of his father and mother. Property is itself an element in prestige,

[7] This is Lloyd Warner's familiar distinction between the family of orientation and the family of procreation. I prefer the terms, "origin" and "marriage"; in the family of origin the individual is a child and a sibling, in the family of marriage a spouse and a parent.

[8] The bilateral form of the kindred is plainly reflected in the terminology. The word σόϊ, kindred, applies, of course, to both maternal and paternal relations; and the words for kinsman συγγενής and relationship συγγένεια are both used in the same way. The terms which are used to describe kinship relationship outside the family do not differentiate between maternal and paternal kinsmen. Thus the term θεῖος, uncle, is used for both mother's brother and father's brother as well as for all male first cousins of both parents whether these are connected through male or female links. The same may be said about the other terms for παππούλης, grandfather, βάβω grandmother, θεία aunt, ἐξάδερφος, ἐξαδέρφη, male and female cousin, ἀνεψιός, ἀνεψιά nephew and niece and ἐγγόνι, ἐγγονή, grandchild, grand-daughter.

while wealth without prestige loses its significance. Individual and family reputation, as I have already indicated, is a self-evident value; without it social life has no meaning. This prestige is inherited both from the father's family and the mother's. It is true that the prestige of paternal connections is greater; but the quality of the mother's family of origin is also critical, for criticism of the mother, who contributes important moral qualities to the characters of her children, is a peculiarly effective method of denigrating a family. The individual, of course, may increase or diminish his reputation by his own acts but it is on the basis of a reputation inherited from both parents that he at first faces the judgements of the community. And if this inherited reputation is unsatisfactory, it will be exceedingly difficult for the individual by his own efforts to redeem it. It is partly for these reasons that the choice of a wife is a matter which is approached with delicacy and deliberation. Many personal qualities of a prospective bride are taken into consideration but invariably the crucial question to be debated is the quality and prestige of the girl's family and close kin. The Sarakatsani use a Turkish word, νταμάρι of which the primary meaning is a vein, to indicate the general quality of a man's immediate maternal and paternal ancestors.[9] And if either the bride or the bridegroom is from a family of lower prestige than the other, it is said that he (or she) "destroys" the νταμάρι of the other partner. For it is thought that in the family which results from a marriage both partners have contributed their blood "to make one blood" which is unique and on whose purity the prestige and honour of the new family depends.

In a similar manner both husband and wife contribute wealth to the elementary family which they establish. The corporate property of a family is a common stock of animals, money, and goods from which sons and daughters must be endowed. Daughters receive their portion as dowry at the moment of marriage, but the married sons normally continue to live in an extended family group where family wealth is still held in common. In the eventual partition of this joint household and its property, which is delayed

[9] The more general meaning of νταμάρι in modern Greek is stone quarry.

until all the daughters have been married, and generally occurs
5–10 years after the marriage of the eldest son, equal shares of
stock and other assets are received by each son; but in the case
of the youngest son an extra half-share is provided for the maintenance of each surviving parent who by custom remains in the
household of this son. When an elementary family leaves the joint
household of married brothers, the husband's family has probably contributed about 100 sheep and goats and one or two mules
while the wife's family has supplied in the form of her dowry,
προικιό, the furnishings of the hut and sufficient clothes and
finery for the bride to wear or display for a period of 10 years or
more. The value of such a dowry is about £150, or the equivalent
of 50 sheep. Since 1945, however, the practice has grown up of
demanding from the bride's family about forty sheep or their
equivalent in gold sovereigns in addition to the traditional dowry.
Thus, approximately under the traditional convention, and
more rigorously today, there exists a certain balance between the
wealth that passes into a new family from the husband's family of
origin and that which is contributed by the wife's family of origin.
It would be wrong to think of the dowry merely as a payment
made by a bride's family to obtain a husband for her. Certainly
there have been cases where girls who had physical or moral
deficiencies, have had to pay large dowries to get any kind of
husband at all. It is also true that calculations of family prestige
are concerned in the size of the dowry. But the implicit purpose of
the dowry is to complement the wealth with which the new family
is, or will be, endowed by the husband's family. In this sense the
handing over of the dowry is the first act of socially regulated
co-operation between two previously unrelated and therefore hostile families. The two parties to the marriage contract co-operate
to establish a new group. Each side contributes one of its members
and a certain amount of property. And, under the traditional
custom at least, the contribution of each side appropriately reflects
the complementary activities of the two partners. The husband
provides the animals, the wife the furnishings of the hut. And this
bilateral endowment of a new family with property from both

families of origin is also observed in the limiting case where a man has no sons and marries his youngest girl to a bridegroom who is willing to live in his father-in-law's home. In this instance it is the bridegroom who contributes wealth at the moment of marriage, bringing with him his share in the flocks of his family of birth, while the property of the wife's family of origin, which may be considerable, does not formally come under the control of the new family until the wife's father has retired from active work.

Just as the elements of wealth and prestige are inherited through both the mother and the father, so the Sarakatsani also believe that a child inherits the elements of its moral character from both parents, although, since the important moral qualities in this community are sex-linked, sons are thought to form their moral character essentially after the pattern of their fathers, especially with reference to manliness, while daughters particularly inherit those qualities of the mother which affect their sense of sexual shame. Nevertheless the pattern of character and behaviour, which a son partly inherits and partly learns from his father, may be modified by elements which he receives from his mother; and in the same way a girl may inherit some character traits from her father. Sometimes facets of character which are passed from or through the parent of opposite sex may be referred to the individual's χουΐ. This is an aspect of personality to which one may attribute those idiosyncratic actions and attitudes which are in some way unusual or even deviant. The Sarakatsani insist that this is as likely to be inherited from one side of the family as from the other. John Charis tears his shirts to shreds when he dances at weddings. This odd behaviour is not approved, but in terms of χουΐ it may, at least, be explained; and it is remembered that his mother's brother, although he did not tear his shirts, used to waste his substance in another way by gambling at cards for high stakes which he could not afford.

It is clear, then, that the elements of wealth, prestige, and character pass into a family from both the families which enter into the original betrothal contract. This not only reflects the bilateral and symmetrical form of the kindred but in some measure helps to maintain it. For, if a man has contracted a judicious marriage with a girl from a family of at least equivalent prestige, the children will be anxious to associate with their matrilateral kin. On the other hand, it is noticeable that where a man has married into a family of lower prestige than his own (that is, where prestige has not been equally inherited from both sides), his children tend to evade obligations to their mother's kinsmen while they carefully cultivate kinsmen of the father. Similarly, if a wife brings a substantial dowry (that is, where a newly established family is equally endowed with wealth from both sides), the husband is obliged to be especially helpful to the family and kinsmen of his wife, and this leads to close relations between his children and their maternal cousins.

The bilateral structure of the kindred implies, of course, that this association of kinsmen is not a corporate group. Its definition must always be relative to a particlar group of siblings.[10] At a wedding, when representatives of all sections of the bridegroom's kindred gather round him in support against the kindred of the bride, the illusion is created that two solidary corporate groups of kinsmen are involved. But in fact they are united only in the particular context of the wedding and by reason of each individual's personal kinship relation to the bridegroom. Indeed since any particular kindred comprises descendants of four pairs of unrelated great grandparents, only the sibling group which is central to this kindred is related to all its members.[11] It is only through the marriages of their own grandparents and parents

[10] This has long been recognized. Vide Bertha Phillpotts, *Kindred and Clan*, Cambridge, 1913, p. 3, 275. However, it should be clear that corporate associations of kinsmen may exist in this kind of community. But other criteria will be involved, not merely kinship relationship.

[11] Any two kinsmen other than siblings have kindreds which to a greater or lesser degree overlap. A man may find himself in a situation where two men, both related to him but unrelated to one another, are in some form of conflict in which both appeal to him for support. In this predicament the only solution is to remain neutral, since it would be sinful to act against a kinsman except under great provocation. But generally such a situation extends rather than restricts the range of kinship obligations; towards a person who, although not a kinsman himself, is closely related to a kinsman, a man ought to act with more consideration and less hostility than is usual between men who are unrelated.

that a man and his siblings are related to the four component groups of collaterals in his kindred. Kindred relations are personal not corporate relations. And the Sarakatsan kindred in no way acts as a property-holding group since, besides the fact that it is relative to a particular sibling group, it has no continuity from generation to generation.

In drawing attention to this bilateral and symmetrical form of the kindred I have been careful to avoid speaking of bilateral descent. In anthropological writings principles of descent normally refer to rules which determine membership in corporate lineal descent groups. Such groups are bodies of kinsmen whose members may be recruited through filiation to a line of descent exclusively through males (patrilineal), or exclusively through females (matrilineal).[12] Descent from a common ancestor or group of ancestors defines membership in the group and identifies the interest of its members, which may concern political and ritual rights and obligations as well as inheritance and succession. It is possible to talk of a corporate bilateral descent group where membership depends upon filiation through both parents but in such an instance the group would have to practise obligatory endogamous marriage. But the Sarakatsan kindred is not an endogamous group. Corporate descent groups imply a principle of perpetual succession, a feature which the kindred entirely lacks; and they also imply that individuals have categorical rights and obligations outside the elementary or extended family, whereas in the Sarakatsan kindred this is not so. Not descent, but filiation of a man or woman to his or her family of origin is the factor which determines status, categorical rights and obligations, and membership in the family group, which is the only solidary kin grouping in this system of kinship and marriage. Hence in a description of the Sarakatsan kindred it seems preferable not to speak, even loosely, of any principle of descent.[13]

[12] There are other possibilities viz. bilineal or dual descent, parallel descent, and alternating descent.

[13] In some general remarks about the concept of descent in bilateral systems Professor Firth has adopted a similar viewpoint. Raymond Firth (Ed.), *Two*

It is true that the kindred of any man includes the descendants of four pairs of great grandparents. It is, therefore, possible to represent the kindred diagrammatically as four interlocking pyramids of cognatic descent. But this kind of abstraction bears no relation to the mental image which a Sarakatsanos forms of his kindred, in which relations are conceived in terms of extension from the family of origin, not descent from a common ancestor. There is mutual affection and moral obligation between my second cousin and myself because my grandparent and his grandparent were siblings rather than because we are both descendants of common great grandparents. I prefer, then, to speak of equivalent bilateral extension, for this describes precisely the constitution of the kindred. The qualification of bilateral extension by the notion of equivalence is intended to underline both the fact that collateral kinsmen are recognized to the degree of second cousin on either side of the family, and also the equipotential character of matrilateral and patrilateral relationships.

The second formal characteristic of the kindred is the definition of its limits, which, in this case, are drawn in a man's own generation at the collateral degree of second cousin, a span of collateral kinship which is calculated by recognizing as kinsmen the descendants of his four grandparents and their siblings. Thereafter, as we have seen, the recognition of collaterals is increasingly restricted in descendant generations. This limitation, considered together with equivalent bilateral extension, leads to a simple process within the kindred whereby the range of collateral relationship which a child may inherit from either parent is severely delimited. The second cousins of his parent are not, in a formal sense, a man's kinsmen and, therefore, he may marry a kinswoman of this degree. In other words, the children of a marriage throw away, as it were, three quarters or more[14] of those kinsmen

---

Studies of Kinship in London, London, 1956, p. 15. Cf. also W. H. R. Rivers, *Social Organisation*, London, 1924, p. 86, and G. P. Murdock, *Social Structure*, New York, 1949, p. 15.

[14] The exact size of this fraction depends upon the size of the various sibling groups in the kindreds.

who are recognized collateral relations of the parents. The father, when he identifies himself with the interests of his own children, at once creates a certain kinship distance between himself and any one of his own siblings, the kindred of whose children only partly coincides with the kindred of his own children. Since the descendants of the father's second cousins are no longer kinsmen of his children, they also cease to be significant for him and are not recognized as kinsmen; similarly in the case of the grandchildren of first cousins, and the great grandchildren of siblings. The same considerations apply in the case of the mother and her collateral kin. With the passage of time parents turn their loyalty and interest from the collateral kinsmen of their own generation to their direct descendants and to only those collateral descendants who remain relevant for their own descendants; these are necessarily fewer in each descendant generation.

From one point of view a man's kinsmen are the descendants of the four sibling groups of his two grandfathers and two grandmothers. Sarakatsan kinship finds its source in the unity of the sibling group born and nurtured within a legitimate family. Collateral kinsmen see themselves as the descendants of such a group and it is this sentiment which provides the basis of the personal moral solidarity with a kinsman. Thus the Greek word for cousins, ,ἐξάδερφοι means literally "from brothers". But Sarakatsani are also conscious that it is through marriages in which the interests of siblings or cousins cannot be mutually identified that kinsmen become separated. For a man is related more closely to a particular kinsman than to the kinsman's child; thus, with the close identification of a father's interests with those of his children and the exclusive concentration of categorical obligations in the family of marriage, the marriages of collaterals inevitably lead to change and a measure of disintegration in the individual's kindred. In a phrase, marriage joins strangers while it separates those who are already kinsmen. The consequences for the children and grandchildren of siblings are that a man has approximately only half his kindred in common with his first cousin and only one quarter in common with his second cousin. It shows with what rapidity in this kinship system the common interests of the descendants of a sibling group disappear. With the passage of only three generations these descendants are formally unrelated and there is no restriction upon the marriage of third cousins. A man says of this third cousin, "The kindred has left the house", *Βγῆκε τὸ σόϊ ἀπὸ τὸ σπίτι.*

The third formal characteristic of the kindred is that a man may not marry within its limits. This means that the two families who form a marriage alliance are unrelated[15] and that the kindred of the groom will not considerably overlap with the kindred of the bride although they may claim some kinsmen in common. A kindred in which maternal and paternal kinsmen normally form mutually exclusive categories naturally has a wider span than a kindred in which these categories overlap; and to that extent, the marriage prohibition is consistent with the need to have many kinsmen in many places.

We have seen that the principle of equivalent bilateral extension together with the defined limits of the kindred acts over a period of time to force collaterals apart. A second consequence of the prohibition on marriage in the kindred is that it makes it impossible to counteract this process by confirming in a later generation a relationship which has already been established. Thus the practice of either first or second cousin marriage such as is reported from Spain by Pitt-Rivers,[16] where it is favoured as a means of conserving property within the family, is not possible amongst the Sarakatsani. This leads to a third consequence of the marriage prohibition. It forces a man who wishes to marry off his son or daughter to face, as it were, outwards from his kindred towards the total community. Thus while non-kinsmen are rivals and even enemies, they are also in a sense potential affines. This is peculiarly significant in a community where men unrelated by kinship are associated mainly through institutionalized forms of hostility and rivalry. A contract of marriage is normally the only instrument which may bring two unrelated families into

[15] Except in the cases of marriage between third cousins.
[16] J. A. Pitt-Rivers, *The People of the Sierra*, London, 1954, pp. 103–6.

positive association and co-operation. Indeed, a sense of the community's endogamy is an important element in their consciousness of being a community at all. Sarakatsani, when they wish to stress their solidarity in opposition to villagers or other outsiders, often claim that, if full records of their marriages had been preserved through the generations, it would be clear that they are all kinsmen, although they are quick to add the qualification that such kinship has long ago "left the house". The same principles of kinship extension and marriage prohibition which from the viewpoint of the individual tend towards the loosening of his relations with collaterals within the kindred, at the same time lead to a measure of cohesion within the community considered as a system of actual and potential kinship relations. Kin and non-kin, actual relations and potential relations are opposed, but also complementary categories.

Of these three formal features of the Sarakatsan kindred the dominant is, without doubt, equivalent bilateral extension. The distinctive consequence of this principle is that the only possible corporate group based upon kinship alone which can exist in such a system over a period of time as long as a generation is the elementary family. For since there is no unilineal principle of descent grouping, there can be no corporate kinship group of higher order, which either includes the elementary family, or cuts across it by including some of its members and excluding others. Nor are there non-unilineal corporate kin groups in which membership is based on optional or alternate filiation or on the choice of residence after marriage.[17] Such arrangements would conflict with the symmetrical affiliation of Sarakatsani to all kinsmen through all lines and the equivalence of obligation to all kinsmen of the same degree. Although the association of an elementary family, for the first five to ten years of its existence, with the husband's extended family of origin may

[17] For a review of non-unilineal "descent" groups, *vide* William Davenport, Nonunilinear descent and descent groups, *Amer. Anthrop.* **61**, (1959), 557–72. Cf. also J. D. Freeman, The family system of the Iban of Borneo, article in *Cambridge Papers in Social Anthropology* No. 1, Cambridge, 1958.

obscure the situation, the newly established elementary family is influenced by both the families of origin of the husband and wife.

An interesting recognition of this occurs on the very day of marriage when in other respects the bride's family feel that they have been defeated and plundered. The Greek Orthodox marriage service is in two parts, the first being the rite of betrothal, ἀρραβῶνας, the second the rite of "Crowning", στεφάνωσις; and normally they are celebrated in church as one ceremony. The Sarakatsani, however, bring a priest to the huts of the bride's family to perform the religious betrothal ceremony which the shepherds name "the half wedding", ὁ μισὸς γάμος, and consider to be equal in importance to the office of "Crowning". The bride's kinsmen will not surrender her to the groom's retinue until this ceremony is performed and equally the marriage ceremony cannot be completed until the bride is brought to the home of the bridegroom. In effect each side celebrates half the marriage service.

This double attraction is eventually resolved by the new family's relative emancipation from both the old families. Once the young family has parted from the husband's extended family of origin, it stands on its own without categorical rights over, or obligations towards, other related elementary families. It neither gives nor receives unconditional support of the kind that involves physical violence or economic assistance. In these important respects the family, even within the kindreds of its members, is, in a sense, isolated.

This isolation of the elementary family is accurately reflected by the kinship terminology, although in this respect it does not differ from the general form of European kinship terminologies. It is significant that the terms for the kinship personalities in a man's elementary families of origin and marriage, that is, in his inner circle of kinship, may not be extended to more distant kinsmen as is the case in many societies with systems of unilineal descent. The family, οἰκογένεια, which may refer, according to context, to either or both elementary families in which the individual has or had corporate membership, and to any surviving grandparents, is part of the kindred, yet at the same time is clearly distinguished from it. In its widest connotation the "family" is, of course, a class of relations and not a residential group. The principles which essentially relate members of the family are parental obligation and filiation while the kindred is based on collateral extension. Between these two classes of kinsmen siblings are the bridge, since at the same time they are directly descended from the same parents and grandparents and occupy, before marriage, a socially equivalent status, but become, after their marriages, the points of departure of distinct collateral lines of descent.

At the beginning of this essay I described the multiform character of the family. It is a domestic group, an economic and property-owning unit, a quasi-political association, a religious communion, and so on. It is now evident that the elementary family group is the only stable solidary unit associated with the kindred and that while it enjoys important support from collateral kinsmen, it is also, in a sense, isolated from them. The immense importance, then, of this social group on the one hand, and its lack of continuity through time on the other, mean that the institutionalized arrangements for its establishment or dissolution, for the transference of categorical rights and obligations from an old family to a new, are of critical importance. Underlying the nature of these arrangements is the simple fact that each individual during some part of his lifetime is almost always the member of two families: one of origin, the other of marriage.[18] A man is a son and brother in one family, a father and husband in the other; a woman is a daughter and sister in the family of origin, a mother and wife in the family of marriage. It is obviously important that the rights and duties of these different roles, when played by the same individual, should not conflict. This is a problem for all systems of kinship but it is especially acute in this community because of all the individual's significant rights and obligations

[18] An individual may have membership in a third family; for the parents, after the father's retirement, normally live as members of the family of marriage of their youngest son.

inhere in the family and in no other group. The individual passes from his first family to his second through marriage. In the case of the woman the solution of the problem of conflicting roles is radical; she leaves the home of her father, who ceases to have any rights over her except the residual right of resuming his power over her if she becomes a widow before the birth of children. The protection of her honour is no longer the concern of her brothers, and her working services now belong exclusively to the husband's family. When later she pays one of her rare visits to her original home, she may not spin even a handful of her mother's wool. The husband does not shed the categorical obligations of his roles as son and sibling quite so rapidly, though it is significant that after his marriage and even before the birth of his children he is unlikely to undertake a vengeance killing for a murdered brother or a dishonoured sister. Eventually, after 5–10 years, but often sooner, he parts from the extended family and from all his remaining categorical rights and obligations as son and brother.

Thus siblings before their marriages are a unity for a person outside the group. If he injures or insults any member of the group, he attacks the whole group, every male member of which is under equal obligation to retaliate. At this stage siblings of the same sex are socially equivalent as to status, there is an almost complete identity of interest, and their mutual relations are governed by a consciousness of their common filiation to the same parents. After the marriage of the brothers and sisters of a sibling group the situation entirely changes. They no longer form a unity against the outsider nor are they socially equivalent; they have become differentiated by their marriages and young families. Their interests are not identified because each new family has its own interests, and siblings both in form and effect are now merely collaterals. There is a growing tendency to isolation from all collateral lines, not only those of the individual's own siblings. The supreme value in a man's life now becomes the economic welfare and social prestige of his children. He is, therefore, not always free to give unreserved and unthinking aid to his brothers and cousins as he used to do. Moreover, he is now forced, also for the sake of his children, who derive the half of their kindred through their mother, to consolidate his relationship with his affines. This he can only do by weakening to some degree the previously exclusive solidary relations between himself and his brothers and sisters.

Always implicit in Sarakatsan kinship relations is the interplay of the two notions of sibling solidarity and parental obligation. Parental obligation, of course, is established through legitimate marriage and the resulting conjugal relationship, but the very strength of the latter relation is founded on the sacred character of parental love and duty. In the elementary family the two principles of sibling solidarity and parental obligation are complementary and together guide its members in their duties and exclusive affections. But in the relations of married siblings and collaterals the two principles are opposed, sibling solidarity being the source and justification of relationship and moral obligation between collaterals, while parental obligation is the principle which, within the limits of a bilateral kindred, isolates the family from other kinsmen and their families. At the risk of some repetition, and in summary form, the critical aspects of these relationships are: (1) before marriage siblings are bound to one another by categorical obligations; (2) after marriage, the purpose of which is the begetting of children, this nexus is gradually dissolved; (3) after marriage the supreme value in a man's life becomes the welfare of his children; (4) parenthood forces a man for the sake of his children to cultivate his affines; this weakens to some extent the relationship with his siblings; (5) brothers after living together for a few years after marriage as a united extended family divide the common flock and the common household; after partition brothers generally continue to co-operate in the management of their sheep, but on a basis of strict accountancy; (6) collateral kinship is conceived by the Sarakatsani themselves as an extension from the family of origin which relates kinsmen to an original pair of siblings; thus collaterals see themselves as united by derivation from a once united sibling group but divided as a result of the marriages contracted by the members of that group and their children.

I must now introduce a consideration which to some small extent qualifies the symmetry which I have claimed to be a feature of the bilateral kindred. The absence of a unilineal principle of descent grouping does not prevent the Sarakatsani from having a very strong sentimental interest in their patriline and a formal preference for those kinsmen who are related through the father, especially those who bear the same name. The cousins with whom a man often shares his early childhood years in an extended family are agnatic cousins. And while the obligation to carry out blood vengeance does not extend beyond the elementary family, it is significant that when a man voluntarily avenges a kinsman beyond this narrow circle it is almost always an agnatic first cousin. Yet it must be said again that outside the elementary family moral obligations to kinsmen of the same collateral degree are the same however the relationship is mediated and the man, who states categorically that "we prefer relatives through the father", may name a maternal cousin as his most trusted friend.

When a Sarakatsanos talks loosely of his "fathers and fore-fathers", he is probably thinking of a vague body of ancestors in the agnatic line. But in fact a man seldom knows very much about his direct ancestors in any line beyond the generation of his grand-parents unless they have some claim to particular fame or infamy. Ascendant kinsmen are only relevant as individual personalities to the extent that they affect the inheritance of physical and moral attributes and social prestige. And it is the families of origin of the man's parents, presided over by his four grandparents, which essentially affect his social standing. The lines of descent from the two pairs of grandparents are the kinship co-ordinates, as it were, which intersect and define the unique position of a group of siblings within the community. Naturally the preference for the kinsmen of the father implies that in this evaluation the qualities of paternal kin have more weight, but this is not to be confused with the presence of a patrilineal descent principle.

A man is more interested in his sons than in his daughters simply because they are males and not because they are specifically agnatic links ensuring continuity in an exclusively agnatic descent line. It is important to a man to beget male children because in so doing he accentuates his own masculinity, extended in time. A man wants sons "so that his name will be heard", νὰ ἀκούεται τ' ὄνομά του, not simply the surname which is inherited patrilineally, but for it to be said that this is George Carvounis son of John Carvounis. Sons bring prestige, daughters do not. When the husband enters the hut for the first time after the birth of a daughter his wife turns her head away and lowers her eyes in shame.

This formal preference for the father's kinsmen is consistent with, and indeed is, in the area of kinship, a reflection of the greater value placed upon the male sex. This is a fundamental value of Greek culture, whose essential masculinity can be re-marked at all stages in its development from Homeric times until the present day. Thus, in the Sarakatsan community it is the behaviour of the ideal man that provides the dominant value patterns of manliness, honour, and pride. The sexes divide the community into opposite yet complementary categories, categories which are moral as well as biological. The behaviour which is considered right for the male and female stereotypes is at many points antithetical, and relations between the sexes are hostile although this hostility cannot generally be given overt expression. The male sex is held to be unambiguously superior not only in power but also in worth to the female, to which the stigma of original sin is closely attached. The female is a constant threat to the honour and integrity of the male, and must be disciplined and dominated. In the absence, therefore, of a unilineal descent principle, it is reasonable to suppose that these attitudes and beliefs of the Sarakatsani concerning the relation of the sexes are significantly connected with the preference for paternal kinsmen.

Patrilocal marriage fits consistently into the pattern of these preferences. A man brings his bride into the household of his father or, if he has retired, into the household of his elder brother. The extended family of origin remains a single corporate unit until such time as one or more of the brothers decide to contract out, claiming then, as is their inalienable right, their equal shares in the flock. A brother begins to press for partition precisely when the claims of his children for special attention begin to be felt. Normally this occurs when the eldest child of the second son in a family is about 5 years old.

But the presence of extended families needs to be explained on other grounds than a preference for paternal kinsmen. Elsewhere in the Greek world, where masculine values and preference for paternal kin are equally strong, the residential pattern is often neolocal, that is to say the newly married couple set up house in a home of their own, independent of either family of origin. Such arrangements are, of course, exactly those we might expect to find associated with a bilateral kindred. Amongst the Sarakatsani there seem to be three important reasons why separation does not take place immediately after marriage. Firstly there is the solidarity of the elementary family of origin built up over a period of about 25 years of mutual devotion and mutual responsibility in face of a hostile and critical world. It is difficult to describe adequately the quality of this solidarity, except perhaps to say that even by the standards of Greek family life it is remarkable—proof against appalling adversities and unyielding to the weaknesses of individuals. Secondly, the marriage ceremony does not set the seal upon an already established relationship, it only creates the necessary legal and religious conditions for its inception. This is a pertinent fact in a community where, although a man may sometimes have seen his bride before the marriage day, it is most unlikely that he has ever spoken to her. It requires the passage of time and the birth of children before it can be said in any real sense that an elementary family has been founded. The third reason introduces an economic factor. The Sarakatsan technique of grazing sheep demands for optimum efficiency the co-operation of certainly not fewer than four adult males. An undivided household means an undivided flock, and generally sufficient shepherds to look after it. It is true that after partition brothers normally continue to run their sheep together, but sheep must then be branded, accounts kept, and in different ways the possibility of friction between the associated brothers is greater than when the flock is undivided.

These, then, are the formal characteristics of the Sarakatsan kindred. Naturally the consequent system of personal relations has various implications beyond the field of kinship behaviour. Two of these I believe to be peculiarly characteristic of Greek society.

As we have seen, the community from the viewpoint of each individual is divided into kinsmen and non-kinsmen, "own people" and "strangers". The division is unequivocal; kinsmen inspire loyalty and obligation, strangers distrust and moral indifference. Yet within the category of kinsmen itself the only stable solidary group is the family. Plainly, the nature of the physical and social environment is such that it forces so small a group, however it may value the ideal of autarky, to cultivate both intensively and extensively the support of kinsmen and affines. But for reasons inherent in the structure of the kindred, which it has been my purpose in this essay to analyse, this support is contingent upon a kinsman's prior commitments to his own family. Thus the family emerges as a social isolate in two associated respects. In the first case, families unrelated by kinship admit virtually no moral obligation towards one another; in the second, families related by kinship nevertheless owe only conditional services. In a community where social relations are marked by such radical discontinuities it follows that the primary values are necessarily particularistic. The mutual opposition of family groups is expressed through the concept of honour with its connotations of exclusiveness, not the morality of universal values such as honesty or fair dealing. Christian virtues such as humility, meekness, and self-effacement suggest only weakness; whereas strength is simulated better by the heroic attitudes of self-assertion, pride, and even arrogance. And strength, individual prepotence, is what each man needs to be an effective protagonist for his family, and the protector of its public reputation and honour against the calumnies of those who are also its judges.

These considerations also affect the external relations of the Sarakatsan community. The local community of shepherds exists within the framework of the Greek state and must accommodate itself to a system of law and administrative regulation. It is, however, a community existing on the margin of subsistence. Any administrative action may disturb the precarious balance of the shepherd economy or even threaten the existence of the community, particularly when it is related to land usage or distribution. With the progressive restriction of the areas of winter grazing the dependence of the Sarakatsani on the agricultural policy of the government and the mercy of its administrators becomes greater each year.

The more explicit this external threat to the community the more necessary it is for the Sarakatsani to establish a form of relationship with these authorities through which they have some hope of introducing flexibility, at least, into government action when it concerns their affairs. They cannot themselves approach the senior officials who refuse to delegate the power of decision to their subordinates even in relatively unimportant matters. For these men are imbued with values which, if they differ considerably in content from those of the shepherd, nevertheless share their competitive form. They validate their position in the service through the display of severity and pride, and by the marking of social distance between rulers and ruled; not by implementing any ethic of public service, or through the treatment of each case upon its merits. Some intermediary, then, must be found to bridge this absence of moral obligation. The persons who fill this role are people who, on the one hand, by occupation or profession, have Sarakatsan clients, and, on the other, are able to number higher civil servants amongst their friends in the local provincial élite. These may be merchants, doctors, and particularly lawyers. The shepherd pledges not only his professional or commercial custom to the patron, but also his political and social support; in return the patron protects his client, so far as he is able, in all his affairs and particularly by bringing any case of hardship to the notice of a friend in the Government service who is able to deal with it. The civil servant may effect this, not because he is impressed by the justice of the shepherd's grievance, but because the political support which the shepherd's patron is able to command makes him a person of some importance on the political scene able to affect the civil servant's promotion or posting; or more simply because the patron is a friend who does more strictly professional favours for the official or for his kinsmen and friends. The more clients the patron has, the greater, of course, his political influence and social prestige; and the more effective the protection he is able to offer. This in paradigmatic form is the structure of patronage that offers the Sarakatsani a measure of protection against uncomprehending administrators and regulations which were framed without consideration or knowledge of the local difficulties of particular communities.

The form and function of these patronage obligations, however, are related to the categorical quality of the individual's commitment to the family, and to the reciprocal hostility and distrust between families unrelated by kinship or marriage. There are few circumstances where his own wishes, or public opinion, allow a Sarakatsanos to honour an obligation outside the family at the expense of an obligation within it. It follows that the protection and prestige which a man enjoys because he has a powerful patron is not to be shared with other unrelated men who envy him this advantage; although it may be extended vicariously to kinsmen and affines, since their dependence is a mark of strength, not weakness. But, in general, to share an advantage is to lose it.

Furthermore the shepherd believes that his world is a closed universe of limited resources. There is not enough wealth, and particularly not enough grazing land, for everybody. Consequently, if one family meets with disaster, it must necessarily benefit the others. Partly for this reason, and partly because the shepherd believes that the official also has a primary obligation to his service, his family, and himself, which prevents him from acting for reasons other than personal benefit or obligation, he has no confidence that concessions are to be gained on a wide front for the whole community, but only as particular dispensations to favoured families. In practice, then, the form of these patron-client relationships associates individual families with particular patrons, and through them with particular officials in the Government service.

It is significant that the group which seeks the patronage connection is the individual family and not the community. In this way the community is related piecemeal with the wider society along lines of personal obligation, and not through membership of a large corporate group capable of attempting an infinitely more effective resistance to the authority of the state. Consequently the structure of patronage is an important means of integrating the Sarakatsan community (and *mutatis mutandis* the village community) into the wider community of Greek society. Within limits, the greater the interference of direct administration into the affairs of the local community, the more pressing is the need for individual protection, and the greater the proliferation of these forms of relationship which are partly influenced by, and further accentuate, the exclusive values of the family.

A Study of French Canadian Kinship*

RALPH PIDDINGTON

1. INTRODUCTION

Anthropologists and comparative sociologists have often been struck by the differences which exist between systems of kinship in "modern" or "civilized" societies and those found in societies which we call "primitive". The most striking contrast concerns the position of the individual family which in modern societies has often been taken to be the only significant socio-economic grouping based on kinship, whereas in primitive societies it is usually integrated with wider groupings of kinsfolk such as lineage, clan, or extended family. And in regard to modern societies a contrast has often been drawn between kinship in rural and in urban communities. It has been widely held that the modern phenomena of urbanization, migration, and industrialization must necessarily weaken or destroy bonds of kinship beyond those existing within the individual family.

Firth (1956) and his collaborators were the first to demonstrate that extended kinship bonds can be extremely important even in such a highly urbanized society as London, and their work has opened up wide opportunities for investigations in which the techniques of social anthropology (which is so largely concerned with kinship) can be of use to the sociologist in the study of modern societies.

One most promising field for such investigations is French Canada, where historic events have set the stage for the testing

* I wish to express my thanks to the Carnegie Corporation of New York for providing a travel grant which made possible the research described here; to Mr. A. B. Hooper for most valuable help in analysing the results; and to my colleagues Mr. Ralph Bulmer and Dr. Murray Groves for reading and commenting on the manuscript.

71

of many hypotheses concerning the role of kinship in modern societies.

The region of the St. Lawrence River was first exploited by France during the sixteenth and early seventeenth centuries, the primary basis of this exploitation being the fur trade. In 1606 Samuel de Champlain founded the city of Quebec, and agricultural settlements, largely self-sufficient, began to grow along both banks of the lower St. Lawrence, though the fur trade continued to flourish and spread westward as the fur-bearing animals were progressively exterminated. The *habitants* of the St. Lawrence agricultural settlements lived in small parishes in which the parish priest played an important part as religious and secular leader—the whole of New France was solidly Catholic, as are the communities of French Canadians today.

This was the situation which the English met after Wolfe captured Quebec in 1759. The subsequent social and political conflicts between the two major ethnic groups in Canada (Wade, 1950; Lower, 1946) are beyond the scope of this paper, but the memories of them are relevant to French Canadian attitudes today. These are marked by a consciousness that they were the first Europeans in Canada; that they were conquered by the English and subsequently betrayed by France by the cession of Canada in 1763; that they must protect their language and their Catholicism against the predominantly Protestant English majority; and that their way of life, especially in regard to kinship, is superior to that of the English.

The settlements of the St. Lawrence *habitants* remained very much as they were until the middle of the nineteenth century, when the growing pressure of population on a limited area of fertile land produced extensive migration to industrial towns in New England and in Quebec itself (Faucher and Lamontagne, 1953). After 1870, with the opening up of Western Canada, a new trend in migration developed: French Canadians from both Quebec and New England established communities in Manitoba (Howard, 1952; Morton, 1957) one of which forms the subject of the study reported here.

Kinship had, and still has, certain important organizing functions among the rural communities of Quebec (Gérin, 1898 and 1937; Miner, 1939; Rioux, 1954). When sociologists became aware of the trends of migration, urbanization, and industrialization mentioned above, they tended to assume that either these trends would produce atrophy of French Canadian cultural elements (including kinship) or that adherence to these "archaic" elements would militate against the successful adjustment of French Canadians to modern conditions. In this they were supported by leading French Canadian churchmen who had always held up the simple, closely knit village community, in which material advantage was regarded as secondary to spiritual values, as the ideal of French Canadian life. They feared that departure from this ideal would mean the collapse of French Canadian values, including those connected with kinship.

Such predictions have not been confirmed by Garigue's studies of kinship in the city of Montreal and in the mining town of Schefferville (1958, pp. 63–76; 88–102) where French Canadian kinship usages, far from becoming atrophied, have assumed new functions which have helped the communities concerned in the social and economic adjustments which they have been forced to make. It is therefore interesting further to test the hypothesis of the correlation of "progress" with degeneration of kinship in a comparatively new Canadian community of a different type. This I attempted to do during a period of 10 weeks' field work during the summer of 1957 in the township of St. Jean-Baptiste, Manitoba. This community differs in several significant respects from the traditional *habitant* parishes of the St. Lawrence: economically, it is far removed from subsistence agriculture and forms part of the largely wheat-based economy of the prairies; its people have not lived there for many generations, most of their ancestors having migrated to Manitoba since 1870; they were of heterogeneous provenance, coming from various parts of Quebec and also from French Canadian communities in the industrial towns of New England; since they have frequent contacts, economic and social, with Winnipeg, they cannot be described as "isolated"; and all the people, except some of the more elderly, are perfectly bilingual.

The parish of St. Jean-Baptiste is a prairie farming community with a population of approximately fifteen hundred, of whom about one-third live in the township. It is situated on the Red River, 46 miles south of Winnipeg and 20 miles north of the U.S.A. border. The population is almost exclusively French Canadian, though there is one English Canadian family in the township and several descendants of the original *métis*[1] settlers who first set up farms along the banks of the Red River about the middle of the nineteenth century (Howard, 1952). Community life centres largely around the Roman Catholic Church and its associated social centre which is used as a curling and skating rink in winter and for wedding receptions, entertainments, and other social functions. The community is solidly Roman Catholic and there is a Central School staffed mainly by nuns.

As a basis for a study of kinship I collected a number of genealogies from people in St. Jean-Baptiste. Unfortunately my informants did not represent a balanced sample of the population of the community, belonging as they did predominantly to the higher social stratum and to the older age groups, ranging from 45 to 75. I made several attempts to obtain genealogies from younger members of the community, but my visit coincided with the busy harvest season. Some told me frankly that they were too busy to co-operate or too tired after long hours of work; others referred me to their older relatives in such terms as: "He knows far more about the family than I do."

As will appear, all my informants turned out to be related to each other, though they were not selected on the basis of kinship. This means that what I in fact collected was one enormous genealogy which could perhaps be written out on a cinema screen. So for the sake of convenience I have selected ten informants as

[1] This is a French term, derived originally from Spanish. In Canada it is used to describe individuals of mixed Indian and European descent. It usually refers to Indian–French Canadian mixed bloods, but one may also speak of a "Scots *métis*" or an "English *métis*".

Egos to act as nuclei for ten genealogies, particulars of which are given in Table 1.

TABLE 1. PARTICULARS OF GENEALOGIES

Reference number of Ego and genealogy	Sex of Ego	Language used	Collected from
I	F	English	Ego
II	M	English	Ego
III	M	English	Husband and wife jointly
IV (wife of III)	F	English	
V	M	English	Husband and wife jointly
VI (wife of V)	F	English	
VII	M	French	Ego, wife and f.b.d. who is wife of VIII
VIII	M	French	Ego and wife
IX	M	French	Ego and half-brother
X	F	French	Ego and mother's sister

The present work does not pretend to be a full study of kinship, which would involve a description of kinship relationships in action. For example, the shortness of the time available and the fact that I was a newcomer to the community made it impossible for me to collect systematic data on the economic aspect of kinship, in particular on the tendency to secure economic advantages for kinsfolk. This is an extremely important phenomenon, because in Quebec it is one of the sources of tension between English and French. The English call it "nepotism" and the French call it "family solidarity" (Garigue, 1958, p. 72). Actually both are right, given a relativist approach to conflicting cultural values.

2. THE RANGE OF KINSHIP AWARENESS

It was originally hoped that the material on kinship collected at St. Jean-Baptiste could be compared quantitatively with certain conclusions of Garigue's study of this subject in Montreal. Garigue analysed thirty genealogies to discover the range of the genealogical knowledge of the informants. "The mean of such knowledge is a range of 215 persons. The smallest range was 75; the ten with least knowledge ranged from this to 120. The next ten ranged from 126 to 243; the highest ten from 252 to a maximum of 484 known kin." (1958, p. 64). These and other facts reported by Garigue establish his contention that urbanization does not destroy the complex web of kinship which characterizes French Canadian society. It would have been interesting to compare his figures with material from another "modern", though rural, community.

Unfortunately it soon became apparent that this would be impossible for several reasons. One is the unbalanced character of the sample, previously mentioned, so far as age groupings are concerned, whereas Garigue's informants ranged from 19 to 72 with an average age of 30½. Again, Garigue collected genealogies from informants with a view to assessing their *individual* knowledge of their kin. In St. Jean-Baptiste it proved impossible to do this. One obstacle arose from the conditions under which several genealogies were collected from two or three informants jointly. In the case of husbands and wives, I was invited into their homes and started asking questions of one of them. The other would prompt from time to time, while one or other would occasionally leave the house on some errand or other. After this had gone on over a series of interviews it was impossible to say how much each of them knew about the range of kinsfolk who were common to both. Again, since all informants were related to each other, they sometimes referred me back, for information on certain branches of their families, to genealogies which they knew I had already collected from their kinsfolk. Several informants, with courteous thoroughness, insisted on resorting to mnemonic aids. One put through, during a single interview, six telephone calls to relatives in order to obtain answers to my questions. Others referred to address books or telephone directories. And I was once handed an obituary notice which gave details of the immediate kin of a deceased kinsman. In such circumstances it was obviously impossible to assess the amount of knowledge possessed by any given individual at the outset. It may be noted that the investigators in the South Borough project in London encountered similar difficulties, but finally reached the conclusion that it was preferable to record kinship awareness in terms of the collective knowledge of households rather than that of individuals (Firth, 1956, pp. 27–8).

Taking the above considerations into account, it would have been both ungracious and tactless to attempt to insist on working conditions which would have made the data comparable with Garigue's. Nevertheless it is of interest to record the range of kinship knowledge revealed in the genealogies, provided that it is clearly recognized that these cannot be regarded as accurately representative of the range of knowledge possessed by individuals in St. Jean-Baptiste. The richer genealogies show a range which is probably greater than that possessed by younger members of the community. Those which show the lowest ranges are attenuated, for various reasons. Genealogy I is incomplete because the informant left St. Jean-Baptiste before I could finish its compilation—it contains no information on the informant's knowledge of her affinal relatives through her husband. Genealogy VIII is a case in connection with which it was pointed out to me that I had already gathered certain information about Ego's family from Ego VI, his f.b.d. The four genealogies collected from two married couples (III and IV, V and VI) reveal that the two couples were able to give the names of 542 and 580 kinsfolk respectively. But it would be quite wrong to assume that each member of the couple possessed the range of knowledge indicated by these figures. They constantly referred to each other for information, and the women were much better informed about their kinfolk than the men (cf. Garigue, 1958, p. 66; Firth, 1956, p. 40). This was in general true of my other informants, though one of the fullest genealogies (II) was obtained from a man.

In spite of the fact that the genealogies from St. Jean-Baptiste cannot be compared quantitatively with Garigue's, one conclusion emerges with striking clarity from the material: the very wide range of kinship awareness among French Canadians, compared with that of most English-speaking societies. For example, twelve genealogies collected in South Borough show a mean of 102 named kin (Firth, 1956, p. 42). The corresponding figure of St. Jean-Baptiste is 256. But if the genealogies of husbands and their wives are lumped together to form household genealogies, of the kind collected in London, the figure rises to 320.

The discrepancy between the French Canadian data and those from London is partly due to the large size of French Canadian families.[2] Generally speaking, the larger the size of families the greater the number of priority kin, both consanguineous and affinal, and the more numerous the chances of acquiring chosen kin (Section 5). But this fact is not sufficient to explain the very wide lateral spread of French Canadian genealogies.

The criteria used here in categorizing the kinsfolk recorded in the genealogies differ somewhat from those of Firth and of Garigue. Kinsfolk are divided into *named kin* and *unnamed kin*. The former are those for whom either the Christian name or the surname (or both) are known, except where the surname could be inferred from a previously recorded marriage. For example, if an informant said "Edouard Duval married a Cartier and they have ten children, though I do not know their names" this information is recorded as two named kin and ten unnamed kin, though the informant would know by inference that all of the

[2] The large size of French Canadian families is well known. The Church is strong in its insistence that people should have as many children as possible, as both a religious and a patriotic duty for members of a minority group whose cultural survival and status in the Dominion depend largely on their numerical strength. That French Canadians should have large families is accepted both as an ideal and an accomplished fact—*la revanche du berceau*, "the revenge of the cradle" against the English who conquered them and subsequently sought on many occasions and in many ways to deprive them of their ethnic rights and identity. A total of 529 families are recorded in the genealogies from St. Jean-Baptiste. Of these, 57 have ten or more children, the highest number being 20. The median number of children is 4, but this undoubtedly underestimates very greatly the true figure—firstly because informants often admitted that they were unable to give the total number of children in certain families and secondly because a large number of the families are those of young married couples who will certainly have more children in the future.

children would have the surname of "Duval". Again, when neither a wife's Christian name nor her maiden name were known she is recorded as an unnamed kinswoman, even though her married name might be known.

It will be seen that our category of named kin corresponds to Firth's "nominated kin". However his "recognized kin" consist of both our named and unnamed kin, with the proviso that the sex, as well as the existence, of unnamed kin must be known.

The total numbers of kinsfolk recorded in the St. Jean-Baptiste genealogies are given in Table 2.

TABLE 2

Genealogy	Named kin	Unamed kin
I	130	56
II	363	234
III	285	134
IV	257	185
V	352	81
VI	228	9
VII	397	149
VIII	123	213
IX	233	210
X	191	33
Total	2559	1304

It is interesting to record how the kinsfolk involved are distributed over the generations of the past century or so. In line with the findings of Garigue, interest in kinsfolk tends to be concentrated on the contemporary and near-contemporary generations. In Montreal, Garigue found that between 50 and 66 per cent of known kin (recognized kin, in Firth's sense) belong to the generations of Ego and his parents (1958, p. 64). In St. Jean-Baptiste the corresponding figure is 62 per cent for named kin and 25 per cent for unnamed kin. The French Canadians of St. Jean-Baptiste—and this is probably true of Western Canada in general —have largely severed their ties with the Quebec of the past.

They often tell of the doings of their pioneering forbears who came from Quebec; they rarely refer to ancestors of earlier generations. Several of them have visited Quebec and have met relatives there, just as they have done in other parts of Western Canada and in the U.S.A. But in the French Canadian settlements on Red River we find a sub-culture of French Canadian culture, not a colony of Quebec. There is even a suggestion of a certain mild antipathy towards Quebec, where people are said to be "less friendly than here".

3. INTERMARRIAGES OF KIN

A characteristic feature of French Canadian kinship is the large number of intermarriages between kinsfolk (Miner, 1939, pp. 70–72; Garigue, 1958, pp. 65–6). This is perhaps more marked in St. Jean-Baptiste and adjoining Red River parishes because of the initial settlement of this region by a limited number of migrant families who took up adjoining tracts of land. Large families and frequent social contacts within and between the parishes made possible the development of a complex network of interrelationships based on marriages. How far this development was stimulated by preferential marriages based on economic considerations, or obstructed by objections to in-breeding (Miner, 1939, pp. 70–72), it is impossible to say. But the prevalence of intermarriage between kin may be judged from the data given below, which certainly under-estimate the total number of intermarriages among individuals recorded in the genealogies. In some instances of married couples either the surname or the Christain name of one of them was unknown to informants. In several such cases the couple were probably related, but in the absence of precise identification I am unable to assert this with confidence.

The most common, and the most easily defined, types of intermarriages of kin are tabulated below. It should be made clear that the figures given refer to the number of *unions* and not to the frequency of *types* of marriage. Thus when two brothers exchange sisters, this is recorded as two marriages.

Type of marriage	Number of marriages
Sister exchange	14
Brothers marrying sisters (including one case of three brothers marrying three sisters)	71
Two brothers and a sister marrying two sisters and a brother	3
Cross cousin marriage	2
Parallel cousin marriage	4
Marriages between more distant cousins	3
Two siblings marrying individuals who were parallel cousins to each other	16
Two brothers marrying individuals who were cross cousins to each other	2
Parallel cousins marrying individuals who were parallel cousins to each other	4

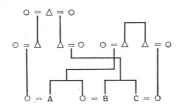

Fig. 1.

In addition to the above, a variety of types of marriage of men with more distant kinswomen were recorded. Figure 1 illustrates one such type. Here it will be seen that each of the three men, A, B, and C, is married to a woman who is related to him in two distinct ways, namely:

A: f.b.d.h.f.f.so.d.
    sis.h.f.f.so.d.
B: f.f.so.d.h.sis.
    b.w.f.b.d.
C: b.w.f.b.d.
    f.f.so.d.h.f.b.d.

The prevalence of intermarriages between kin means that for each genealogy it is possible to compile a chart showing the intermarriages among Ego's kinsfolk. Figure 2 shows, for Genealogy II, the kinship relations of 90 individuals. Comparable charts for other genealogies are of the same general type. The number of individuals shown on similar charts for the ten genealogies are as follows:

Genealogy I:	35		Genealogy VI:	23
Genealogy II:	90		Genealogy VII:	48
Genealogy III:	37		Genealogy VIII:	26
Genealogy IV:	45		Genealogy IX:	57
Genealogy V:	69		Genealogy X:	24

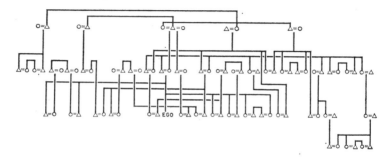

Fig. 2.

It should be noted that whereas Genealogy II was an individual one, others, showing a smaller number of intermarried kin, were collected from more than one informant. Thus Genealogies V and VI give a total of 92 intermarried kin for the husband and wife jointly.

One consequence of this network of intermarriages is that it is possible to find in each genealogy the names of individuals who are related to all other informants in various ways. As stated in Section I, informants were not selected on a basis of kinship, but they all turned out to be related to one another in at least two ways. The charts and tables demonstrating this are too complex to reproduce here. But they are vividly reminiscent of the informant in the small St. Lawrence community of l'Île Verte who, in pointing out another man to Marcel Rioux, said: "He is my brother-in-law because his second wife is my wife's sister; he is also my uncle, because his first wife was my mother's sister; and he is also my cousin, like everybody else." (Translated from Rioux, 1954, p. 36).

The material presented above from a limited range of genealogies suggests, though it does not prove, that everybody in St. Jean-Baptiste, apart from a few recent arrivals, is related to everybody else in a complex network of kinship relationships. The more distant of these relationships do not necessarily involve personal associations, apart from those arising from accident or individual preference. But their existence does tend to produce a sense of unity in the community—almost a sense of belonging to one big family. This principle was explicitly stated in the words of a memorandum prepared by the Trustees of the Central School at St. Pierre, a parish not far from St. Jean-Baptiste, to which they would also apply: "It is not surprising that this village and its neighbourhood provide a remarkable example of community life—a community life in which the family spirit is the fruit of colonization by groups and of marriage between members of these groups. It is a community life in which the close co-operation of Church and home infuses into all activities a single spirit and a common vigour." (Translated from *La Liberté et Le Patriote*, 18 October 1957, p. 3).

4. MIGRATION OF KINSFOLK

The genealogies include records of kinsfolk who have migrated from one place to another. Some of this information was volunteered by informants. Some of it was obtained by direct questioning after the basic data on kinship relations had been recorded, but it was impossible to do this systematically for all the individuals named in the genealogies.

The data provide a paradigm of the migrations of sections of the French Canadian population over the past eight decades or so, though they must not be regarded as giving more than a rough quantitative indication of migration trends. This reservation is necessary because the data were all collected in St. Jean-Baptiste from a limited number of informants who were all related to each other. The direction of migration of individual French Canadians is largely determined by kinship; a man will tend to migrate to a place to which his brothers or other relatives have already migrated, a tendency which is reflected in the material from St. Jean-Baptiste.

The unit of migration is taken as either an unmarried adult individual or a married couple, with or without children. Thus if a married couple migrate with their ten children, this is counted as one migration. It would obviously distort the real pattern to count it as twelve migrations. When, as happened in a few cases, an individual migrated two or even three times during his lifetime, each migration was counted separately.

The data of 310 migrations are presented in Table 3. In addition there were 54 migrations from one Red River settlement to another, 2 to South America, 4 from the Red River to various states of the U.S.A. (Oregon 1, Florida 2, Colorado 1) and 5 from the Red River to unknown destinations in the U.S.A.

It is interesting to consider in detail the migrations to and from Red River settlements in terms of the generations recorded in the genealogies. These migrations reflect the movements of a population which came originally almost entirely from New England and Quebec to Manitoba during the years immediately following the opening up to settlement of the Red River region in the mid-seventies of the nineteenth century. All the land became occupied, the mechanization of agriculture meant that a much smaller labour force could be employed in cultivating it, and the rapid increase of population, resulting from the size of French Canadian families, made emigration inevitable for a number of younger people.

It is important to note the direction of this process. A substan-

TABLE 3. MIGRATIONS OF KINSFOLK

Migrations from	MIGRATIONS TO							Total emigrations
	New England and Quebec	Montreal and Ontario	Red River settlements	Winnipeg and St. B.	Canada west of Winnipeg	Central states	California	
New England and Quebec	—	0	36	2	6	0	1	45
Montreal and Ontario	0	—	5	0	3	0	0	8
Red River settlements	2	34	—	71	78	9	25	219
Winnipeg and St. Boniface	1	8	3	—	3	3	4	22
Canada west of Winnipeg	0	2	1	2	—	1	2	8
Central states	0	0	1	4	0	—	1	6
California	0	0	0	0	1	1	—	2
Total immigrations	3	44	46	79	91	14	33	310

tial proportion of migrations were to Canada west of Winnipeg, about one-third of them to centres of French Canadian population in Western Manitoba. Others were mainly to centres in other western provinces where there are substantial numbers of French Canadians.

The high incidence of migration to Winnipeg and St. Boniface can be explained by geographical proximity and economic openings in these urban centres. St. Boniface lies on the other side of the Red River from Winnipeg, only a few minutes walk from its commercial centre. But whereas the population of Winnipeg is predominantly English, St. Boniface is a French Canadian town with its own radio station, a cathedral, a college, a French Canadian archbishop, and a weekly paper *La Liberté et Le Patriote*. There is much mutual visiting between French Canadians in both centres and their kinsfolk in the Red River settlements to the south. The significance of this is that Winnipeg and St. Boniface have been able to absorb a substantial proportion of the surplus rural population without doing much damage to the social structure or divorcing too many migrants from French Canadian institutions.

The U.S.A. receives comparatively few migrants. In view of the complete freedom of travel between the two countries, this must reflect personal preference. There is among French Canadians, particularly in Quebec, a fairly strong feeling against the "materialism" of the United States. I have the impression that the feeling is not so strong in St. Jean-Baptiste, probably owing to geographical proximity, more frequent personal contacts along the Winnipeg–St. Paul railway and highway, and certain common Red River traditions going back to the days of buffalo hunting and early conflicts with the Indians (Howard, 1952, parts I–III).

We have discerned certain trends in the migrations centering historically around the Red River. But it is important to note that there have also been countertrends, small numbers of atypical migrations in various directions in the U.S.A. and Canada and also between the two countries. It would appear, however, that these tend to take place between a limited number of places, presumably in most instances places where French Canadians are already located. These atypical migrations cannot be explained, as the major trends can largely be explained, in terms of regional economic pressure. Undoubtedly personal circumstances do lead individuals to migrate in order to "better themselves". But there appears to be also a positive liking for geographical mobility among many French Canadians, a value orientation very different from what we would expect to find in a "folk culture" (cf. Section 6).

5. SOME CHARACTERISTICS
OF KINSHIP IN ST. JEAN-BAPTISTE

Raymond Firth has drawn attention to certain significant contrasts between the kinship systems of primitive peoples, with which anthropologists are familiar, and those of modern Western societies as exemplified in South Borough) 1956, pp. 13–14). We may consider the system of St. Jean-Baptiste in relation to these contrasts, and also to other features which give it a distinctive character. For this purpose a useful classification of kin, based on concepts developed by Firth and Garigue, is as follows:

A. *Effective kin:*   Those with whom significant contacts are maintained, consisting of:

  (i) *Priority kin:*   Members of the individual family and kinsfolk closely related to it, particularly parents of the spouses. Here there is a greater or lesser degree of recognized moral obligation to enter into appropriate social relationships. In the case of the husband–wife and parents–children relationships, some of the obligations are supported by legal sanctions.

  (ii) *Chosen kin:*   More remote kin with whom there is no moral obligation to enter into social relationships. However such relationships are in fact initiated and maintained on a basis of individual or family choice.

B. *Non-effective kin :* Those kin who are known to be genealogically related to the individual, but with whom he maintains no social relationships.

The first contrast between primitive and modern Western societies is that among the former there is usually a much wider range of priority kin and a larger number of prescribed social relationships between them. In Western societies the priority kin are fewer, being in some particular cases restricted to the individual family. For more remote kinsfolk the establishment of social relationships is permissive, not obligatory. But this does not mean that such relationships are unimportant. For example in primitive society it is often obligatory for a man to marry a kinswoman, aboriginal Australia providing the most striking example. There is no such obligation in Western society, though Section 3 suggests that there is in St. Jean-Baptiste a significant tendency towards intermarriage between kinsfolk.

Here, as elsewhere, the regularities of kinship behaviour in modern society are statistical rather than normative—kinship relationships provide bases on which other social relations may be and often are established, but they do not make mandatory their establishment. Yet regularities arising within such permissive systems may be significant for comparative purposes. Thus in the South Borough study, intermarriages between kin do not seem to have been frequent enough to merit discussion by the investigators, and none appear in the specimen genealogy given by them (Firth, 1956, p. 47). In St. Jean-Baptiste intermarriages between kin are a striking feature of every genealogy and are frequently commented upon by informants.

Another contrast between primitive and western societies is that in the latter there is a separation of economic relationships from those of kinship, outside the individual family. This contrast is necessarily not so marked in the township of St. Jean-Baptiste. As we have seen, its population is largely descended from a few original families who have intermarried extensively. Though the record is not complete, it appears that practically all the proprietors and employees of shops and other business premises are related to one or more of my informants, sometime closely. For example the Post Office is conducted by a married couple. The husband is a brother of Ego X while his wife is h.sis. to Ego I. And since all informants are related to each other, it will be seen that it would be impossible for them to avoid having business dealings with kinsfolk, even though the relationship involved might be a distant one. It must be emphasized, however, that this still differs from the articulation in primitive society of economic with kinship systems, since the latter do not in St. Jean-Baptiste dictate obligatory economic relations between kin. Such relations arise as a result of the pervasive character of genealogical connections within the community. But this also means that special economic favours, of the kind mentioned in Section 1, are in fact from time to time rendered to kinsfolk.

Another contrast, previously mentioned, is the prominence in Western society of the individual family, in contradistinction to primitive communities in which it is often embedded in wider kinship groups such as the extended family. This contrast also applies in St. Jean-Baptiste. Most of the houses are not large enough to accommodate more than one family, though in a few cases one finds affinal kin or unmarried relatives residing as members of the household. But I have no reason to think that such cases are more frequent than in other Western societies. What does distinguish the individual family in St. Jean-Baptiste is that though it is a discrete residential and economic unit, it is the centre of widely ramifying constellations[3] of kinship relation-

[3] I have chosen the term "constellation" from several suggested by Firth (1956, p. 16) to apply to aggregates of effective kinsfolk centred around a given individual. They are structurally quite different from discrete social groups into which the community as a whole is divided—for example the clans or extended families found in primitive societies. Membership differs from one individual to another and can only be defined in terms of relationships to the individual concerned. When, as with the *kano a paito* of Tikopia (Firth, 1936, p. 226), it is feasible for them to come together regularly on ceremonial occasions they may perhaps be called a kinship group. But when, as in St. Jean-Baptiste, such reunions are often made impossible by the geographical dispersal of kin, their continued existence depends essentially on more or less *ad hoc* personal contacts which various members have with the individual who forms their nucleus. In these circumstances it is better not to describe them as "groups".

ships. And the bonds existing within these constellations are multiplied and reinforced by the high incidence of marriages between kinsfolk.

The importance attached to such constellations of kin—many of their members are remote from one another both genealogically and geographically—is reflected in the large number of names of kinsfolk known to informants. And even when they have to resort to mnemonic aids or to relatives for information, this is in itself significant: though they may not have the information at their fingertips, they know where it can be obtained. They realize that the range of their kinsfolk is far wider than that which they can call to mind at any given moment. This may be important when travelling, an activity which practically always involves calling on kinsfolk. One informant told me that when he visited Montreal he consulted the telephone directory to find the names of people having the same surname as himself with a view to getting into touch with them. He was astonished to find that "there were four pages of them" (I quote his statement verbatim; it may be an exaggeration). Mutual visiting is an important activity of kinsfolk, both within St. Jean-Baptiste and outside. The latter kind of visiting is largely conditioned by geographical proximity. As we have said, visits between kinsfolk in Winnipeg or St. Boniface and those in St. Jean-Baptiste are frequent; in the case of the western provinces of Canada and the U.S.A., contacts tend to be more occasional. But in such cases, the existence of kinship bonds provides a social *pied à terre* for the traveller. Thus one informant and his wife went to Chicago for their honeymoon and stayed at a hotel. On the day of their arrival a murder was committed in an adjoining bedroom. The wife said: "I don't like this place; we have relatives in Milwaukee; let's spend the rest of our honeymoon there"—which they did.

The preceding remarks may be compared with Garigue's observations on the significance of kinship in Montreal and in the new mining town of Schefferville in northern Quebec; and particularly with the statement of one informant in the latter community that he had fourteen kinsfolk in the town and that their presence made him feel "at home" there (1958, pp. 68–9, 98–9).

Just as the knowledge of the existence of kin may be useful when travelling far afield, so travelling serves to keep alive knowledge of kin and their doings. One individual who was well-informed about related families in California, several of whom she had not seen for many years, told me that her sister, who lives there, pays regular visits to St. Jean-Baptiste and so keeps her abreast of family news.

Another means by which people may keep in touch with the doings of their geographically remote kinsfolk is the weekly paper *La Liberté et Le Patriote*. Each issue contains items of personal news from various places in Canada west of the provincial border between Ontario and Manitoba. These places are settlements with a majority or substantial minority of French Canadians. Occasionally items from the U.S.A. are included. The news items, usually from a quarter of a column to a column in length, contain accounts of births, marriages, deaths, wedding anniversaries, appointments to office, and various social functions. I have myself found the journal extremely useful in keeping in touch with my friends at St. Jean-Baptiste and in learning of events among the French population of Western Canada generally. Incidentally it is worth noting that personal news items in *La Liberté et Le Patriote* frequently include, under a sub-heading *Va et Vient*, references to comings and goings to and from particular centres. The news presented reflects the mobile character of the French Canadian population of Western Canada, both in regard to migration and casual travel.

Though ties with kinsfolk may be maintained in the ways described, they are sometimes broken. One factor which tends to cause individuals to sever themselves, wholly or partially, from their French Canadian connections is the occurrence of marriages with persons of different ethnic origin. Differences of language, culture and sometimes religion may cause the alien spouses and their families to drift away from French Canadian associations. But this does not always occur. I have no quantitative data on what happens, ethnically and culturally, in these mixed marriages, but my impression is that the alien spouse and his or her children are drawn into French Canadian society quite as often as the family is lost to it.

The genealogies collected at St. Jean-Baptiste record 71 cases of French Canadians (33 men and 38 women) who are or were married to alien spouses, representing an extraordinarily wide variety of ethnic groups, as follows: 25 marriages with English Canadians or with migrants from England (informants were often unable to state which); 12 with Americans; 6 with Germans; 5 with Ukrainians; 4 each with Belgians and with persons of mixed European (including British) extraction; 3 each with Scots and Irish; 2 each with migrants from France and with *métis*; 1 marriage each with a Cuban, a Swede, a Czech, a Pole, and an Italian.

Apart from the disruptive effects of some mixed marriages, there are other instances of French Canadians who simply drift away, as recorded in such statements as: "He went off to the U.S.A.—I don't know where", and "He went out west somewhere". But such vagueness is comparatively rare. Of all the recorded migrations to the U.S.A., only 5 were expressed in terms of the first of the above statements. Again, I questioned two informants (husband and wife) about the extent to which they visited, or received visits from, kinsfolk who had migrated further afield than Manitoba. Here unmarried individuals, or married couples, were taken as the units—children who accompanied their parents were not counted. The kinsfolk concerned were located in Quebec, Ontario, all the provinces of Canada west of Manitoba and also in California and the Central states. Contacts were reported as follows: regular visits, 16; occasional visits, 22; no visits, 31. The last figure includes six cases in California, previously mentioned, in which the informant received regular news from her sister.

It is clear that, in spite of geographical distance, considerable contact is maintained with migrant kinsfolk. This is even more marked in the case of those who have not migrated so far afield.

But it must be emphasized, in line with what was said above, that the regularities involved in social contacts are in both cases statistical and not normative. When informants reported that they had not seen or heard of a certain relative for a very long time, I never detected any note of regret or resentment in their tone. The relatives concerned had chosen to move out of the kinship constellation, and that was all there was to it. There were always plenty left.

6. KINSHIP AND FRENCH CANADIAN CULTURE

The main features of kinship in St. Jean-Baptiste are similar to those found in other French Canadian communities. It has long been recognized that the character of the French Canadian nuclear family is an important factor in the survival of the French Canadians as an ethnic group. It appears that extended kinship, in the form of the constellations to which we referred in the preceding Section, is also of the greatest significance for the persistence of French Canadian culture. But in connection with this statement it is necessary to ask just what is meant by "French Canadian culture".

Discussions on this subject have been confused by certain mistaken assumptions, briefly mentioned in Section 1. These assumptions are sometimes explicitly stated, but more often are implicit in the argument. One of them is that the quintessence of French Canadian culture is to be found in the pristine organization of the rural parishes along the banks of the St. Lawrence River and in the traditional way of life of the *habitants* of that region. These have been described as "folk societies" possessing "folk cultures" in terms of Redfield's classic definition. They certainly have exhibited in the past—and to some extent still exhibit—most of the characteristics of folk cultures as these are known to anthropologists (Piddington, 1957, p. 753). But what is definitely incorrect is to categorize French Canadian culture as a whole in these terms, and to suggest that such factors as migration, urbanization, industrialization, the loss of economic

self-sufficiency in rural communities, and the economic dominance of Anglo-American interests in large business enterprises
will necessarily mean the radical disorganization or even disappearance of the French Canadian way of life. Such statements
involve the assumptions (a) that the static folk culture of the
habitants was the only true French Canadian culture, and (b) that
such a culture was quite incapable of standing up to the impact
of the factors mentioned above without undergoing radical
disorganization. The first of these assumptions involves what
Bennett and Wolff have called "the fallacy of the microcosm"
(1955, p. 340). The culture of the *habitants* represented but one
phase of French Canadian culture, both geographically and
historically. It was not the original culture of New France, the
main activity of which was trade, pre-eminently the fur trade,
and not agriculture (Wade, 1950, p. 13; Garigue, 1953, p. 18).
People engaged in the fur trade rather than the *habitants* were
the first French Canadians. The subsequent rural settlement
along the banks of the St. Lawrence went on *pari passu* with
exploration of Canada and the westward expansion of the fur
trade. Commercial undertakings and educational institutions
developed in Quebec city and in Montreal. There were always
political leaders and administrators, first as servants of metropolitan France and, after the conquest, as increasingly active
agents in developing relations with the English. And in the region
with which we are specially concerned—Canada west of the
Precambrian shield—agricultural settlement was not a mere
transplanting of the self-sufficient rural life of the *habitants* to the
banks of the Red River. Agriculture, like the bison hunt, was at
first a "service industry" to the fur trade (Morton, 1957, p. 88).
Moreover, as we have seen, many of the original Red River
settlers came not from Quebec, but from the industrialized
regions of the New England States.

The second assumption—that the social culture of the St.
Lawrence settlements must necessarily disintegrate as a result of
technological and economic changes—seems to be refuted by
Miner's 1949 re-study of St. Denis (1950, pp. 1–10). He describes

the economic factors which produced changes in material living standards, particularly the Government provision of family allowances and subsidies for livestock and dairy products. These stimulated the economy and introduced into the community a whole range of items of agricultural machinery, household electrical appliances, and the like. Increased transport and a greater use of postal facilities also led the people of St. Denis to have more contacts with the outside world.

But facts of this order do not prove—nor does Miner suggest that they prove—that there has been any radical "disintegration" or "disorganization" in the value system and interpersonal relations of the people of St. Denis. On the contrary, some at least of the innovations conduce to the preservation of these essential features of the local way of life; for example, the raised standard of living has made easier the family life on farms. There is no evidence that the social culture of St. Denis is disintegrating; rather is it becoming better integrated by providing a higher standard of material welfare and by becoming more integrally connected with the culture of French Canada as a whole, a culture of which the traditional way of life in St. Denis represents one subculture.

In view of what has been said, it is interesting to note how it has come about that the life of the Quebec *habitant* has been regarded as epitomizing French Canadian culture. In the first place many French Canadian *littérateurs*, historians, and publicists have held up the rural parish of Quebec as representing the highest ideal of French Canadian society, as a way of life to which it is a duty of piety and patriotism to conform. Secondly, there has been the influence of the scientific descriptions of rural life in Quebec, given by Leon Gérin and Horace Miner. These have attracted well-deserved attention through the thoroughness of their description and analysis; and also because of the exotic, even idyllic, appeal which their subject-matter has for members of more sophisticated societies. Descriptions of other forms of French Canadian society, though of equal scientific importance, are less spectacular and less "different". Everett Hughes' well-known study of Cantonville (1954) describes the effects of industrialization on a formerly rural population; but the way in which such populations can, after a period or re-integration, adapt themselves without drastic disorganization to the problems of industrial life is indicated in the essays on the strike at Asbestos and in Garigue's study of Schefferville (Trudeau, 1956; Garigue 1958, pp. 88–102). In both these cases we see an industrialized group becoming adapted to new conditions without ceasing to be French Canadians. Finally, Garigue's work on St. Joseph's Oratory and on kinship in Montreal (1958, pp. 63–87) has shown that in two of its major aspects—religion and kinship—French Canadian culture is not destroyed by urbanization but merely assumes somewhat new forms.

We have seen that French Canadian society as a whole has always been a differentiated one. At different times and in different parts of Canada, it has undergone profound changes and has adapted itself to a variety of new developments—political, economic and social. This leads us to question the assumption which manifests itself in much of what has been written about contemporary changes and possible future developments—the assumption that French Canadian culture cannot at the same time survive and adapt itself to the demands of modern conditions.

French Canadian society today provides a modern example of the process which I have termed emergent development (Piddington, 1957, p. 732). It is becoming more differentiated, though not necessarily in the direction of closer approximation to Anglo-American standards. There is in fact a conscious opposition to the "materialism" which would be implied in such a development. Standards of living are rising and material amenities increasing. But these facts need not mean the abandonment of the fundamental organizing principles of French Canadian society—the Church with its many associated institutions, educational and otherwise; the French language; political and moral attitudes towards *les Anglais*, exacerbated from time to time by the repercussions of minority status; and French Canadian conceptions of kinship, with all that these imply. These characteristics permeate the various subcultures which have differentiated themselves, the Red River settlements providing one example.

It is of course true that certain individuals, both in Canada and the U.S.A., become completely severed from French Canadian life. But such cases, even if they were numerous, would not affect the survival of French Canadian society and culture. An army at war can, and indeed must, lose individual members as casualties. But so long as it receives reinforcements and is not decimated or demoralized, it continues to function as a system of human organization.

Quite apart from this consideration, it must not be assumed that the loss of individual French Canadians into the wider society of North America must necessarily have a disruptive effect. On the contrary, it serves in many cases the useful function of removing divorcees, atheists, and other misfits and deviants from French Canadian society. As Everett Hughes states the position: "French Canada has never had to swallow its own spit. Its balance of population has long been maintained by spilling the excess into a continent until recently thirsty for settlers and agricultural labour. Its malcontents and heretics have been able to find companions and a place to exercise their peculiar talents somewhere in North America. How much relief from inner pressure of number and of psychological and social tension French Canada has been afforded by being part of something larger than herself, no one can say." (1948, pp. 481–2).

To sum up, French Canadian culture continues to survive, though in a variety of new forms which are themselves constantly changing. In this process of survival, kinship plays an important part. It serves to integrate the local community by providing a complex set of interlocking kinship relationships. These provide channels through which significant social activities can be organized; in particular, they facilitate marriages between kin, which in turn strengthen the system. Outside the local community, kinship does much to offset the disruptive effects of migration by maintaining links between migrants and the communities which they have left; it also provides facilities for social contacts and economic opportunities for people who travel. The material from St. Jean-Baptiste suggests that over the whole of Canada and large areas of the U.S.A. there spreads a network of recognized kinship relationships which helps to keep French Canadians aware, despite geographical dispersion, of their identity as a distinct ethnic group and of the advantages of belonging to such a group.

BIBLIOGRAPHY

BENNETT, J. W. and WOLFF, K. H. (1955) Toward communication between sociology and anthropology, *Yearbook of Anthropology*, edited by Thomas, W. L., New York, Wenner-Gren Foundation.

FAUCHER, A. and LAMONTAGNE, M. (1953) History of industrial development, *Essais sur le Québec Contemporain*, edited by Falardeau, J. C., Quebec, Presses Universitaires Laval.

FIRTH, R. (1936) *We, The Tikopia*, London, George Allen and Unwin.

FIRTH, R. (1956) (Ed.) *Two Studies of Kinship in London*, London, Athlone Press.

GARIGUE, P. (1958) *Études sur le Canada Francais*, Montreal, Faculté des Sciences Sociales, Économiques et Politiques, Université de Montréal.

GÉRIN, L. (1898) L'habitant de Saint-Justin, *Proceedings of the Royal Society of Canada*, 130–216,

GÉRIN, L. (1937). *Le Type Économique et Social des Canadiens*. Montreal, Fides.

HOWARD, J. K. (1952) *Strange Empire*, New York, William Morrow.

HUGHES, EVERETT C. (1948) The study of ethnic relations, *The Dalhousie Review*, vol. 27:477.

HUGHES, E. C. (1954) *French Canada in Transition*, fifth impression. Chicago University Press.

LOWER, A. R. M. (1946) *Colony to Nation*, Toronto, Longman, Green & Co.

MINER, H. (1939) *St. Denis*, Chicago University Press.

MINER, H. (1950) A new epoch in rural Quebec, *Amer. J. of Sociol.* **56**, 1–10.

MORTON, W. L. (1957) *Manitoba: A History*, Toronto University Press.

PIDDINGTON, R. (1957) *An Introduction to Social Anthropology*, vol. II, Edinburgh, Oliver & Boyd.

RIOUX, M. (1954) *Description de la Culture de l'Île Verte*, Ottawa, Musée National du Canada.

TRUDEAU, P. E. (1956) (Ed.) *La Grève de l'Amiente*, Montreal, Cité Libre.

WADE, M. (1950) *The French Canadians*, 1760–1945, London, Macmillan.

Relations with Neighbours and Relatives in Working Class Families of the Département de la Seine

A. Vieille

THE following observations were made during a survey carried out among working class families of the Département de la Seine living in lodging houses, and workers employed by various firms in the suburbs of Paris. We have put the two sets of observations together because in both cases we have noted that relationships with neighbours become exceptionally close, often fulfilling functions which, in other social environments, are entirely the care of the family. An analysis of relations with neighbours both at home and at work reveals the considerable degree of importance which these relations have assumed in the day-to-day life of Parisian families and Parisian workers.

RELATIONS WITH NEIGHBOURS AND RELATIVES IN WORKING-CLASS FAMILIES LIVING IN FURNISHED ROOMS

Our survey was concerned with that section of the lodging house population which is sedentary because of the housing crisis: families with children, self-supporting women with or without children, old workmen. Unmarried people make up an element of the population which is mobile, and thus less easily observed. In studying each category, we have noted that very often relations with neighbours have taken over wholly or partially areas which, in other social environments, are reserved for intra-family relationships.

Families with Children

In middle class families and farming families, responsibility for the children's material and moral welfare, and the safety and upbringing of the young children, is usually assumed by the parents, sometimes by the grandparents or other relatives living with the parents. It is very unusual for neighbours to be responsible for children in the same block of flats. Notwithstanding the development of facilities for pre-school children (home help services, day nurseries, and infant schools), the parents are answerable for their children's welfare to the Tribunaux de Défaillances (tribunals for child neglect), which can intervene in these matters.

In country families, the accommodation is of a size to allow the grandparents to live with their children and grandchildren. Thus it is very often the grandparents who look after young children while the parents are at work on the farm.

Among working-class families in furnished lodgings, living with grandparents or other relatives is usually rendered impossible because accommodation is restricted to one room: thus the family is reduced to husband, wife, and children. Moreover, distance constitutes an obstacle to frequent contacts with those relatives who have remained behind in the region of origin. On the other hand, the extreme overcrowding of tenants, cooped up in rooms which are too small, and the common facilities for water, washing, and so on, bring neighbours into some degree of close contact with the life of the family.

From our survey we ascertained that approximately 40 per cent of parents are forced to part with one or several children because their accommodation is so inadequate, putting them for periods of several years in the charge of a foster-mother, who is not related to the family. Many of the parents then notice that the children often form a deep attachment to the woman who brings them up. It is not unusual for a child to show more affection for the foster-mother he sees every day, than for his mother who visits him at infrequent or irregular intervals.

Sometimes relationships are even formed between the child's family and the foster-mother's family, persisting after the child has left her care. Although this is not a relationship of proximity with neighbours in the same lodging house, it would still be true to say that it is the child's day-to-day proximity with his foster-mother which gives rise to the new situation between him and her.

Relations of proximity are in evidence when children live in lodgings with their parents. In this case, they are cared for by the parents to begin with, but the community life of the lodging house broadens the circle of adults concerned with the child. It is very unusual for a birth to pass unnoticed by women neighbours in the lodging house. If there are no relatives or they live at a distance and do not come forward, neighbours generally offer small gifts to the mother in honour of the occasion. When a child is christened, and relatives or relatives by marriage are lacking, the godfather or godmother is often chosen from among near neighbours. As many neighbours as relatives attend the ceremonial meal. All these practices indicate that parents are more anxious to secure for their child the goodwill of the neighbours with whom they have daily contact, than of distant relatives whom they occasionally see.

When the child takes his first steps in the common courtyard of the lodging house, he begins to belong to some extent to the small community of neighbours who have seen him born and raised. If his mother goes out shopping or on an errand, he is looked after by a neighbour who will keep him till she returns. He rarely plays alone or within the family, because the lodgings are not usually big enough to accommodate children's games; he generally plays in the yard with a small group of neighbours' children. When he is 5, it will be one of the older children from the lodging house who sees him to and from infant school, if he has no older brother or sister. He scarcely ever does his homework on his own, but rather with a neighbour's child who has reached the same stage at school.

Thus the child does not live his life wholly within the framework of family, but within a wider framework, as a result of which the functions of protection, upbringing, and supervision usually undertaken by the parents are shared by them with the people who come into contact with the child within the communal framework of the lodging house: the neighbours.

But in addition to this, in certain cases neighbours even share with the parents the function of providing for the children. To cite one example, Mme D. is living in a lodging house with her husband, a machine operator in a furniture factory, and three children. Two others are placed in foster homes. The family lives in the same lodging house as the husband's parents, following the bombardment of Noisy-le-Sec in which their former residence was destroyed. The young woman, a Parisian, keeps in contact with her mother, her aunt, and her godmother who live in the Departments of Seine and Seine-et-Oise. A typical French working-class woman, Mme D. balances the family budget: out of allowances and her husband's wages, she must pay the rent, and the keep of her sons in foster-homes, give her husband spending money, pay for her purchases from the local shops, and supply all the family's needs. When she runs short of money, she borrows from neighbours on the same floor, not from her parents-in-law or her own family. This is very often found in lodging houses: proximity creates relationships within which exchange in all its forms is more frequent, more "familiar", than with the closest relatives.

Examples of this kind are not isolated instances, yet neighbours participate even more in providing for the child, and in his life generally, in cases where he is being brought up by a woman who is on her own, having been widowed, divorced, or deserted by her husband.

Women Supporting a Family

According to the French civil code, a man when he marries assumes an obligation to provide for his wife and children. In a case of desertion by the husband, the wife can always claim from him a pension for herself and her children. Even if she were not married, the law would still allow her to proceed against the father of her children, provided that she could prove paternity. However, these measures envisaged by the law only take effect in the event of the wife bringing an action against her husband. The formalities involved are long-drawn-out and costly, especially for working-class women whose salaries are usually low. As a result, many mothers weary of the pursuit. Nevertheless, if the father evades his responsibilities, and relatives are distant or lacking, it is observed that near neighbours often proffer support which the wife herself had neither hoped for or looked for.

The following example shows the spontaneous association which has sprung up between two young women neighbours in a lodging house. Nadia is a young woman, a metal worker, who has been left by her husband with a 3-year-old child; she is out of work, because her state of health has prevented her from continuing the harsh work of spray-gun operator which she formally did. Simone, also a metal worker, is a young divorcée with a child in a foster home. The spontaneous association operates as follows: Nadia spends her time keeping the two rooms in order, shopping, and cooking the evening meal. Simone works all day at the factory, so it is she who provides Nadia with the money necessary for the functioning of what could be called the "home" of the two young women. Dinners are served and prepared in Nadia's room. In the evenings, Simone and Nadia spend their free time together talking or playing cards. Nadia's child has been "adopted" by neighbours in the lodging house, who have a paternal attitude towards him. Nadia's only relative is a brother whom she visits at irregular intervals.

Here too we note that relations of proximity based on life in the same lodging house play a greater part in the life of mother and child than relationships with relatives: the neighbours fulfil a role of providing (in the broadest sense) which is more important than the role played by the family and relatives.

The second example I have chosen is of interest because it shows who is selected as godfather or godmother for a child deprived of one of its parents, and born in the lodging house. This family consists of five people: the mother, separated from her husband, and four children: Roger (18), an apprentice plumber; Liliane (16), a hairdresser; and Jacqueline (10) and Claude (5), school children. The family lives in a small room measuring just over 12 by 16 feet—but only theoretically: in reality, their residence has been extended through relationships with neighbours. Communal meals are partaken in the single room, but some of the children do not sleep with their mother— Liliane sleeps with her aunt living in the same block, Jacqueline with her godfather's family on another floor. Jacqueline's family and her godfather are not related in any way by family ties; the choice of godfather arose out of the neighbourly contact between Jacqueline's mother and this working-class family. Similarly, the mother's choice for a godmother for her daughter fell upon another neighbour, a foreign immigrant who is not related to her in any way. As a result, Jacqueline spends more of her free time round at her godfather's or godmother's than she does with her mother; they also feed and clothe her, and she sleeps with their families. It should also be pointed out that for more than a year, the family has had the use of accommodation which neighbours on the same floor have put at their disposal while they are away. This case clearly shows that family ties had nothing to do with the choice of godparents for the child, and that proximity was the determining factor. We also see how the small community of neighbours shares with the mother and her sister (in the absence of the husband, who is providing no pension following the separation), the task of bringing up, providing for, and even housing the children.

Finally, Claude, the youngest of the family, was placed in a foster-home by his mother when she was working at a factory. Through the "proximity" of the child and the foster-mother's family, her daughter and son-in-law became Claude's godparents, although they were not related to him. His mother then made the bitter discovery that her child preferred the foster-mother. When she was out of work, she took him back, but he keeps up what could be called "family" contacts with his godparents, being invited by them, with his mother, on national holidays and during the school vacation, as if they were close relatives. The case of Claude demonstrates how, in addition to the contacts of proximity based on a common dwelling, other relationships imitative of family ties grow up from the "proximity" of the child and his foster-family. Whatever the circumstances whereby the proximity is brought about, it is very often the source of deep social relationships between working-class families.

Old Workers

A study of this type of tenant confirms the importance of contacts by proximity, already revealed in the day-to-day life of families, wives, and children living in the same tenement. Most of the old workmen in lodging houses have lost track of their children, who are often far from their father's town. Moreover, their meagre resources are scarcely sufficient to pay the rent. Who fulfils the function of assisting them, making sure they are tended in illness, and giving them a decent funeral when they die?

In all these contingencies, we find once again that the community of neighbours takes on the task when relatives are lacking. Very often, adult tenants provide these old workers with small jobs which will help them to keep alive. More often, they share with them some of the food they have cooked for themselves. This custom is performed so naturally that it arouses no comment; the practice is taken for granted. Here too proximity, when relatives are absent, entails a sort of tacit obligation to provide food for the old men. Other practices, equally widespread, concern the ill, the dead, and the dying—practices very different from the usual procedure in middle class or country families, where help for the sick and dying, funeral arrangements, and the upkeep of the graves, are generally the responsibility of the family or of close or distant relatives. People often travel great distances to care for a close or a distant relative, or see him buried.

It is most unusual for neighbours to intervene in such cases. In a lodging house or workers' block, a death or an illness no more passes unnoticed by neighbours, than a birth, and they generally intervene.

Here is one example. In a lodging house, Simone, a factory worker, died suddenly of heart disease. Her husband, a North African workman, was not there at the moment of death, because he was convalescing from pulmonary tuberculosis in a sanatorium. Simone's parents were dead, and she had no close relatives, so it was a woman neighbour, the oldest woman in the lodging house, who did what was necessary, informing the husband, sitting up with the body, and making a collection from the tenants to cover the immediate expenses. After the funeral, when the husband had gone back to the sanatorium, it was she who undertook the up-keep of the grave, which she visited regularly. An instance of this kind is by no means exceptional: when the family is lacking, it is the neighbours who care for the ailing, assist the dying, and tend the graves.

We shall not deal with the relationships with neighbours of the Kabyle[1] workers living in lodging houses, because these relationships might be influenced by family ties, in the case of their own compatriots, and by customs specific to their own cul-tural environment, in the case of European neighbours. Never-theless, none of these factors intervenes in the metropolitan workman's neighbourly contact with the Kabyle workers, since in this case it is the Parisian who takes the initiative. Here, we have repeatedly found that proximity creates a situation within which the relationships developed by the Parisian workmen to-wards the Kabyle workers are devoid of anything even remotely suggestive of racial discrimination. One example is that of an R.A.T.P. mechanic (Parisian transport company), who is teach-ing his neighbour on the same floor, a Kabyle worker who is making an effort to attend evening classes, to read French in his spare time. Actions of this kind are usually accompanied by

[1] Kabyles: Algerian immigrants from the hills near the north coast of Africa, and east of Algiers.

explicit affirmations of the equality of Kabyle workers with other workers. "They are just like the others", is a sentiment often expressed by the French neighbours of Kabyle workers, who are unaware that this appreciation is a result of neighbourly contact which has grown up between them, often without them being conscious of it, through living in the same lodging house.

One could ask whether the behaviour described above is found only among these particular tenants, because of the often excessive proximity bordering on promiscuity which results from the living conditions in lodging houses. However, it is found also, though sometimes in attenuated form, among families living in H.B.M.s (*habitations à bon marché*) and workers' blocks, because the facilities in these are still partly collective, and conditions are always fairly crowded. In H.B.M. houses, the children play communally in the courtyard, relations between neighbouring tenants on the same floor or staircase are often formed. Workers' blocks, with their frequently small living space, very densely populated, and often with a single courtyard and communal facilities for water and washing, provide a framework within which relations of proximity arise which are identical to those described in lodging houses.

Does the behaviour we have described relate especially to the non-working members of the working-class—mothers, children, old men, and the unemployed—who, because they have more time free, more readily form relationships with neighbours in lodging houses? Taking the common dwelling as a basis, the non-working population does indeed appear more active in forming relations of proximity, but these do, we find, definitely occur just as often and intensely between members of the working population employed in industry.

RELATIONS OF PROXIMITY AMONG INDUSTRIAL WORKERS

Just as it can give rise to promiscuity, proximity of positions at work within the same workshop or the same firm also creates conditions favourable for the formation of neighbourly relations. This is definitely a question of proximity rather than like sex, like age, or similar qualifications, as demonstrated by the following examples, intentionally chosen from a factory employing both men and women, another whose employees are semi-skilled women, and a third with highly trained male employees.

Relations of Proximity in a Mixed Sex Factory

The factory employs 350 workers of both sexes, housed in three workshops. In the "machines" workshop, the women machine pieces for the manufacture of toys, and the men fitters fit the machine tools appropriate for the process being carried out. In the tool workshop there are only professionally trained toolmakers, turners, and metal shapers, who make the tools. The third workshop contains women "fitters", who piece the toys together from the components manufactured in the "machines" section.

We found that in this factory relations of proximity spring up between employees who are placed close together in their work (for instance, in the same workshop), not between workers of the same age, the same sex, or similar qualifications. For instance, between 12 and 2 o'clock small leisure-time groups are formed including both the skilled women machinists and the skilled men workers from the same workshop. It is the custom for each member of the group in turn to pay for coffee all round.

These relationships extend beyond the rather brief and superficial contact of the lunch-hour: every possible opportunity is taken to celebrate events concerning individual members of the group, or the workshop as a whole. When Colette B. was 20, a collection was made to buy her a present, and Colette herself invited all her workshop neighbours, men and women, old and young, to have "a drink on her". When René V. was 50, the men, women, and girls in his workshop gave him a present and held a birthday celebration, though usually the converse rule applies—the person whose birthday it is must either take his workmates to the café to have a round on him, or regale them in the factory with some choice bottles of wine. Usually, no one opts out of these practices, which consequently reinforce the little community which has arisen through proximity. The workshop also celebrates more or less noisily the events which punctuate the workers' year: New Year's Eve, the day before the Works holiday, la Fête des Catherinettes (25 November, St. Catherine's Day, which in France is a special occasion for 25-year-old unmarried girls)—each has a small celebration attached. We also found that, within the workshop, proximity entails obligations which, in other social environments, concern the family and relatives.

When Roger T. fell ill and went into hospital, a collection was made throughout the workshop to pay his rent, and a small delegation was dispatched to see him in hospital. Exactly the same thing happened when a young widow with two children fell seriously ill.

During this same year of research spent in the factory, we noted dozens of similar cases showing how relations in the workshop produce new customs and feelings of responsibility which imitate the relationships arising from family ties or ties by marriage.

In the course of the year, the men and women workers donated the equivalent of several thousand working hours in order to fulfil effectively and in concrete terms responsibilities which they felt towards their neighbours at work just as imperatively as if they had been members of their families.

Relations of Proximity in a Factory employing Women

The employees of the Dreyfus works are almost all women: 200 women workers are employed there, and a few men, mostly North Africans, do unskilled jobs about the factory. There are three workshops—the cutting-shed where pieces of metal are cut out, the assembly shed, where they are made into tins and drums, and the printing shed, where the trade marks and designs are printed onto the metal tins.

In the canteen, some of the tables are reserved for the workers from the printing shed, who always get together at lunch-time. The contact in the canteen between the relatively few workers from the cutting shed, and the larger numbers from the assembly shed, also gives rise to little lunch-hour groups.

In the cutting shed and the assembly shed, proximity contact has repercussions on the women's ideas of what it is good or bad to do at work. Everyone accepts the rule that "the good jobs" which yield high earnings on a piece-work basis, should be shared about in turn. If one of the women accepts a "good job" several times running, without letting her neighbours take their turn, she is unanimously condemned, ostracized from the community, and suspected of having an understanding with her employer; she is even said to have been "bought by the boss".

It is also this proximity contact in workshops which produces the feeling of a need for a strictly egalitarian attitude to all workers in the factory, without exception, or racial or national discrimination. This attitude was demonstrated by the women at the Dreyfus works under the following circumstances. When an overseer from the assembly shed died, the women collected money for a wreath and sent representatives to the funeral, and received from their employer the payment for the lost working hours, plus the bonus for regular work which depended on the hourly wage. The following year, on the death of Salah, a simple North African labourer, a collection was made, and representatives designated to attend the funeral; the manager was asked to pay for the working hours lost by the delegation. He refused, and there was unanimous protest from the women workers. They elected Louise F., representative of the personnel, to go and talk with the management. These are the words she used in the course of the interview: "You can't buy us off with your bonus. You payed for the lost hours when it was an overseer, so you must pay for them for Salah. He's only a labourer, but everybody is equal in the face of death; you mustn't make distinctions." When the management continued to withold its consent, the women made another collection to pay for the hours lost by their workmates, who found that they had been more generously compensated than if the management had paid them at the usual rate. This is an example of how contact by proximity at work had given rise to the feeling of a need for homogeneity among members of a group racially and culturally very heterogeneous, whereas the management had seen in these factors a basis for discrimination.

Friendships which grow up through this contact by proximity in the workshop are so close that they eventually eclipse family ties either partially or wholly. Such is the case with Louise F., a very specialized metal cutter who has been with the factory for 30 years. Louise, now 60, left her native village of Corrèze at the age of 15, and now lives in a pretty little suburban villa built by her husband while he was still alive. Although a widow, she has numerous relatives, cousins and nephews who like herself set out from the country in Auvergne to make their fortunes in commerce. In spite of this, she prefers to spend her free time with her old working companions. Although she was invited by her nephews for Christmas and the New Year, Louise F. declared that she still preferred to have her friends from work round to her house to see the New Year in. Thus festivities which, in middle-class or farming families are special family occasions, often become for the workers occasions to be celebrated with friends from the factory.

Relations of Proximity in a Factory Employing Men

The Ratti works, unlike the factories in the two preceding examples, employs a great majority of highly skilled workers. Out of 120 workmen, only 4 are unskilled labour: the rest are qualified turners (30), fitters (25), toolmakers and metal shapers (30), mechanics (10), and 21 others (painters, a storeman, and so on). There are 100 workers in the main factory workshop, and only 20 in the one upstairs. Since 1902, this factory has been turning out automatic machines for biscuit-making and sweet- and chocolate-wrapping.

There are a few youths and some old men among the workers, but most of them are of mature age. Each time a young man goes off to do his military service or gets married, a collection is made. Those who do not contribute incur the disapproval of the group, but they are few. Other practices besides these are current: very often money is borrowed and lent in the factory—borrowed from workmates, not from members of the family.[2]

In this factory, the union handed round a list of workers' representatives for the workshops both up and downstairs. When Germain H., a fitter from upstairs, took it upon himself to present a list of representatives for the upstairs workshop only, without informing all the workers, the reaction towards this move, which split the syndical unity of the two workshops, was one of deep suspicion. The previously elected representatives organized a meeting for all the workers to examine the case. The majority came out against Germain's modification, which had been introduced without their knowledge; they suspected a move to destroy the unity which had always prevailed in the factory.

CONCLUSION

We could give dozens of other instances illustrating the depth and prevalence of relationships between neighbours either on an industrial or a domiciliary basis. Without prolonging the discussion, we can sum up our observations as follows:

(a) This behaviour arises out of a "setting" or situation created by living conditions which at the present time, both at home and at work, are those of most working-class people living in industrial neighbourhoods and working for a wage. In lodging houses, more than in any other form of workers' housing, it is evident that the collective facilities there, and the crowded, not to say grossly overcrowded conditions, promote all forms of contact between neighbouring tenants.

In factories, the fact that people are placed close together in

[2] As in the toy factory, birthdays are celebrated here by little gatherings at which alcoholic refreshment is partaken.

their work, and in some cases the functional interdependence of certain tasks, means that workers are entering daily into close and friendly relationships. These relations of proximity form the basis for small communities limited either to the tenants in a lodging house, or to workers in the same workshop, or the same factory if it is a small one.

These small groups usually include members of very heterogeneous race and culture. But proximity prevails over racial prejudice; behaviour is in fact the same towards all members of these communities, be they Parisians or North Africans. Nevertheless, a conscious realization of equality only comes when precipitated by some external obstacle to it. Thus, when the management of the Dreyfus works introduced an element of discrimination in its distribution of "good jobs" or in its attitude to deceased employees, the members of the community rebelled against these measures with a very explicit affirmation of the equality of all the women workers, and the equality of the dead, whatever their race or professional qualifications.

(b) Is there an explicit awareness of the existence of the small community as such? It does indeed seem that in the majority of cases the members of these sub-groups experience emotionally the existence of this "We". The awareness of the community as such does not become strongly explicit until it encounters an obstacle to its continuing existence.[3] For example, Germain H.'s attempt to introduce a division within the Ratti works gave rise to a clearer realization by the workers of the existence of the community as such, at least in so far as its members proclaimed its unity, and condemned Germain H.'s purely "personal" endeavour.

Within the communal "We", solidarity between members of the community is just one aspect of day-to-day life; for the outside observer it is the most spectacular manifestation of the existence of this "We", but it is not the only manifestation. An individual

---

[3] To adopt the expressions of M. Georges Gurvitch, it would seem that in this case there is a transference from the "Virtual" to the "Actual" We (*le Nous virtuel, le Nous actuel*).

may be capable of gestures of solidarity with neighbouring tenants or workmates, yet show a pronounced preference for solitude. However, all the observations we have made demonstrate how much enjoyment the members of these working-class communities derive from spending their leisure hours together, and organizing them by devising countless small celebrations. Thus, in the toy factory, individual birthdays or occasions involving all the workers furnish pretexts for merry-making which consolidate and foster the community life of the workshop.

In lodging houses, it is not unusual for mothers of families, in spite of their very limited living space, to invite women neighbours round with their children on Thursday afternoons,[4] when the presence of the children prevents the mothers from doing house-work. Communal leisure is usually preferred to family leisure. Some people, like Louise F., celebrate what are traditionally regarded as family occasions with neighbours rather than with relatives, even when they are in a position to choose.

These attitudes and ways of behaviour express a way of thought peculiar to the working classes. In particular, the preference for spending leisure time not alone or in the family, but within the small community to which one belongs as a tenant or worker, seems to be very specific to working-class life.

(c) Are there in certain cases customs which correspond to behaviour models? Workers assured us that this was so, when we questioned them on the origin of certain practices. Thus, when we asked Marcel Y. about the practice prevalent in the Ratti works, of making a collection every time a young worker goes off to do his military service or gets married, he replied "It's a custom: I've been at the factory thirty years, and we've always done it".

When Robert L., a spray-gun operator, and Denise G., a varnisher, started work simultaneously in a varnishing workshop, some of the women workers informed them discreetly that it was "the custom" for newcomers—if they were able—to offer drinks around to the old hands in the workshop. Men offered red wine,

---

[4] In France, Thursday is a half day for schoolchildren, who usually have classes on Saturday morning.

women white. These drinks were the occasion of a little gathering of all the workshop members, where the new people were asked about themselves, and a welcome extended to them.

The examples we have given were taken from the metal industry, but in the course of a conversation we held with a militant old builder about these customs, he retorted that "these traditions" were much more firmly established in building, which was a corporation of longer standing in the wage-earning world.

In lodging houses, on the contrary, we have never heard tenants justify the behaviour we have described by citing already existing customs. The present population of lodging houses is, in fact, of recent date, having settled in since 1945. Before that, the great majority of people in lodging houses were passing out quickly into normal accommodation. Customs could not arise within this mobile population. The behaviour which we see being established now among the forced "residents" in lodging houses has not had any model in the past. At the moment it is merely the drastic consequence of a situation arising out of the living conditions which are imposed upon them. If it were possible to make a comparison, we should liken the behaviour of the lodging house tenants to that of the prisoners of war interned in concentration camps during the last war. The behaviour which grew up in these camps, and which has been made known through numerous accounts after the war, was the consequence of a situation resulting from conditions of existence imposed upon those interned, and not an imitation referring back to previous models.

Situation and custom are not mutually exclusive. "Customs" referred to in factories to justify current practice are maintained and reinforced by communal working conditions imposed on the workers in the workshop. In lodging houses the behaviour of tenants which arises out of the situation, might well provide models for behaviour if the accommodation crisis were to continue, so that families were constrained to stay in the lodging houses longer than they normally would.

(d) Having completed this study, we are in a better position to analyse the relationship between contact with relatives and contact with neighbours in the life of the working classes, and situate the working-class family in this respect, in relation to farming families and middle-class families.

In so-called middle-class families, contact with relatives usually eclipses contact by proximity, which is practically non-existent on a domiciliary basis. Relationships arising out of work are often based on rivalry and competition. Although solidarity may sometimes be apparent, intimacy is absent from contacts at work. The most stable and prevalent relationships are above all with *les proches* ("the near ones")—relatives by blood or by marriage, irrespective of distance or the exact relationship within the family. It is towards these "near ones" that obligations are established by law, reinforced by custom, and approved by moral opinion.

With working-class families and wage-earning labourers, the importance of relatives or relatives by marriage has become considerably less through the living conditions imposed upon these families. Their inadequate living-space often reduces the family to wife, husband, and children, and the household is isolated by emigration from grandparents, aunts, uncles, and cousins.

The most prevalent, the most vital relationships, and the most stable, operate within the small communities which have been formed by proximity in the same lodging house, or proximity at work in the same workshop. These relationships generate new customs, and feelings of responsibility towards "near ones" who are not relatives. One observer[5] has remarked that these relationships appear so natural to the working man that he does not comment on them. When they come to live in industrial cities, and work as wage-earners in factories, rural immigrants from the country in Britanny, the Auvergne, and other regions of France assume responsibilities for their lodging-house neighbours or their workmates which were generally limited to the circle of relatives in the peasant families from which they came. As for the Parisian workman, he is brought up to this behaviour from an

[5] P. Chombart de Lauwe, *Paris et l'agglomération parisienne*, Paris, P.U.F., 1952, p. 106.

early age, as from childhood on he lives within an environment extending beyond the family.

Nevertheless, these responsibilities are not felt to be imposed from the outside: they spring from emotional involvement in the small community to which the worker belongs. In his *German Ideology*, Marx already noted the absence of all ideology (in the Marxist sense) and alienation from the relationships between members of a working-class family: "Where a family has really decomposed, as in the proletariat, the idea of the family does not exist at all, while we observe, only in places it is true, a propensity to family life based on relationships which are entirely real." Is it not also this absence of alienation and of stereotype which characterizes the "entirely real relationships" occurring within the relations of proximity which, as we have shown, hold a place of considerable importance in working-class life, both at home and at work?

The Functions of Kinship

The Family in a Greek Village: Dowry and Inheritance; Formal Structure

E. Friedl

THE dowry and inheritance system in Vasilika is primarily a mechanism by which property is transferred from one generation to the next. It is this kind of mechanism, but it is also more. By reason of the context of values in which they operate and because of their specific characteristics, dowry and inheritance patterns as they function in Vasilika have ramifications not only for the Boeotian countryside but also for Greece as a whole.

INHERITANCE BY SONS

Both the Greek laws of inheritance and village custom require that property be divided equally among all the children, sons and daughters alike. Some receive their shares through inheritance or by gifts while the parents are still alive, but the daughters of a family are entitled to their share at marriage in the form of a dowry. Since, from the standpoint of the villagers, a man's most compelling obligation is to arrange for the successful marriage of his daughters, and since no girl in Vasilika can normally expect to marry without at least a token dowry, the girls have first lien on the family's property. For most of Vasilika's families, land holdings are the most valuable assets, and dowries are, therefore, calculated ordinarily as a transfer of a share of the land from parents to a daughter and through her to the jurisdiction of her husband. However, if a family's land holdings are such that it is obvious that by giving daughters their share of the land at the time of their marriage, the shares remaining for the sons will be too small to enable them to support their future wives and children, the family recognizes the problem and tries to make some adjustment that will prevent the threatened poverty. The villagers are well aware of the dangers of land fragmentation under a system of equal inheritance. The average land holding in Vasilika is already only one-third to one-fourth of what it was at the time the village was settled. Thanks to the introduction of irrigation and improvements in agricultural techniques, both the bulk of yields and the cash value of the crops in the area have increased to the point at which the farmers maintain a higher standard of living on the smaller holdings than their grandfathers did on the more extensive ones. But the process has its limits, and the future possibility of economically useless small holdings is a real hazard for Vasilika's families.

One kind of solution to its problem is for a family to try to train or educate its "surplus" sons for a nonfarming occupation; if possible, one that will send them to the towns and cities as white-collar workers or as professional men. This effort, however, is more than merely a solution to a recognized problem. Status as an urbanite has very high value for the villagers in its own right. The families of Vasilika try to import urban ways into the village; their efforts to send their own sons and daughters directly into the towns and cities may now be discussed. For quite apart from the necessities of their situation, the people of Vasilika act as if they assumed that life in towns and cities is superior to life in a small village. This judgement is not based on a belief that there is necessarily greater economic well-being in the towns. On the contrary, the villagers believe it is more difficult to achieve a respectable standard in the larger centers and, indeed, that the plight of the poor is worse in the town than in the village. They say it is harder to have little when one is tempted by so much. But the villagers respect an educated man; education enables a person to pursue occupations which the villagers believe have greater prestige than farming, and the preponderance of these occupations are practiced in towns. Not only white-collar workers but also journalists, lawyers, doctors, writers, gymnasium and university professors congregate in the provincial towns and in Athens (cf. Antonakaki, 1955, p. 93). Even if a young man from Vasilika is not fortunate enough to work in one of these favored occupations—even if he is a tailor or a barber or an artisan of another type, or a small merchant—he is believed to acquire some aura of prestige simply by living in the more populous center.

The young girls of Vasilika want to marry into the towns because they are well aware of the greater physical ease and comfort available there and contrast these conditions favorably with the arduous and endless labor they are accustomed to in the village.

Still another incentive for gaining the status of a town dweller is the belief, in Vasilika, that life in town is more full of adventure and less monotonous than life in the village. Besides, the towns and Athens have crowds, and *polis cosmos* (many people) are enjoyed by the villagers for their own sake. A *paniyiri* or Easter is considered successful in proportion to the number of people the village attracts, and the villagers comment on their satisfaction at seeing some different faces.

A caveat may be in order here, however. No matter how much the villagers like the variety of life in the towns, and no matter how much they dislike the tiring and messy work on the farms, when they actually live in the village and are engaged in the work in the fields and at home, they work hard, steadily, and with a will. The people of Vasilika do not believe work is ennobling in itself; they seem to have no compulsive need to work to achieve self-respect, but they accept the need for hard labor as a means to the end of support for the family. Therefore, the villagers expect the farmer and his household to work hard and for long hours if an agricultural existence is their immediate fate, but do not condemn some farmer if he tries to arrange a different fate for his children. If he is unsuccessful, and all his sons stay on the farm, or if his daughters are married off to farmers, there is no disgrace in that either, as long as he did the best he could. And if a farmer can bequeath a good farm to any of his sons and the son manages the property skilfully, the economic success of the farm brings a measure of prestige, in Vasilika, to father and son alike.

Within the context of these values let us consider how the dowry and inheritance system functions in Vasilika. Sometimes after a farmer marries and has had at least one child, it would appear that he and his wife consider the question of how many more children it would be sensible for them to have. The parents recognize that the more children they have, the harder it will be to provide adequately for the future of each of them. Therefore, regulation of the size of families is accepted in the village as obviously prudent and sensible. The villagers explain that more children survive nowadays as a result of modern medical care, and that this obviates the need to have a large family in the hope that at least two or three of the children will reach maturity. In Vasilika, some prenatal care and confinement in one of the proprietary hospitals in Levadhia is recognized now as the safest kind of maternity care and also has the most prestige (Friedl, 1958). Such care immediately increases the cost of childbirth and is a drain on the family's resources. But even those families whose babies are born at home with the aid of a traveling government-trained midwife are expected, as we have seen, to provide better food and finer clothing for their children than earlier generations provided for theirs. The added expense of rearing children has not been counterbalanced by any increase in their economic value on the farms. On the contrary, less labor is regularly needed.

The trend to smaller families seems to have started back in the 1920's. Genealogies show that the parents of the marriageable young adults of the middle and late 1950's had already limited the size of their families to a mode of four children in contrast to their parents who typically had had eight. The overt statements made by married men and women of all ages including the 60- and 70-year-old widows indicate that the change is deliberate and coincides with their expressed attitudes. Parents who have more children than they can adequately feed and care for are accused of behaving like animals; they are said to have neither brains nor self-control. Parents with marriageable children were, therefore, in 1961, contemplating the division of their estates into fewer portions than their parents had done before them.

As his children are growing up, a farmer calculates approximately what he must give his daughter or daughters for dowries and how much will be left for each of his sons to share. If it is fairly obvious that the share left for the sons will be insufficient to support each of them, the farmer tries to make some other provision for one or more of the boys. Any boy who shows promise as a student is encouraged to continue his schooling beyond the compulsory sixth-grade elementary school in the village. Education is so highly prized that sometimes even an only son who might inherit an adequate farm is allowed to continue his education if he shows ability in academic subjects. The next step after elementary school most commonly chosen by the villagers is the 6-year classical or humanistic gymnasium which serves as a necessary base for any civil service or white-collar post, and also for further study in the university or in specialized advanced technical schools. Although there are some private gymnasia, most of the farmers of Vasilika have sent their sons to the virtually free public institutions (Antonakaki, 1955, p. 39). These are in the provincial towns or in Athens, so that although there is little tuition charge, the farmer must pay for his son's board and room, for his school supplies, and for adequate clothing. Whenever possible, children are boarded with an aunt or uncle who lives in the town, but even under these conditions, farmers pay a fee to the relatives to cover the cost of their children's care. Sometimes, to keep food costs down, a mother prepares a basket of bread, cheese, and perhaps a vegetable stew for her son, places it in the bus bound for the town in which the boy goes to school, and the boy picks up the basket at the bus depot.

Whatever the particular arrangement, schooling involves an expenditure of current income, and the farmers consider that the cost of educating a son is about equivalent to a major portion of his share of the inheritance. The Greek Civil Code makes a specific provision for this view by declaring that educational expenses beyond those normally to be expected from the economic position of the family may be counted as part of the inheritance (section 1895). In Vasilika it is assumed that a gymnasium-educated young man will spend the rest of his life living in some town, and that he will receive only a token share of the land after his father's death or at the time of the division of the estate. His parents, brothers, and sisters remaining in the villages as farmers gain in social stature and in potential actual advantage from his residence in town in a prestige-giving occupation. Both the legal code and village custom, then, involve the recognition that when farmers or shepherds undertake to educate their sons beyond the village school, they are striving for an improved status position in the nation as a whole, and that if sons succeed in the new prestige-giving occupation, they are the agents of upward social mobility for the family. Among Vasilika's land-owning farmers, an educated son gives the village the added advantage of a larger amount of land to divide among the remaining children. For farmers and shepherds who have very small land holdings or none at all, the sacrifices necessary to keep an academically talented son in the gymnasium are undertaken with enthusiasm, because such a son gives promise both of increasing the income of his family and raising its social position.

Although not all of Vasilika's boys who start the gymnasium have sufficient talent or self-discipline to complete the course, a majority of them do so and give observable evidence of the feasibility of sending boys for advanced schooling. In 1959, of the thirty-four boys and young men who were between the ages of 12 and 30 and who were also sons of farmers, sixteen had attended or were then attending gymnasium, and three of the sixteen had received or were still receiving some education at a higher level. By 1961, as we have seen, a shepherd's boy had completed a year in gymnasium. Whether all these sons will succeed in finding employment commensurate with their educational qualifications depends, of course, on the economic development of the nation, and especially on the increased possibilities for employment in the towns and in Athens. In Vasilika each educated young man and his family hope that he will not have to return to the village to live.

The pattern of educating sons is not a new one in the village. With few exceptions, the groups of middle-aged brothers and of young adult brothers and sisters in the village in 1961 could boast of one additional brother who was living in a town or in Athens, and each of these men had had some education beyond the village school. There were also two men in this age group who were living in the village but had had some gymnasium training.

A second solution to the problem of surplus sons well known in the history of Greece has been emigration out of the country itself. In the decade between 1910 and 1920 about four young men left Vasilika for the United States. One of these returned to fight in the Balkan Wars of 1912 and has lived in the village ever since. The other three are still in the United States. In the 1930's, one man left with his wife and child for Tanganyika. The extent of continuing association with these overseas relatives is different in each case; one man returned to Vasilika to visit his brother in the early 1950's and stayed for only a year; another wrote sporadically; a third disappeared and his son knew only that he had died in the States. The Tanganyika relatives, however, continually sent packages to their village cousins, and the son of the original emigré, who had died, returned to the village with his mother in 1959. The villagers always referred to the packages from Tanganyika as gifts from America and referred to the Tanganyikan, even after his return, as "the American". Apparently, the word "America" in the village is a generic term for an El Dorado abroad. However, emigration out of the country is not currently of interest to the villagers; no one in the village ever asked us for help in arranging the emigration of one of their sons to the United States, though joking references to our taking young people back with us were not uncommon.

Up to this point, then, we may conclude that the system of equal inheritance of property and the villagers' approval of urban living have led to an actual geographical movement of young men out of Vasilika and to a social movement into occupations other than farming for young men who have grown up in the rural settlement. Another aspect of the situation is that income from land directly supports boys who live in towns both during their years in school and until they find a job. The possible importance of this for the urban economy of Greece will be discussed again in connection with dower wealth that is transferred to the cities.

DOWERING THE DAUGHTER

The dowry wlll be discussed first as the social mechanism by which daughters inherit property at marriage, and second as a mechanism for social mobility. In Vasilika, parents are obligated to arrange marriages for their children, and with few exceptions they do so. They most frequently look for spouses outside of the village. They expect that a girl will leave the village to live with her husband and that a farming son will bring his wife to Vasilika to live with him (technically, patrilocal residence). In Vasilika, when the villagers speak of the engagement of a man or a woman, they say, "He (she) has become engaged in Mirali": or in Sfaka, or in Athens, or in whatever village or town the prospective spouse comes from. They explain the prevalence of exogamy, to which the phrase just quoted gives linguistic expression, by saying that it is too difficult to find, inside Vasilika, anyone who is sufficiently distantly related to be eligible for marriage.

The custom of the village prohibits marriage between relatives on both the mother's and father's side to the degree of third cousin. In a village with a total population of 216, in which there are six sets of adult brothers and one group of three men whose fathers were brothers, there will certainly be limits to the number of boys and girls eligible to marry each other. The number of families connected by kin ties in the village is even larger, however, because in each generation there are some marriages that do take place among fellow villagers and this, of course, relates some of the village's children to each other through their mother's line, even if their fathers have no paternal relatives in Vasilika.

Kinship connections are further extended within the village by the ceremonial kinship ties of godparenthood. On the ground that any godparental relationship between two individuals automatically places not only the individuals concerned but both their elementary families into close kin relations, the Greek Orthodox Church prohibits marriages between the two families to the same degree that would be necessary if they were consanguineal; that is, were blood relatives.

When a daughter is to be married, the father of the girl is believed to have ultimate responsibility for giving the dowry. However, the brothers' interests are involved, the mother is deeply concerned about the future of her daughter, and certainly the girl herself wants to know something about her prospects. In the informal discussions that go on within the family, everyone participates and expresses his point of view. The father alone, however, has the formal responsibility for conducting the negotiations, which are always carried on with the aid of a *proksenitis* or *proksinitra* (marriage intermediary). In the Boeotian countryside, this person (either a man or a woman) is a friend or relative, either from the village or from the community of the prospective spouse, rather than a professional. On the groom's side, the father participates in the negotiations, but the prospective groom himself is present and active in the proceedings. His decision as to the minimum value of the dowry and the form in which he will accept it is the crucial one.

The dowry negotiations and the final marriage contract can be usefully discussed, therefore, as analogous to a commercial transaction in which each side tries to get the most value at the least cost. For the bride's father, the material costs include the land and cash he must give as part of his daughter's dowry. She is, of course, legally and customarily entitled to her share of the patrimony, but except for the cash, the determination of just how much is her share is not easy to arrive at. A farmer, as we have seen, holds land in scattered parcels of different quality; some of the parcels are in the immediate vicinity of Vasilika, no more than an hour's walk away from the village; others may have been part of his wife's dowry and may, therefore, be near her village; his house has value, but since his daughter will not live with him, he cannot give her part of it. The problem is solved in Vasilika by making a rough estimate of the money value of the parents' property in terms of gold sovereigns (*lires*) and then determining how many *lires* a girl is entitled to. Since the end of the Greek Civil War in 1949, the drachma has been stabilized, and the villagers as well as the rest of the Greek population are gaining confidence in the currency. However, the belief that gold sovereigns, worth approximately $10 each in 1961, are the only trustworthy form of cash is still common in Greece, as is the hoarding of the sovereigns and the requirement that bills be paid in them. The villagers evaluate property in terms of *lires* and always speak of a dowry as one of so many *lires*, regardless of whether the property transferred is cash or land or both.

Besides the property costs of the dowry, a farmer loses the labor of his daughter both on the farm and in the household. Finally, there is an emotional cost to the parents, particularly to the mother, at the marriage of a daughter. A mother loses the companionship of a friend, a confidante, and a working partner in the house and the fields. Among the more prosperous farmers, girls marry in their middle or late twenties. As a result mothers frequently have had many years of cooperation with grown daughters. The wrench at parting is seriously felt. Mothers in Vasilika openly lament the loss of their daughters and speak frequently of how much they miss their absent girls.

When a marriage is contemplated between families of equal wealth and social position, for example, when the daughter of a farmer is being married to a man who expects to stay on his father's farm, and when his share of the farm has approximately the same value as what the girl brings in as a dowry, the negotiations are relatively straightforward. Each side can then limit itself to checking on the claims the other is making and to surveying the total situation. Is the yield of the land the girl is bringing what her father says it is? Will the son-in-law be entitled to the share of the land he claims he will have? Does the boy have so many sisters that his father may die before they have been married off leaving the boy with the responsibility of dowering them? Is the father-in-law's house well enough equipped so that the girl will be able to live at approximately the standard she had at home? How many brothers does the groom have who are also going to be farmers and who will, therefore, have to share the house itself, or for whom some housing provision must eventually be made? Because personal qualities of the prospective groom will influence the success with which he manages his own and his dower properties, a father asks whether the groom has a reputation for industriousness. Is there any danger that the groom will "eat" the dowry properties, as the villagers phrase a propensity for using capital resources for current needs or for luxuries? Are the groom's father and brothers sober men who will conserve property and work to get the best income from it?

In short, the bride's father wants to assure, insofar as he is able, the future well-being of his daughter and of her children. He also wants the emotional satisfaction of having been successful at making a good arrangement for her. One village father pointed to a field we were passing and explained that he had given it to his daughter as part of her *prika* (dowry), so that all the cotton from the field was for his grandson. He then went on to say that he had married his daughter well and said of his three-year-old grandson, "Who knows, one day he might become a lawyer or a doctor. He has a brain, the little one". The implication was that he, the farmer, had contributed to whatever the final destiny of his grandson might be by having supplied such good fields for his daughter's dowry.

A girl's parents also want assurance that she will live in a congenial household. They hope that the new mother-in-law and the groom's sisters will accept the girl with good grace and that she will be decently treated. A man's wife and daughter will always remind him of the resources the family has already expended on the trousseau and the skill with which they were woven. From the women's point of view, these are important parts of the cost, and they want a girl to go to a family which will appreciate both the quantity and the fine workmanship of the *rukha*. Some friction between a girl and her mother-in-law and sisters-in-law is accepted in Vasilika as part of the condition of marriage to a farmer. The severity of friction is mitigated, however, by the independent dignity a girl acquires by having brought her husband a dowry and by the pride her husband's family takes in their own skill at having helped arrange a good marriage for their son.

The groom's interest, on the other hand, is to supplement his patrimony with as much land and cash as he can get from his wife's dowry. After their marriage, the husband and wife will have jurisdiction over her dowry properties. Unless the marriage contract states otherwise, and it rarely does in marriages between a farmer and a village girl, the husband has the right to the management and control of movable and personal property that he received with his wife and the management of the real estate given as part of the dowry. The alienation of movable dower property requires only the informal consent of his wife, while the alienation of real estate requires a formal notarized consent statement from his wife and the permission of the court (Civil Code Sections 1416 and 1417). (The groom's father, therefore, is interested only from the standpoint of the general welfare of his son. He himself will have no direct control over his daughter-in-law's land or money.) From the groom's point of view, an industrious young girl also has high value, and if she is healthy, good-looking, modest, virtuous, and amiable as well, she is of still additional worth. Therefore, an ugly older girl with a bad reputation would have to bring a large dowry to compensate for her personal deficiencies. Conversely, an attractive, healthy, virtuous young girl might be able to marry a slightly wealthier man than her dowry would normally be expected to command. Greek folk songs often lament the story of a young girl who attracted a wealthy older suitor to whom her family married her because he was willing to take a smaller dowry. The songs, in this instance, reflect actual situations known on the Boeotian countryside, although they do not occur with any great frequency.

NEGOTIATIONS, COURTSHIP, AND MARRIAGE

For the families involved, the marriage negotiations have the quality of participation in a kind of ritualized contest. A young man may have been recommended to a girl's father; the father sends an intermediary with information as to how much dowry he is willing to give; the intermediary then goes off to the groom and his father, to whom he exaggerates the size of the dowry and the qualities of the girl. The villagers assume he will also exaggerate the qualities of the groom to the girl's family. The enjoyment of the game lies in each group's efforts indirectly to get accurate information about the other side. This is done by making inquiries among one's own relatives living in the prospective spouse's village and by asking questions of others who know the family. Secrecy about the very existence of the negotiations is helpful at this point, because the villagers do not believe they can get accurate information if anyone knows they have a direct interest in the matter. Many times a sister in another village will act as informal intermediary for her brother and try to find out how much of a dowry some of the better young men are asking for. Tentative questions of this sort may be asked for years before a serious negotiation is finally fully launched. These tentative steps may be terminated at any time without loss of honor on either side if the young man informs the intermediary that the dowry is not quite enough, or if the girl's father uses the excuse that his daughter is not yet ready to marry because she has not accumulated sufficient *rukha*. In fact, the grooms are not interested in the *rukha*. As one villager phrased it, "It is land and money they burn for around here".

In Vasilika, both in the previous generations and at present, it has been possible for a young man and woman never to have seen each other until the first formal occasion for meeting. However, a young man may have seen an attractive girl at a *paniyiri* or other festival, and may have asked his father to investigate her situation. But, since unmarried village boys and girls do not talk to each other in public unless they are related, the chances are that he has never talked to her. A young girl may, in her turn, know a great deal about the young men in the surrounding villages and may also have had opportunities to see them at the local festivities, but may never have talked to any of them. In any case, it is village custom for both boy and girl to act as if they know nothing about the discussions going on. At the first formal meeting, both the boy and girl have the right to express any personal antipathy they may have for the prospective spouse. But if the marriage is otherwise an advantageous one, they are likely to be persuaded to overcome any but the most extreme feelings of repugnance. The villagers are not callous about the matter of personal compatibility between spouses; they assume, however, that if the marriage conditions are right, a harmonious relationship will develop, and if it does not, the successful economic or prestige conditions of the marriage will help to allay sufferings arising from the lack of personal contentment.

Once the major provisions of the marriage contract are agreed upon, the machinery for the formal engagement gets under way. This involves, first, a visit by the groom, his father, and several of his other relatives, but not his mother, to the home of the bride. Here the men again check on the agreements, the father of the groom pins a single *lira* on the bride, the bride's mother pins a *lira* on the groom; there is food and drink, and the bride gives gifts of small items such as socks, stockings, pillow cases, or towels to the groom and his entire group. For the women, this process is important; what is given on the one hand, and what is received on the other, is discussed by the women on both sides with great zest and frequent criticism. If this affair raises no issues which lead to the dissolution of the agreements, about ten days later, the bride's father invites his own relatives and those of the groom from wherever they are in Greece to a large engagement party which lasts from a Saturday night through to Sunday. The bride's neighbors and the groom's friends also come.

From the time of the ceremonial exchange of the *lires*, the young couple are considered formally engaged. They are now free not only to see each other but to travel anywhere together, and the groom may even come and stay at the girl's home for some time. In the villagers' view, if the young couple have proper respect for both sets of parents they will refrain from sex relations during this period. Certainly if the girl becomes pregnant before the wedding there is disapproval not only because of the moral stigma, but also because it requires an immediate wedding at a time when the accumulation of the agreed-upon dowry property may not yet have been completed. A premature ceremony is therefore not advantageous to the groom. Engagements lasting a year or more are frequent, and the villagers speak of unfortunate situations in which this status has been protracted for as long as ten years.

Weddings in Vasilika in recent years, the villagers say, have become less elaborate and less of a village event than they once were. As later sections will show, many of the village girls marry men in the towns, and this frequently results in having the wedding in the town church rather than in Vasilika. Moreover, the villagers say, this system obviates the necessity of inviting large numbers of villagers to the wedding feast and so cuts down on the cost to the bride's father.

At weddings held in the village between children of farmers, however, much of the tradition is maintained. For example, the groom's male relatives come to the house of the bride on the Saturday afternoon before the Sunday wedding to take the *rukha* and the house furnishings she has received as gifts to the groom's home. The groom hires a truck to do the job, not because there is so much furniture, but because of the quantity of *rukha*. A Vasilika girl is expected to have woven at home approximately thirty sheets, six light blankets, two heavy woolen carpets, five lighter woolen floor coverings, five coarse woolen blankets, four mattress covers, ten carry-all bags or sacks, two heavy ornamental table covers, one red-and-white striped and one blue-and-white striped tablecloth with twelve napkins to match each of the cloths, six cotton face towels, and two long cotton towels for the tray in which loaves of bread are left to rise before baking. To this accumulation she will add several pieces that are bought from itinerant merchants and embroidered at home. Also purchased, usually in town, are white sheets, pillow cases, and turkish towels as well as the material for about six pairs of curtains. Furniture consisting of a wooden wardrobe, a bed, a table, and some chairs may be added, as are the cooking and serving utensils given to the girl as gifts. The colorful collection fills a small pick-up truck, and the sight of one of these on the road with laughing and singing young men crowding whatever space is left is a sure sign of a wedding. On Sunday morning the groom's party, including his marriage sponsor (*kumbaros*), arrive at the house of the bride. The *kumbaros* leads the group to the house, only to find the door closed and locked. He begs that the door be opened. The girls inside giggle and demand 1000 drachmas to open the door. After some bargaining, the *kumbaros* gives a five-drachma piece and the party comes in. It is the *kumbaros* who rents the bride's white wedding gown, provides the wedding crowns, the large white candles which are held at the ceremony, and the *kufeta*, the sugar covered almonds arranged in small packages of white netting, tied with a white ribbon, which he distributes to each of the guests after the ceremony. After the wedding feast, for which musicians are hired so that the guests can sing and dance, the bride is accompanied to the groom's home by her brothers and sometimes a sister. The women, including the bride, all cry as they leave the girl with her new husband.[1] But even among farmers these customs are changing, and in recent years the bride and groom have taken to leaving the wedding guests to go off on a short honeymoon.

DISPOSITION OF DOWER PROPERTY

After the marriage of a farmer, the couple is settled in the man's village, usually in the home of his parents. The groom has acquired some parcels of land in his wife's village and a small hoard of

---

[1] The description of the engagement and wedding ceremonies is not complete. The details selected are meant to give only an impression of the nature of these affairs.

cash as well. For the first few years of his marriage, he may go to his wife's village to work the land himself, or he may contract with his father-in-law or with one of his brothers-in-law to work it for him on shares. Either way he will have occasion to visit his wife's village and to have some association with her father and brothers. In the meantime, he is likely to be looking for an opportunity to exchange land with a farmer who lives in his wife's village and has married a girl from his own settlement and, therefore, has land near the groom's village. A farmer husband may even be willing to consider the sale of the land in his wife's village to make a good purchase nearer home. Neither of these possibilities may come to fruition for years, so that they may remain subjects for long-term discussion between a man and his father- and brothers-in-law. To summarize the situation, land given as one part of the dowry and village exogamy have the consequence of stimulating land exchanges and sales in the Boeotian countryside, of stimulating the visits of men among the villages in the region with a consequent exchange of views and ideas, and of providing an economic focus for maintaining some kind of relationships between affinal relatives, that is relatives by marriage. The system of transferring land as dowry has the effect also of permitting a man to utilize his wife's property throughout his married life instead of having to wait to do so until after his wife's father's death.

The actions of the villagers and the tone in which they discuss these questions suggest that although there is some sentiment attached to the land inherited from a father and to the land that were parts of a mother's dowry, the symbolic value of particular parcels of land as a link between generations does not usually take precedence over the economic value of the land as an income and food producer.

We have still to consider the question of the ultimate disposition of dower properties in marriages between farmers. The Greek Civil Code states that dower property must be accounted for separately from that owned or eventually inherited by the husband, and as we have seen, stipulates that the consent of the wife is required before dower property can be sold or exchanged. If there is a divorce, the wife is entitled to the return of the dower property or of its equivalent. In the house of the groom's father, the newly married couple is given a room in which they and, later, their children sleep. Here the bride's trousseau gives the room a personal touch. Both the young people work on the farm holdings of the groom's father along with his father, mother, and brothers, and unmarried sisters. They also work on the young wife's dower lands. The income from these may be pooled with that from the paternal holdings but need not be. The young husband's father has jurisdiction over the ordinary living expenses of the entire household and distributes the cash needed for purchases of clothing, food, and household equipment. During the lifetime of his father, the cash portion of the dowry may be invested by the son in additional land or in some other capital equipment such as a diesel pump. Under no circumstances do the villagers consider it proper to sell dower lands or to use dower funds for ordinary living expenses. Only the need for money for a very serious illness or for some other emergency is felt to justify such action. In whatever form, the dowry is considered capital which may be invested or saved to add to the estate available for the newly married couple's children.

After the death of the husband's father, the young man continues to live with his brothers, most of whom are likely to be married by now, until they decide to separate and divide the patrimony. This now consists of the property their father inherited from his father's patrimony, the dower property of their mother, and any additional properties acquired by their father in the course of his lifetime.

DIVISION OF THE PATRIMONY

The division of the property is always a dramatic event in the lives of the villagers. They believe that the separation of brothers is necessitated more by human than by economic considerations. They explain that brothers should be able to get along with each other and work together under the supervision of the eldest. Harmonious relations between brothers are highly approved in the village, and their maintenance is considered a moral obligation. But, the villagers will add, "What can you do?" When the wives and children of several brothers are part of the same household, inevitably they quarrel. One wife complains that her children's shoes are all worn out while her nieces and nephews are wearing new shoes. The matter of the work contributions to the joint household causes dissension; each wife tries to convince her husband that he works harder than the others. The children of one brother may cry at night and keep another brother and his wife from getting proper sleep. There also may be some envy ift he dowry received by one brother is larger than that of the others.

The decision to divide the property may be delayed in spite of considerable disharmony in the household for several reasons. First, division implies a kind of moral defeat. Second, there are economic factors which favor the maintenance of a joint household. It cuts down on the consumption expenditures for each of the families; more women are released for work in the fields because the young children may be cared for at home by the grandmother or by only one of the wives; and the amount invested in farm animals and equipment can be held down because they are cooperatively used. Then, too, as one farmer puts it, before brothers divide the patrimony, it seems as if they have a lot of land and are earning a good living, but once the property is divided, each brother has little and then one sees that the family was not so wealthy after all. Appearances are important to the villagers, and a group of brothers may be reluctant to reveal the details of their economic condition. But the most important impediment to the separation of the brothers is the house itself. For the house is part of the patrimony, and if the brothers separate, the housing must also somehow be divided among them. There are several ways in which the villagers have solved this last problem.

When there are only two brothers involved, the house may be

physically divided simply by building a wall between two sets of rooms both upstairs and downstairs. The brothers work together to improve both parts of the house so that each is of equal value and then draw lots to determine which brother gets which part (Levy, 1956). Such houses are thenceforth called *dhipla* (double houses), and two or more families live in them as in entirely different establishments. Once the households are separated, a brother who has received cash in his wife's dowry is now able to make further improvements in his side of the house without regard for the other. There were four double houses in Vasilika in 1961. None were then occupied by brothers; their occupants were second and third generation descendants of the brothers who had originally put in the wall. The houses showed the effects of the long separation. In one of the houses, one side has been inhabited by a branch of the family that is losing its lands; that side has no additions and is in poor repair. The descendants of the other brother have prospered and have added some rooms and a terrace to their side of the house. In another case, both parts of the house have been expanded and modernized but in different ways.

Vasilika's houses are not ordinarily large enough to be divided into more than two parts. If there are more than two brothers, or if the paternal house is small, another solution to the housing problem exists. Here, the brothers agree to refurnish the ancestral house which one of them will continue to inhabit, and to build, in addition, new houses to the number of the remaining farmer brothers. The significance of the agreement is that the cost of the new houses and the repair and modernization of the old will be borne by the patrimony. Moreover, the brothers do not decide in advance which one is to have which house. That decision is made by drawing lots after the new houses are habitable and the old one has been improved. In a sense, the brothers agree jointly to improve the father's estate before they take their shares. The process is not different from that involved when the men in a joint household buy land which is added to the estate and is eventually divided among them. The process of building the new houses takes years (in one case where two new houses were built, the actual work took seven years) and during that time the brothers and their wives watch carefully to make sure that no one house is less well equipped than any other; for no man knows which of the houses it will fall to his lot to own.

The drawing of lots and thereby the division of the property does not have to await the completion of the new houses. As in the towns and cities in Greece, a dwelling is considered habitable at what to an American view is an early stage in its construction. Villagers will live in a house in which the ground-level rooms still have earthen floors, in which there is no ceiling to hide the rafters and to exclude the earth and dust that the wind sends through the roof, in which only the outer stone walls have been completed and the inner walls have not yet been plastered or stuccoed. Even at that, the cost of labor and materials for the basic stone or brick shell of a two-storey house in Vasilika can absorb the surplus cash from joint holding of some eighty *stremata* for 2 or 3 years.

Once it is agreed that the new houses are ready for occupancy and that the old house has been sufficiently improved, the moment for the separation has come. The farmers are then joined by any town brothers they may have and they sit down together to evaluate the patrimonial property. No women participate in the deliberations. First, the men examine their land resources and make up sets of holdings of equal value. For example, if there are three farming brothers, virtually all the patrimonial land will be divided into three parcels; one parcel may have an extra *stremata* of vineyard as compared to the other two parcels, but that will make up for the fact that the second and third parcels consist of cotton lands which are slightly more fertile than those assigned to the first group of holdings. Once again, no brother knows which parcel of land will become his until after the drawing of the lots. Each man, therefore, has a strong incnetive to see to it that the partition of the land holdings is as equitable as possible. If the mother of the men is still living, the brothers set apart several *stremata* of land which will become part of the share of whatever brother she elects to live with. This represents her dower right. Still other small parcels of land, of the order of five to ten *stremata*, are assigned outright to the brothers who are no longer farmers and do not live in the village. The token land is kept in their names "so that they may remember their father", as one villager puts it. The conferees next turn their attention to their animal holdings and once again group these into parcels of equal value. Farm equipment and the outbuildings are treated in the same way.

Once the shares for each kind of property are decided upon, an enumeration of each share for each type of holding is written on a piece of paper and rolled up to resemble a cigarette. At that point, the women and children are called in and the time for drawing the lots has arrived. A neighbor or one of the children (never any of the adults in the family) is invited to draw the lots, first for the land, then for the farm animals, then for the equipment and out-buildings, and then for the houses. The moment is a tense one, for in spite of all efforts to equalize the shares some will be considered more desirable than others. The old house, for example, is not desired as much as one of the new houses, and the family that draws it may be disappointed. After the lots are drawn, the mother decides where she will stay. In one recent instance, she stayed with the brother who won the old house (he was not the eldest) because she felt more comfortable there. In another, the mother went with her younger son who had drawn a new house because his child was still small and her services as a baby-tender were needed.

When the whole procedure is completed, the personal effects of each brother and his wife and children are moved to the appropriate house, the furniture is distributed, and that night, for the first time, each family sleeps alone in its own establishment.

Descriptions given of the drawing of lots always convey the strong emotional involvement the participants have in the proceedings. The occasion heralds a change in the routines of life and in each family's attitude toward his property. The women tell of their tears and wails as they bid each other farewell before leaving to spend their first night in separate houses. They also describe their sensations of loneliness and strangeness under the new circumstances. The fact that the houses are almost always close together because they must be built on family-owned house sites in the village seems not to lessen the sense of dispersion as far as the women are concerned. The brothers continue as neighbors. They cooperate in agricultural activities much as unrelated neighbors in the village do: they borrow plows, draught animals, and other equipment from whoever owns it. In the meantime, the sisters-in-law may call on each other for help in the housework, they draw water from the same well, and their children visit freely in each other's houses. In other words, face-to-face associations continue at only a slightly diminished rate. But the villagers' conception of the separation as a drama of great significance is based on the change in point of view which accompanies it. Henceforth, each small family is free to develop its own resources as it wishes. The different personalities of the brothers and their wives manifest themselves in the way they administer their property and raise their children, and, most importantly each brother can now freely give his entire loyalty to his own wife and children and consider all new situations from the standpoint of how they will affect the smaller unit. He is now at liberty, in the village view, to make decisions advantageous to himself, even at the expense of his brothers. The burden of consideration for the welfare of others has been lifted and the brothers are now as free as the rest of the villagers to be rivals of each other. This is not to say that all kinship rights and obligations towards one's adult brothers and sisters and their children disappear, but rather that the emphasis of most intense concern shifts at the time of property division. Indeed, it is generally agreed that the longer harmonious relations among the brothers can be maintained, the better. As a matter of fact, it is just for the sake of keeping good relations that the villagers claim they draw lots for the patrimony. They explain that by so doing, they can manage the business of dividing the property *me aghapi* (with love). No brother can blame any other for the particular share he happened to draw.

The villagers take it for granted that neither impartiality nor altruism is possible in situations which involve one's own interests. They do not believe that anyone, even one's own brother, can act fairly out of principle. Therefore, they feel, some mechanism is required to enforce equity. The strength of their mistrust of the fairness of others is illustrated by a villager's response to a question as to why the mother was not invited into the deliberations. (Mothers who are still active normally have the respect of their adult sons and participate in other kinds of decisions.) The son explained that it was because she might show favoritism toward one of the sons. This explanation was given in spite of the fact that the lot system effectively makes it impossible for anyone to implement favoritism. It is chance that makes the decision as to who gets which share and when faced with the operation of uncontrollable forces of the universe, the Greek villagers say, "*Ti na kanume*", "What can we do?" From their point of view, adverse decisions left to chance are easier to bear than decisions made by self-seeking humans. Therefore, in situations over which they could have control, they prefer, if possible, to rearrange the situation into one in which chance, or fate, if you will, makes the final decision.

In the late 1950's, the number of households in which any married son was still living with his father and mother was small, and there were none in which several married sons were living this way. The reasons for this are first, the decreasing number of sons who are remaining farmers; second, the age distribution of Vasilika's male population (relatively few men in the marriageable age group); and third, the increasing age for marriage even of farming sons. Five of Vasilika's elementary family households were the result of the separation of two sets of brothers in the early 1950's. In Vasilika, therefore, the existing composition of the households is a deceptive base for understanding the principles of organization of households in the village. The existent situation is one in which elementary family households predominate, but the mental construct which influences the formation of new households does not seem to have changed from the old expectation that several married farming brothers will live together. It remains as a latent principle, available for implementation whenever the circumstances warrant it.

CONSEQUENCES OF THE DOWRY SYSTEM

The discussion of the dowry as a mechanism of inheritance for children of farmers who remain farmers may now be summarized. The dowry is part of a system in which children receive property through the parents of both their fathers and their mothers. Property from two sources merges in each generation and is redistributed in the next generation. Although patrilineally inherited lands (those passed from a father to his sons in each generation) have some continuity in space and have some continuity of ownership in the male line, such lands always constitute only one part of the total holdings of any particular elementary family. Therefore, in Vasilika and its vicinity, the pattern of land and money circulation through inheritance has two facets: one portion that is patrilineally inherited straight down the line of males; a second, distributed at marriage, that eventually circulates among unrelated elementary families. The system cannot be described as one in which women inherit from women, in spite of the legal residual control of a woman over her dower properties, because brothers have equal rights with their sisters to their mother's dower lands. In Vasilika, at least, there is neither an explicit nor an implicit pattern of giving daughters only dower property and sons only patrilineally inherited lands.

The combination of practices including the function of the dowry as inheritance, land as a major form of property, and village exogamy have some further consequences for the relation of property to groups of kinsmen in the Boeotian countryside. In spite of patrilocal residence and some patrilineally inherited land, the descendants of a male line are not associated with any particular landed estates. Since no man owns or farms exactly the same holdings as his father farmed before him, nor the same holdings his brothers have, and since he himself will expect to work different lands in different communities even in the course of his own adult life, the permanent association of certain estates with certain lineages is obstructed (Friedl, 1959b). Moreover, since dowries move down the generations and not across to a man of one's own generation who might use the property to marry off one of his daughters, there is no economic advantage to brother-and-sister exchange marriages. This situation is congruent with both the Greek Orthodox Church's and the Civil Code's (section 1357) prohibitions on marriages between sisters and brothers-in-law and between cousins to the third degree. This rule, as well as the bilateral reckoning of kin in Greece (section 1356), prevents the transfer of property at marriage from resulting in either a series of equal exchanges between two sets of kin groups or in a regular pattern of circulation through several generations among particular sets of such groups. The control of property establishes social links between a man and his wife's relatives not only in the ways we have mentioned, but because his wife's parents and brothers and sisters have a legal and customary right to be consulted before the final alienation of dower property (section 1418). These links last only one generation, however, so that in each generation a new network of relations between elementary families in the neighborhood develops, clustering around the management of dower properties. These matters are important because they reveal some of the economic and social structure of Vasilika and its neighborhood that is congruent with the type of relationships people, both kin and non-kin, have with each other.

One other situation occurs frequently enough in Vasilika to be worth mentioning. When a farmer has no sons to inherit his land and his house, but has a daughter, the father may acquire a man's assistance on the farm by importing a son-in-law. Such a man is called a *soghambros* in Vasilika; he is a husband who moves into his wife's household instead of vice-versa. The importation of a *soghambros* is also a solution to the problem of a young widow who has no grown sons to run the farm left by her husband and arranges a second marriage for herself with a man who is willing to work her first husband's holdings and her original dower lands. Since a *soghambros* is always a manager of, and the laborer on, property belonging to others and is expected to bring no property of his own with him, there is a slight social stigma attached to the status of Vasilika. The villagers say also that a *soghambros* is not "master in his own house". Certainly, the lot of a man who is not a master in his own house and comes as a stranger to a village where most of the other men have known each other all their lives is not a happy one. But a *soghambros* is not really dishonored by this position; the villagers, in this situation, as in so many others, recognize the practical necessities which brought about the arrangement and do not strongly condemn a man for making the best of his difficulties.

The dowry in Vasilika enters into the life of the villagers in other ways besides inheritance at marriage. It has long served as a means of upward social mobility for girls. Since, as we have seen, the marriage of a daughter is among the most important obligations of parents, the dowry comes into the consciousness of the villagers more often as a property requirement for marrying off their daughters than as a means of transmitting inheritance. When, in addition, the high value placed on upward social mobility is translated into an effort to find urban sons-in-law for one's daughters, the dowry emerges as a mechanism for increasing the social prestige of the family. Farmers are willing to give larger dowries in exchange for the great satisfaction they derive from having town sons-in-law. In Vasilika, the education of some sons has released land to add to the girls' dowries. Improved agricultural income has also enabled the farmers to give larger dowries. In the decade ending in 1959, every marriage of a Vasilika daughter whose father was in the upper half of the village's income range had been one with a man of respectable occupation who lived in a provincial town or in Athens. The husbands are tailors, small retail store-owners, or civil service workers. One young man is a photographer, another is a gymna-sium professor who has become the principal of his gymnasium. In 1961, however, the son of a rather prosperous village farmer became attracted to a daughter of another Vasilika farmer with good land holdings. The young man asked his father to arrange the marriage for him, and, since all the conditions were entirely suitable, the young couple were engaged.

The trend in favor of town husbands prevails, however, among most of those who can afford it. Once a few girls had married urban men, the rivalry between village families led to greater efforts to secure town husbands for the others. Consequently, there has been an inflation in dowries which is alarming the villagers themselves. In the early 1950's, a *prika* worth $3000 was enough for a town husband of no special prestige; by the late 1950's, the same kind of man was asking for one worth $4500.

The inflation has had several consequences. Often the value of the dowry can no longer be limited to the share of the inheritance to which a girl is entitled. Farming sons are willing to give up some portion of their shares so that their sisters can "live well", as they put it. The brothers gain also from the added prestige and influence of the family. These in turn may make it possible for them to find a girl with a larger dowry than their property qualifications might warrant. A farmer so situated may make higher demands on the ground that his and his wife's children will have an urban aunt and uncle. The town sister might provide board for her nephews and nieces (girls are increasingly being sent to gymnasium) while they are in school and can also be expected to help them find jobs.

Another consequence of the dowry inflation is the increasingly late age of marriage for the village girls and the town men. It takes farmers longer to accumulate the larger amounts of cash for the dowry, and the prospective grooms longer to attain a position or income at least partially commensurate. Vasilika's girls who marry town men are usually between twenty-five and thirty. Those whose fathers have few land holdings, and consequently can offer only small dowries, have been marrying farmers from other villages or within Vasilika itself and have been in their early twenties at the time of the engagement.

Now let us consider the disposition of the dowry which goes with a girl marrying a town husband. First, if he accepts land as part of the dowry, he will of necessity have it worked by his wife's male relatives. In time, however, often by the end of the first decade of the marriage, the son-in-law may wish to expand his shop, or may wish to start building a house for himself or for his daughter's dowry, or may hear of a good investment opportunity. He will want money for these purposes, and so he begins, with his wife's consent and after consultation with her father, to arrange for the sale of dowry lands. Since the 1950's, prospective town grooms have been less willing to take land which they know they will eventually want to sell, and have been asking for cash or for a house in town. Anticipating this situation, several of Vasilika's farmers who have small daughters have begun to use their savings and even to sell a little land in order to build houses in Athens or in a provincial town so that by the time their daughters are ready to marry, the houses will provide the main portion of the dowry. Rents are high and earnings relatively low in cities so that houses are a good investment. However, since building materials must be bought, and contractors paid, in cash, the houses may take many years to build. The young couple may then move into the habitable shell, and the rest of the dwelling will be completed out of the farmer's then current income. This kind of dowry-on-the-installment-plan becomes part of the marriage contract. It is often a source not only of continuing long-term discussions between a farmer and his town son-in-law, but also a source of quarels—what in Greece are called *fasaries*.

The rate of movement of farmers' daughters into the towns and cities has been accelerating in the last decade, but marriages to urban husbands are not a new phenomenon. Between 1930 and 1950, at least five of Vasilika's woman married "into Athens".

This type of marriage, like those discussed above in which both bride and groom are members of farm families, accelerates land sales and exchanges. The network of association which develops between Vasilika's residents and their relatives in Athens and the towns, is, however, perhaps the most important consequence of the urban marriages of village women (Friedl, 1959a). In addition to the economic reasons for continuing relationships, there are several customary patterns which increase the frequency of contacts between the two groups. Lonely village mothers are grateful for visits from their married daughters and their grandchildren, and the midsummer season not uncommonly finds city women with their children back in the village visiting their parents, often for as long as a month or two. A return to one's village for Easter, sometimes for most of the Holy Week as well, is a well-known pattern in Greece. *Paniyiri* in one's *patridha* (home village) is another occasion for visiting.

Journeys in the opposite direction also occur with some frequency. Village men and women, when ill, may enter hospitals in a town in which they have sons or daughters, or brothers or sisters. Village men visit their town brothers and bring their children; occasionally a child spends a summer with his town aunt or uncle. Visits to the village or to the town usually last several days. They are made possible by still another congruent pattern of Greek culture. Neither the villagers nor their town relatives seem to have any strong need for personal privacy. Visiting relatives are bedded down on pallets when there are not enough regular beds, and it is not considered either indecent or especially uncomfortable for one or even two families to sleep in the same room. It is through this intervisiting process that so many urban traits of culture are introduced to the villagers and, indeed, that some village patterns are conserved in urban areas.

An additional consequence of the town marriages of village girls is that rural wealth derived from land flows into the cities. This wealth is an addition to what the productivity of land normally contributes to urban centers in the form of food, taxes, and the export of rural produce. A portion of the farmer's profits, through the dowry, is being used, it would seem, directly to support a part of the urban population. When the dowries are invested in housing or in small commercial enterprises, many low-salaried employees, civil service workers, or economically marginal entrepreneurs find it possible to support themselves and their families in the town and cities. Without the aid of dower wealth, they might not be able to do so.

ATTITUDES TOWARD THE DOWRY SYSTEM

Let us now turn from the nature and consequences of the dowry system to a renewed examination of the villagers' attitudes toward the dowry. They unquestionably think of the dowry as a burden. Raising daughters is called *vasana*, a task full of tribulations. The people of the village know that daughters are, in the long run, a net economic loss to the family. They strongly emphasize the burdens of having to give large dowries with daughters, and they rarely mention the size of the dowries sons will receive with their wives. When a girl is born to one of the more prosperous villagers, other men say with a certain suppressed glee, "*Tha plirosi*", "He will pay", and they rub the fingers of the right hand against the thumb in a gesture of money payment. But the men who act this way have no corresponding phrase or gesture for what a son will bring in, and dowry inflation is always looked at from the standpoint of what must be paid out. Young prospective bridegrooms tend also to emphasize their roles as contributors to their sisters' dowries, rather than their roles as recipients of their bride's property.

In spite of their lamentations over the burdensomeness of the *prika*, the villagers regard it as a fixed feature of their lives. They invariably express puzzlement in conversations with Americans as to how any people can exist without it. Identifying the dowry with the trousseau, women ask how any girl can set up a household without one. They also ask how a dowerless woman can have any sense of economy, security, or support; how she can guard against the dangers of a shiftless husband.

The men say Greece is a poor country, and that therefore young couples need a double source of land or capital to assure the economic welfare of the new family. But at least of equal importance to the men is their feeling that their own self-respect depends upon the knowledge that they have provided for the future of their daughters—that they have enabled their daughters to "live well". When asked whether girls who did wage labor or who earned money from dressmaking used their earnings for their dowries, the villagers, men and women alike, looked shocked and displeased. They would say no, only fathers or brothers give dowries. Then they would explain that the girl gives her earnings to her father who uses it for the family's living expenses and may, if he wishes, return some to help in the collection of the trousseau, which, as we have seen, the men consider an insignificant part of the dowry. That the girls' earnings enabled the family to save other current income was a concept the villagers neither had *a priori*, nor understood when it was suggested to them. Neither did the villagers like the suggestion that by working in the fields the daughter of a farmer was contributing to the family's income and, therefore, indirectly to the savings accumulated for her dowry. As we have seen, in the context of farm management, they recognized the work of their women as contributing labor value, but in the context of the dowry, they did not see the situation this way.

The villagers act and talk as if they felt that it is the obligation of men to care for women, and that the obligation is largely fulfilled by the provision of a dowry for a daughter. The provision of the dowry is thus, in a sense, an outward manifestation of masculinity. By village custom, when a father dies or is incapacitated, a girl's brothers are considered responsible for marrying her off, and they are usually expected to fulfill this obligation before they themselves marry. This point of view does not correspond with the legal requirements. In the Civil Code (section 1496) the mother is responsible for furnishing dowries for her daughters in the event of her husband's death or incapacity. The village attitude, however, I believe, is based partly on the feeling that most women are not capable of managing their estates and on the congruent custom of appointing male guardians to manage for them until their sons are grown, but more importantly on the basic notion that the provision of dowries is a male prerogative.

The emotional overtones accompanying the dowry system may be understood as a possible shift of emphasis from one kind of expression of male honor to another. Anthropologists who have worked in Greek Cypriot villages and in shepherd communities[2] report that the males in these settlements, almost all equally poor, based their sense of manly prestige not on wealth, but on the degree of honor they achieved by the protection of the chastity of their women. It would seem as if, in Boeotia, male honor depends not only on male protection of the chastity of women but also more explicitly and obviously on the provision by the men of adequate dowries for their women. The sense of satisfaction a man gets from dowering a daughter becomes more intense and compelling because the action is also an expression of his masculinity.

The shift of emphasis can be demonstrated in the village. Among the shepherds and landless or land-poor families in the village, girls marry earlier, with small dowries and trousseaus, and acquire correspondingly less prosperous husbands. The fathers and brothers involved, and the other villagers, comment on these unions by saying that early marriages are essential because otherwise the girls might run wild and disgrace the family. In other words, then, when economic means are limited, men can maintain their honor and self-respect only by protecting their women, and this becomes the paramount concern. The villagers seem to recognize that when there is no hope for even the modest degree of economic security and material well-being that the dowries of Vasilika's land-owning farmers can provide, there is less impetus for the girl herself to remain virtuous or for her prospective suitors to respect her situation without the added emphasis on physical retaliation by her menfolk. However, flamboyant behavior and clandestine affairs could destroy the hope of a decent marriage for a girl whose father can provide a reasonable dowry. Or such

[2] John Peristiany and John Campbell, respectively.

actions might require an exorbitant dowry to overcome the effects of her bad reputation. For these girls, the rewards of waiting are great enough for them to be willing to postpone both marriage and affairs, so that there is less danger that they will allow themselves to be compromised and less need to claim male protection.

Yet, with all the difficulties and sacrifices required by the dowry and arranged marriage system in Vasilika, there have been very few young people who have "gone to the mountains", as the villagers phrase elopements of couples who have fallen in love. One or two such affairs seem to occur in each generation, at a time when the girl's male relatives are dead or not in the village; and among young people each of whose families have relatively few economic resources. The subsequent standard of living of the couples has been among the lowest in the village, and the men never fully recover from the stigma of such senseless behavior, from the villagers' view. Observable examples reinforce the villagers' argument that there is no hope for a decent life without a dowry, and reinforce their admonitions to their sons to wait for properly arranged marriages and not to be *trelos* (crazy) and run off to the mountains with a girl. The admonition gains force from the further observation that if the eloping young couples have little, their children will have still less. Any man who accepts a girl without a dowry is thought to be cheating his children of their rightful inheritance from their mother.

Yet, as we have had occasion to remark in other connections, the structure of marriage arrangements in Vasilika is not quite as rigid and as precise as the foregoing generalized description might imply. One Vasilika brother, in speaking of a sister who had become his responsibility after their father's death, remarked "Glory be to God (and he crossed himself) she met a man who liked her and was willing to take her with nothing but the *rukha* and what we had in the house". The unexpected can happen in Vasilika, and infant girls are still dandled with songs about how their beauty will some day attract a husband without a dowry.

FAMILY AND KIN STRUCTURE

The foregoing discussion of family activities and of the forms of property inheritance and circulation has by implication involved questions of family structure. By giving a newly married couple property of its own to manage, the dowry serves as a mechanism to separate the newly married couple structurally from either of their two sets of parents. This is true even when the farmers bring their brides back to their fathers' households. Such patrilocal residence produces the temporary situation of a functioning, cooperative, extended, patrilineal kin group, but one that is continually aware of its distinct component elementary families. We have said temporary because there is no contemplation that the several elementary family groups concerned will live out their lives in a joint, cooperative household.

The kinship terminology used in the village is congruent with the structure underlying the realities and expectations of the situation just described. Greek terms of reference for mother, father, grandfather, grandchildren, cousin, aunt, uncle, niece, and nephew are directly translatable into the English words, except that the linguistic forms vary for males and females, and that, in fact, the villagers refer to distinctions between first and second cousins more frequently than Americans do.[3] Like ours, the system is characterized by the distinctness of elementary family terms, the separation of generations and the equal consideration of both father's and mother's line of descent in the terms for all consanguineal (blood) relatives. So far the Greek terms are also entirely congruent with the actual functioning distinctiveness of the elementary family and the existing bilateral descent in the country. There is special interest for us, however, in the Greek terms for affinal relatives (that is, relatives by marriage) which, in some instances, differ from those in English and are, in turn, congruent with the particular significance of marriage in Greek social structure.

Petheros (masculine) and *pethera* (feminine) are equivalent to

[3] See Andromedas (1957) for a complete list of modern Greek kinship terms.

English father-in-law and mother-in-law, but there is an additional, reciprocal Greek term which two sets of in-laws use in referring to each other: *simpetheros* and *simpethera*. In English these must be rendered as "my son's or daughter's father- or mother-in-law". The Greek terms, then, group together the parents of a husband and wife with a term of reference roughly translatable as "co-in-laws". The Greek word for son-in-law, *ghambros*, is also used to mean groom, and that for daughter-in-law, *nifi*, is also used for bride. Moreover, all the members of a man's elementary family, not only his parents, but also his brothers and sisters, all refer to his wife as their *nifi*, and all the members of a woman's elementary family refer to her husband as their *ghambros*. The term *nifi* and *ghambros*, then, are not equivalent to any English kin terms, but must be translated as "that man or woman who has married a member of my elementary family". At least two generations, that of parents and their children, use the same terms to refer to people normally in the younger generation. In other words, the generational distinctiveness characteristic of terms for blood relatives is replaced by the status designation for a person who has married into an elementary family. This disregard of generation is not reciprocated, however, by the spouses of one's children or by one's brothers and sisters. As we have seen, mother and father of one's spouse are called *petheros* and *pethera;* now we can add that brothers and sisters of one's spouse are referred to as *kunyadhos* and *kunyadha*, that is brother- and sister-in-law.

The status category of marriage into a particular elementary family appears again, however, in the existence of distinct terms by which men who have married two sisters refer to each other, *badzanakidhes*, and by which women who have married two brothers refer to each other, *sinifadhes*. Men who have married sisters and women who have married brothers have to deal with the same sets of in-laws and this constitutes a common bond which is signalized by the terms just given. Another way of saying this is that those women who are referred to as *nifi* by the same actual kin, also have a name for each other, *sinifadha*, and those men who are referred to as *ghambros* by the same actual kin, also have a name for each other, *badzanakis*.

There is a reciprocal term equivalent in meaning, but not at all as technical in its connotation as the English word "spouse", whereby husbands and wives refer to each other: *sizighos*. Apart from this, there are no Greek words with the specific and exclusive significance of English "husband" and "wife". For husband, *andras* (man) is used; for wife, *yineka* (woman) or *kira* (lady).

The remaining terms in the Greek system that are related to marriage are those which refer reciprocally to a couple's marriage sponsor and the latter's spouse: *kumbaros* and *kumbara*. Moreover, the terms are extended on both sides to refer to the parents, brothers, and sisters, and children of the original sponsors and their spouses when they marry.

Marriage sponsors may, but need not be chosen (and in the majority of instances in Vasilika are not chosen) from among one's biological kin. The term *kumbaros* is, however, properly considered part of the system of kinship terms because of a very weighty customary prohibition which the status of *kumbaros* imposes: the prohibition against marriage in the same degrees as those appropriate to blood relatives.

The same reciprocal terms, *kumbaros* and *kumbara*, with the same extensions to the kindred of each of the original parties and the same marriage prohibitions, are established between the parents of a child and his baptismal godparent (*nonos* or *nona*). Here again, parents may choose those with whom they wish to enter into this relationship, and individuals may or may not accept the request to sponsor a godchild (*vaftistikos* or *vaftistikya*).

Vasilika's inhabitants make use of the possibilities of the *kumbari* system in such a way as to parallel their search for affinal kin (in-laws). Just as the people of Vasilika select marriage partners for themselves and their children with an eye to the augmentation of material resources and social prestige, so they try to find *kumbari* whose wealth and position will be a source of potential help for themselves and their children. The similarity in functions of the two types of relationships is paralleled by their similarity in structural effects. Just as affinal connections preclude the possibility of marriage between any of the relatives of the two elementary families involved, so do *kumbari* connections. Moreover, since the people of the village apparently prefer to select *kumbari* from non-kin (they must do so with affinals), they succeed in augmenting their network of associations with what, from the standpoint of kin connections, is a random collection of elementary families and their bilateral kindred. Non-kin are more likely to be in other villages, and people of greater prestige in the towns and cities. Here again *kumbari* associations tend to lead out of the village, and there is frequently a disparity in the economic and social positions between villagers and their *kumbari*. On the one hand, some prosperous village farmers serve as godparents for shepherd families, and on the other, the aspiring farming families choose an urban merchant, or a professional man, as *kumbaros*. The parallel with relatives by marriage is most striking between *kumbari* through godparenthood, and the mutual obligations involved are larger in number, last longer, and are more likely to be fulfilled than those with marriage sponsors.

Still another parallel between in-laws and *kumbari* is that the individuals who fill these statuses are freely chosen, in contrast with consanguineal (blood) relatives who are, of course, automatically acquired by birth. Certainly this is a real distinction between the affinals and *kumbari*, on the one hand, and consanguineals on the other, but, in Vasilika at least, it is not a difference of preponderant functional importance. In practice, any significant relationships established even between consanguineal kin outside of the elementary family are voluntarily arranged, and this element of the situation is more important than is the fact that the pool of blood kin from whom a man or woman can make the choice is predetermined.

Let us summarize the situation this way: A man and his elementary family can normally provide all the personnel needed for the year-round functions on his farm. At peak periods the farmer hires the necessary additional labor. However, from time to time he may need temporary help. He may need an extra horse for plowing, or he may want to join with someone to fill a truck with grain for a trip to the mill or with cotton for a trip to the gin; or he may need an extra hand or two to string tobacco or to separate cotton from the pod, or he may want someone to help with irrigation, or he may wish to join with another family for the Easter feast. For both giving and receiving assistance of this kind, Vasilika's farmers seem to consider all the village's inhabitants, kin or non-kin, *kumbari* or non-*kumbari*, neighbor or non-neighbor, as almost equally suitable candidates. A farmer may choose one non-neighbor villager who has a good horse, and exchange plowing assistance with him, a next-door neighbor with whom he joins in sending grain to the mill, a village sister to help with tobacco stringing to whom he gives a bottle of wine or the like in return, and so on. Moreover, none of these arrangements is necessarily permanent; the personnel may vary from year to year and from season to season. Indeed, shifting relationships of this kind are more common than permanent ones. From our point of view, the significance lies in the fact that whether or not kin are involved, the type of association is the same.

There is one notable exception. No matter how valuable assistance might be, it is not sought after if the individuals capable of rendering it belong to a family with whom there is an acute, even if temporary, disagreement. For example, although one of the village girls was adept at giving penicillin injections, a woman from a family which was on bad terms with that of the girl preferred to leave the village for a week to live with a town relative who was also capable of giving the injections. The trip was inconvenient for the ill woman's family, and since she was not fond of her relative, the visit was actually distasteful to her. But neither of these considerations was compelling enough to have her choose what in her and her family's opinion was the worse alternative—to ask assistance from a village family with whom they were currently in acrimonious rivalry. Feuding of this kind can occur among kin as well as among neighbours.

Apart from the agricultural production cycle and other predominantly village-centered activities, Vasilika's farmers need help in arranging marriages, in educating their children, in finding employment, in dealing with government officials and with merchants to whom they sell their produce. They also want some urban associations simply for prestige, and to provide a place to stay if they visit towns and cities. For these extra-village purposes, a farmer is more likely first to survey his consanguineal kin, his affinals, and his *kumbari*. From among these, he may choose one of his first cousins with whom his son will board while he goes to the gymnasium, one of his sons-in-law who is a civil servant to help with tax problems, one of his *kumbari* to recommend a merchant, and so on. Again, the farmer chooses different individuals from among those potentially helpful to him by virtue of their statuses and need not ask any one person to help him in more than one way. Once more the relationships need not be permanent; if for any reason they prove unsatisfactory, a man shifts to another individual. Moreover, the farmer reciprocates these favors in various ways, for example by taking his cousin's child for the summer, by offering hospitality to *kumbari* at festival times, or by getting information about village girls from among whom his urban connection may want to arrange a marriage. If a farmer can find no one among his group of consanguineal kin, his affinals, and his *kumbari* who is willing to enter into an agreement with him for these extra-village needs, he turns to his fellow villagers and neighbors and attempts to attach himself to their network of extra-village associations.

What Vasilika's farmers do not do is attempt to establish new and direct relationships with complete strangers, that is, persons or agencies outside the network of their own or their fellow villagers' extra-village associations.

In sum, then, outside of the elementary family, a Vasilika farmer expects to establish voluntary relationships with a number of different individuals from each of whom he expects the fulfillment of a limited set of obligations to himself, and toward each of whom he will fulfill an equivalent but usually not identical set of obligations. Each man is the center of a series of varied relationships in which those with whom he associates himself have no necessary connections with each other. He is the hub of a wheel that has no rim. George Foster has called paired relationships of this kind "dyadic contracts" (Foster, 1961). He believes they will occur in societies in which the number of people to whom a man can have culturally defined obligations is so large that it is not possible for him to fulfill them all. Men and women, therefore, choose from among their many kin, godparents and the like, those with whom they will make dyadic contracts. The people and the situation in which the contract is enforced vary from time to time. Foster suggests that such sets of paired relationships deter the development of factional groups. The idea of the dyadic contract is an extraordinarily useful concept for understanding the relationships I have just described for Vasilika, and Foster's analysis illuminates the consequences of what I have just called a situation in which each man or woman is the hub of a rimless wheel.

REFERENCES

ANDROMEDAS, J. (1957) Greek kinship terms in everyday use, *Amer. Anthrop.* **59,** 1086–8.

ANTONAKAKI, K. D. (1955) *Greek Education*, New York, Teachers College, Columbia University.

FOSTER, G. M. (1961) The dyadic contract: a model for the social structure of a Mexican peasant village, *Amer. Anthrop.* **63,** 1173–92.

FRIEDL, E. (1958) Hospital care in provincial Greece, *Hum. Org.* **16,** 24–7.

FRIEDL, E. (1959a) The role of kinship in the transmission of national culture to rural villages in mainland Greece, *Amer. Anthrop.* **61,** 30–8.

FRIEDL, E. (1959b) Dowry and inheritance in modern Greece, *Trans. New York Acad. Sci.* **22,** 49–54.

LEVY, H. L. (1956) Property distribution by lot in present-day Greece, *Trans. Amer. Philolog. Assoc.* **87,** 42–6.

The Family in a Spanish Town

C. Lison-Tolosana

THE word "family" can, of course, refer to anything from conjugal unity to any wider group of people. When a resident says *mi familia*, the real meaning of the word has to be inferred from the context of the conversation. It may be equivalent to the nuclear family, composed initially of the spouses, and later of the spouses with offspring.... In the second place family is synonymous with kinship. Kinship is the bond which, in respect to an individual, unites each one of the ancestors, descendants, and co-laterals of his family by consanguinity and affinity. Taking "ego" as a basis in practice kinship embraces these two zones: (a) from the grandparents to the grandchildren through its line, i.e. five generations on the one hand, and on the other, collaterally to second cousins and the sons and daughters of uncles and aunts in second degree. (b) Kinship by affinity is more restricted. It includes the family of orientation of the husband or wife. The remaining members who constitute kin of the husband or wife of "ego" in the sense first defined fall into the category of "the family of my wife" or "of my husband".

The cohesion of kinship in general is weak and flexible. It acquires a certain expression in mutual assistance—the lending of agricultural tools, for instance—which generally though not according to any clearly defined pattern follows the ramifications of kindred. The *rites de passage* are occasions when the fullest implications of kinship are realized. Also people tend to favour their kindred when selling plots or houses; they give them first refusal. The relations of kinship are effectively recognized towards uncles, aunts and first cousins who are addressed as "uncle" or "cousin"; with uncles and cousins in the second degree the ties are weaker and the appellation is frequently omitted. At weddings all the first cousins but not necessarily all the second cousins are invited, although they are notified of the wedding. However a man would join a fight to defend a cousin in second degree.

Deudo is another word which signifies kinship. From the Latin *debitus—debere*—it is equivalent to being a debtor which brings into relief the network of obligations and duties involved by kinship. Nowadays the word has been divested of its initial content and the functions which used to be part of the bonds of kinship have undergone a process of development along other lines so that its cohesive force has been diminished. Familiarity of intercourse can be deeper among families only united by bonds of friendship. Both families express their relationship with the phrase: *nos tratamos como familia* (we treat each other as family). The popular proverb says: "close friendship makes kinship". In this case there may be more friendly co-operation between the families concerned than with their respective kin. Between kindred most people have more in common with some of their relations than with others; economic power, temperament, similarity of ideas and personal likings sometimes exert a stronger force than kinship itself, and the same happens through associations with neighbours and friends made in the bar or café. To all this it is necessary to add that the fiercest hatreds and the most violent quarrels occur among members of a family. This prompts a sketch of the flexibility of family affection through another meaning of the word family, a meaning which completely identifies the family with the land, with property, with the economic.

The third meaning of the word *familia* refers in a wide sense to a constellation which encloses three nuclear families together with the spouses of all the married members: the families of orientation and procreation of "ego" and the family of orientation of his or her spouse. This constellation can be symbolized by Fig. 1.

Secondly, and more narrowly, it refers to the family of orientation and of procreation of "ego", but as "ego" is married, his or her spouse includes another social cell, i.e. her or his family of orientation, in the nuclear family sphere.

The marriage of the son or daughter alters the unity of affection, the economic unity, and in most cases the unit of residence of the family of orientation. If this step in the life of an individual were a purely personal one it would not be relevant sociologically; but the transition is invested with structural characteristics which automatically incorporate and adjust it first of all to the system of relationships of kindred, and secondly to the pattern of inheritance. This last in its turn unites the three families owing to the

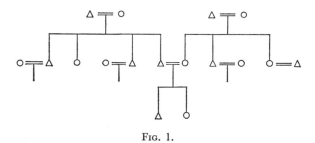

Fig. 1.

fact that there is now a bilateral system in the sense that "ego" inherits from his own family of orientation and then from the family of orientation of his or her spouse. To this right of inheritance corresponds the obligation of both families of orientation to provide economically for the incipient family of procreation. What really matters here is that each spouse occupies a key position due to a simultaneous membership of three families. Through him, or her, the three are interlocked in a complicated structure of relationships, rights, obligations, and tensions.

The marriage of a son or daughter includes an economic readjustment in the respective families of orientation of the spouses. The *donatio propter nuptias* demands that the family of the husband provides him, if not with legal ownership, at least with the use of one or several plots or with some other means of living. The wife must contribute an *ajuar* (furnishings and linen), with which to set up the new home even if the newly wedded couple are not going to live by themselves in a house of their own. The bestowal of one or more plots on the daughter at this point is optional. By custom it is the husband who has to afford a means of subsistence for the new family. But frequently if his parents give him something her parents will offer her something of equal value *por no ser menos* (not to be outdone). This emulative tournament reaches its height when the marriage has offspring, because if the paternal grandparents regale the grandchildren with toys or clothes, the maternal grandparents consider themselves obliged to enter the lists with more gifts for the grandchildren.

The early symptoms of tension between the three families stem from the two old families of orientation, both of whom in turn stir up the family of procreation. Here the main part is played by the temperament of the respective parents or rather of the respective mothers, the more or less pronounced tendency to interfere in the affairs of the new home, the reaction of the spouses, etc.; but the key to the incipient friction between the three families is usually economic. There are two focuses of friction: the parents—especially the mothers—of both families of orientation, and the spouses of the family of procreation in relation to their brothers and sisters through whom they affect their parents. The first series of conflicts arises in the first year or even in the first few months of marriage. The second assails the married couple when they attempt to divide the inheritance definitively and legally.

The first phase largely depends on the value that the two original families of orientation attach to the arable land transferred to the son or the goods brought by the wife. The husband's family may think that his wife is *muy gastadora* (very extravagant), that she does not manage her household budget efficiently and that her house could be better ordered and cleaner. If the woman fails to provide any arable land it will be a weapon brandished repeatedly in any family altercation, since whether or not she does so is not regulated by traditional norms. The wife's family of orientation will most probably retaliate: the husband's parents did not provide him with sufficient lands to support his wife, his brothers and sisters obtained the best part in the initial parcellation of the land; he could work harder, spend less money in the bar, etc., because *para lo que le han dado* . . . (an untranslatable expression implying that the husband's family are in no position to criticize their daughter-in-law as they failed to provide their son with adequate means).

Thus in this initial period the relationships of the family constellation are the consequences of an economic fact, springing in the last resort from the plots, from the land. The new home involved in these frictions is normally a passive focus because it is not likely that differences are going to emerge between the newly wedded couple in the first months of marriage. Finally the lines of tension originate from the respective mothers of the spouses and passing via the son or daughter through the wife or husband are directed against the other mother. Here we can detect again the preponderance of the mother in the life of the family.

The fathers endeavour to keep outside such dissensions. The respective mothers-in-law exercise their interference through their son or daughter and very rarely do they dispute the matter directly between themselves.

Though relations between the spouses are normally harmonious, one or both tend to look upon the family of the other as a source of inopportune meddling. In many cases these first disagreements are resolved by the birth of grandchildren. By then, too, the parents of the wife have probably given her some land, which is customary when all her brothers and sisters have married. The transfer of land acts as a lubricant and a reinforcement of good relations. Again, the constellation can have a cohesion *sui generis*. The young couple keeps up a certain degree of intercourse with the other two families, which may, however, have broken off all possible relations with each other, not even exchanging greetings in the street. The relations of the husband with his wife's family and vice versa have not yet been severed but are cool. If the young couple reckons that the husband's parents have not dealt properly with them in the economic sphere it is possible that the daughter-in-law will not speak to her parents-in-law, renouncing all contact with them. In these circumstances the parents-in-law never go to the son's home; the grandchildren are the ones who visit their grandparents. The son–husband preserves a precarious relationship, if any, with his parents.

A last point in relation to the first of the two focal points of tension. A situation of particular strain arises when "ego" resides with the parents/parents-in-law. The choice is dictated by the room available in the houses of the families of orientation. Although in the shared home the finances of both families are almost always distinct, there is frequent friction for economic reasons. Both women use the same kitchen and cooker and both families eat at the same table and at the same time. Each wife prepares her own meal, but if the young wife makes use too freely of the salt or oil which belong to the older woman there will soon be trouble. The same happens in the work of the men. The use of even the smallest agricultural tools belonging to the father/father-in-law may provoke the latter into selling them in order to prevent his son/son-in-law from making use of them; otherwise he would find himself in the disagreeable position of having to refuse to lend them, such is the degree of economic separation reached by the two families.

In the diagram of the three families the brothers and sisters of "ego" are included with their spouses. All are caught up with "ego" in a well-defined subsystem of relationships. As before I am only going to analyse the zones of friction of the subsystem, beginning by the mildest ones and taking Fig. 2 as a point of departure.

A, due to special circumstances, i.e. a university education, married C whose family of orientation was of an economic power vastly superior to that of A. His brother B married D, whose family was economically on the same level. B did not have a university education. The circle of friends of AC is of superior social standing to that in which *BD* move; the style of life of the first couple is higher than that of the second couple notwithstanding all *D*'s efforts to compete with *C*. *D*'s expenditure in first communions, clothes, or jewelry surpasses that which would normally correspond to her "estate" because it is in this sphere, not in the social one, that she can attempt to emulate *C*. *D*'s jealousy of *C* makes for coldness and hostility between *BD* and *AC* on the few occasions on which they mix socially. Once again the woman appears as the axis of family tension; though what matters here is the difference of economic power and social status· It is this that brings about the rupture, and prevails to some extent over family ties of the first degree.

Fig. 2.

I have already alluded to some of the norms governing the inheritance which I call "initial" in the sense that it has these characteristics: (*a*) it is the *donatio propter nuptias* which is a private and not a formal settlement, with no effect before the law; it is a personal arrangement between the father and children. (*b*) The *donatio propter nuptias* is temporary and reversible because it expires the moment the definitive inheritance takes effect, when "ego" may receive plots or paternal property which till then had been worked by one of his brothers or sisters. (*c*) The parents distribute the initial inheritance as they wish, and the children must conform to their wishes, because the parents have generously disposed of part of their property and directly control the economy of the remainder. While the parents run the homestead, two lines of tension are possible, on which I have already commented:

the interference of the family of orientation of "ego" in his family of procreation, and the inherent tension in the relations between "ego" and his/her parents if "ego" feels that these have been partial to his/her brothers and sisters in the initial distribution of the inheritance. As "ego", however, has not got any customary right on his/her part to claim a bigger or better portion of inheritance, he/she takes care not seriously to offend the parents before the definitive inheritance is drawn up.

The fiercest family conflicts ensue when the legal and definitive inheritance takes effect. Sometimes elderly parents or the surviving parent dispose of their property and transfer it legally to their children. The norm which regulates the inheritance is simple in

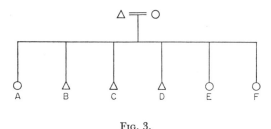

Fig. 3.

principle. The property is divided equally between all the children. The practice is more complicated, because it is not always easy to divide equally plots, domestic animals, furniture, chattels, agricultural tools and houses. The parents, or parent, allot a portion to each child according to their own criterion of evaluation, which naturally does not always coincide with the one held by the heirs. If the parents die intestate the same problems arise. From these practical difficulties violent fights spring up between the children, together with the extraordinary efforts made by some of the sons or daughters to persuade the parents, if they are still living, to revoke the will, whether it is already consummated or still in the process of consummation. Figure 3 is an example.

The parents built a house with the manual co-operation of

their sons, B, C, and D, two of whom were already married. In return for the help given, the parents promised the house as an inheritance for the sons to the exclusion of the daughters. C, who was married, lived with his parents in the newly built house. The mother died a little before D married and he and his wife went to live in his father's house (in which C was not living at that time) to take care of his father. D's wife died and later he contracted a second marriage. The father, of advanced years, found it difficult to get on with D's second wife and demanded that both left the house, but D categorically refused to go. A, B, C, E, and F judged it necessary to intervene in the affair—but each from his or her point of view, with an eye fixed on the inheritance of the house. A violent argument followed and the children split up into two fiercely antagonistic bands: one consisting of the brothers with the right to the inheritance of the house, and the other of the sisters with their claim to a share. The daughters took their father to one of their houses to look after him. After a week of better treatment they persuaded him to leave them the half of the house which belonged to him. The other half had belonged to the mother already deceased, who had expressed her desire that the sons should inherit it. Having been persuaded, the old man was furtively escorted to the city by his daughters to make his will. In the face of this *fait accompli* the brothers' reaction was extreme. From words they passed to blows and D beat A. A's sons went to D's house, and when D saw them coming he prepared to meet them with a knife. Fortunately his wife managed to shut him up in a room, and pacified her nephews. Eventually one of the brothers suggested selling the house and dividing the proceeds between all of them; in the end, therefore, nobody got the house. The brother preferred to forgo his share in the house rather than see his sisters enjoy something to which according to "justice" they had no claim. Later I will comment upon this sense of justice.

An old widow, gravely ill, recommended a friend who went to visit her: "Don't divide your things before dying; my children's dissatisfaction, not my sickness, is killing me." The old lady had been submitted to every kind of pressure by her children in an attempt to persuade her to modify her will according to their personal requirements. As a rule when aged parents have made their will they take pains to keep it absolutely secret, so that they may live their last days in peace, respected by their children.

After a major altercation over the inheritance brothers and sisters or parents cease to be on speaking terms. This means absolutely shunning each other always, which in a small community imposes a series of heavy restrictions. Those involved even shrink from physical proximity, choosing a different path in the plots or crossing the street if they see a brother or sister approaching. They take care never to coincide in the bar or cinema. They disentangle themselves from membership of a religious association if there is the danger of meeting one of the *personæ vitandæ* (odious persons to be avoided), because the sight of them is abhorrent. Their names are avoided as true tabus, never mentioned unless to be execrated. They are never invited by their brothers and sisters—or by their sons and daughters—to any kind of *rites de passage*, nor would they accept if they were. If one of the *vitandæ* persons, trying to diminish family tension, sent a present it would be returned. If the *vitanda* sister or brother is seriously ill nobody visits them; if they die no one goes to the funeral. Sometimes, however, such circumstances do provide a starting point for the resumption of relations, and if the parents are the *vitandæ* they are generally visited if gravely ill. Sometimes the duration of the *vitandæ* relations ends only with the death of one; at other times a *rite de passage* can terminate the family avoidance if only one of the families can climb down sufficiently to issue an invitation which the others can accept without loss of face. Finally in many cases such *vitandæ* relations lose their vigour gradually after several months or a few years, and the families renew the threads of kinship. Other factors, such as religion or temperament, play their part. This *vitanda* relationship does not affect the children of the families involved, although their relations may reflect a certain strain during the worst periods of family passion.

In the two examples above the quarrels were centred round

the house and the plots, the principal causes of dissension over an inheritance. But there can be other grounds. Three old chairs have occasioned a violent family rupture which finished in the most obstinate *vitanda* relationship. One insignificant agricultural tool, the yoke, practically unusable since mechanization, has been the cause of a similar conflict. After hours of heated argument one of the heirs to the yoke hacked it in half so that each could inherit "his" part. This incident was followed by a *vitanda* relationship of the same intensity as if it had been caused by an inheritance of several hectares of arable land. Of course the dispute over such objects is in certain cases merely the spark which sets fire to a latent antagonism.

Figures can give us an approximate idea of the extent of these *vitandæ* relations. In 1958 there came to my knowledge sixteen cases which involved directly at least thirty-two brothers and sisters and indirectly, because all were married, sixty-four people. This was only among one age-group, both consorts being in the region of 40, when the definitive inheritance is likely to occur. I know of no case in which this has not provoked real family storms, at least momentarily, because naturally not all of them end in the *vitanda* relationship described. Common sense on the part of the heirs, the desire to avoid publicity about disagreeable internal affairs, religious sentiments, can lead to a peaceful settlement with mutual concessions.

Conflicts develop because the same objects—houses, plots, tools, furnishings—constitute the focus of the families' interests. Discussion far from being conducted on a purely objective basis involves people not only as possessors of a right to a common inheritance but also in their more intimate, subjective aspects. Their physical defects and personal failings may become the objects of attack, so that although the inheritance has been definitively divided the personal antagonism aroused by these altercations persists. These, the most serious rupture in the life of the community, originate from and acquire their fullest expression of odium within the family circle. The family thus offers two opposing facets: it is the centre of the deepest affection and integration, and the focus of the most virulent hatred and discord.

This supposes, then, two radically different senses of the word family. Competition and conflict in the family, in the sense of the family of constellation, does not affect the cohesion of the nuclear family, the solidarity of which is preserved at all costs. The parents' insistence that their rights to the inheritance be respected by everybody are prompted by consideration for their children's welfare, to whom in due course they will bequeath the inheritance. The *pietas erga liberos* forces the parents to count scrupulously the smallest particle of the inheritance, and repeatedly to weigh up their rights to the same. "They have stolen a plot from my children", the mothers comment when displeased with the final result of an inheritance. The conflict surges up when one of the children leaves the nuclear family to form another one, when the children achieve economic, legal and social independence. When all the brothers and sisters have formed so many unitary cells through their marriages, breaking up the old family of orientation, so many nuclear families have been consolidated, creating the family constellation of which I spoke. Within this constellation each nuclear family tries to maintain its own cohesion, which means cohesion against the other families within the constellation, because these are the ones which, having a common basis of interest, can affect it more directly. The family tension described is thus limited to the conflict between nuclear family and the family constellation, which in turn reinforces and integrates the former.

The early Middle Ages saw the development, especially in Aragón, of an extensive domestic community composed of parents, married children and their offspring, and uncles and cousins in first degree. This domestic community was called *germanitas*, a community of co-heirs, and its principal aim was the common exploitation of the land and enjoyment of the parent's patrimony.[1] The post civil war agrarian economy has led to similar results among some *pudientes*. This patrimonial community

[1] L. Valdeavellano: *Historia de España*, vol. I, part II, p. 207 ff. (Madrid, 1955).

provides the last meaning of the word family to be analysed. It denotes the parents, their married children and the grandchildren. The simplest form is in Fig. 4.

A *pudiente*, because economic affluence is the *conditio sine qua non* of this type of family, divides his arable land into two or more parts according to the number of children, assigning to each child his respective lot when he marries or shortly after. The legal ownership of the land remains the father's, but the children acquire the use and enjoy the fruits of it. The division of lands may correspond to what each child will eventually inherit, though not necessarily so. The father moreover places all the

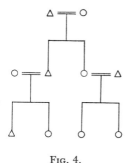

FIG. 4.

agricultural instruments he possesses, from the smallest hoe to the tractor and harvesting machine, at the disposal of his children. Whilst one child, usually though not always the daughter, lives in the same house as the parents, the father provides the others with a house of their own. The economic settlement upon which the solidarity of the family relies is very simple: the agricultural exploitation is a family exploitation and the equipment is domestic. The father, who holds final authority, provides the lands, the house and farmbuildings attached, and the agricultural tools kept there. Usually he does not work himself but supervises and inspects everything. For every farmer this is the ideal status.

The children contribute with their work, each child preferably on his own portion of land. The benefits obtained by each child are divided into two equal parts, one for the father, the other for the child. Thus the father takes half the profits, while each child benefits by a fourth of the total.

Such a father enjoys great prestige in the town. First of all this appears to be the best way of treating one's children; secondly his position is envied because his profits increase considerably *viviendo sin trabajar* (living without working); in the morning he is seen reading the newspaper, seated at the door of his house while the others go to work. He relaxes listening to records on his gramophone, he goes to the opening performances of new films in the city and he travels. All these are essential signs of a man of his status. These *pudientes* take a prominent part in the charitable activities organized by the parish and the Council. Their children venerate them because their parents have treated them so generously, saving them from the initial problems of most young families. Moreover the other parents of the children may feel compelled to emulate their opposite numbers in generosity, so that the gifts of both converge to create a state of economic prosperity for the children. Every Sunday and feast day the *pater familias* presides at his table surrounded by his children and grandchildren. At the same time his children are united by harmonious fraternal relations because their respective interests oblige them to work together in close collaboration. Son and son-in-law use the tractor together in the cultivation of both their lots, they carry out in partnership any task which requires co-operation in any part of the land of the *pater familias*. There is not much place for tension because each one administers his own lot; what they share is the work and the use and care of tools. Finally this type of family reconciles two opposing psychological problems. The father wields undisputed authority, advising the sons about their work and supervising the arrangements of the plots; but the sons too enjoy wide personal initiative because they operate the modern farm machinery about which their fathers are often technically ignorant.

It seems then that bonds of kinship and family cohesion are specific attributes neither of affection nor of feelings but of property. The *pudientes* most clearly exemplify family cohesion and harmonious relations because of the type of domestic community they can afford. To a great extent the family solidarity is a consequence of the common interests involved in an extensive ownership of land.

To sum up:

(a) The specific spheres of action of the husband and of the wife are so closely modelled on traditional norms and patterns that the moralists of the sixteenth century would observe only slight deviations from their precepts in the family theory of today.

(b) The social and legal authority of the father of the family is more than counter-balanced by the feminine influence, that is of the wife–mother, in all the doings of the family. The woman who in the early part of her life was the least significant element in the house, becomes on her marriage not only the minister of finance but the prime minister as well.

(c) Authority on the one side and familiarity of intercourse on the other govern inter-family relations. To the former corresponds the reverence due to the head of the family; the latter is characterized by a lack of tabus. This duality expresses the institutionalized form with which the nuclear family contends with disruptive forces.

(d) The markedly economic character which has left its impression on all family relationships has been the key point for understanding the integrating and disintegrating forces of the family community in all its different meanings. Economic considerations always underlie questions of social status, tensions, conflicts, *vitandæ* relations, and inheritance, and their various repercussions in the family.

(e) The domestic community of the *pudientes* positively corroborates the presence of the economic as an essential ingredient in family relationships, producing a special type of family which has had much to do with the recent mechanization of agricultural methods.

Composite Descent Groups in Canada

E. Leyton

In the past decade anthropologists have turned their attention to the study of kinship in "bilateral societies": in particular, interest has been aroused in the nature of kin groups in urban Western industrialized society. Previous to these investigations, sociologists had assumed the functions of kin groups in Western society to be minimal. Kingsley Davis (1956), for example, wrote:

> Modern society, characterized by an elaborate industrial technology, a high degree of urbanization, and a great amount of geographical and social mobility, has sheered away the extended kinship bonds. The sole effective kinship group is now the immediate family, and even this unit has lost in size and function.

While Firth (1956), Mitchell (1961), and Williams (1963) have modified this view, there is still little published material on complex networks of kin in Western society.

This paper[1] is an attempt to demonstrate that complex kin groups with important social and economic functions do exist in Western society. It is argued briefly that in those sectors of the society which value the maintenance of close family relations, the control of a specific resource[2] makes possible the formation of a kin group with important social and economic functions. Further, the isolated position of immigrants makes them particularly reliant upon kin for social and economic contacts.

The material presented below is a study of a Jewish family business in a Canadian city, Cherbourg.[3] The study shows that

[1] The author would like to thank C. S. Belshaw, J. R. Fox, S. B. Philpott, and Raymond Firth's 1963–4 L.S.E. seminar for their criticism and advice. Opinions expressed are the responsibility of the author.

[2] See Firth (1963).

[3] "Cherbourg" and personal names are fictitious.

kinship—*i.e.* consanguinity and affinity—can be the principle of recruitment to corporate groups in Western society; further, that the activities of these groups, termed here "composite descent groups",[4] are economic as well as social.

The "family" studied here is really the combination of two "families", the Ostroffs and the Allans (Fig. 1). From approximately 1939 to 1955 they existed as a single composite descent group, each member possessing corresponding rights and duties in the economic, social and religious spheres. In 1955 the group

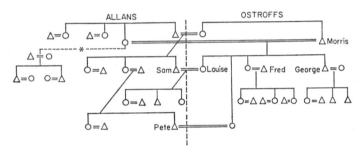

FIG. 1. The Allans and the Ostroffs. (Only adults are shown on the chart. Everyone on it, except Morris Ostroff, was alive in 1963. The broken median line shows the line of segmentation in 1955. Full partners in segmented corporations are named; all others are either directors or salesmen. *Exact relationship unclear.)

segmented along agnatic lines into two composite descent groups, and they continue as such as of 1963.[5]

Both the Ostroffs and the Allans were small shopkeepers in Russia at the beginning of the twentieth century. *Circa* 1920, Morris Ostroff and Harry Allan exchanged sisters in marriage. In the early nineteen-twenties, Morris emigrated with his wife and children to Canada, settling in Cherbourg. During the following

[4] The term "composite descent group" was suggested by Professor Raymond Firth. It is used here to refer to a group using both cognatic and affinal ties as the basis for recruitment.

[5] The material in this paper suffers, of course, from the inevitable distortions and inaccuracies of oral history.

decade Morris brought the rest of the family shown on the chart to Canada, but deposited the Allans in London, Ontario.[6] Harry Allan was a poor businessman and his family struggled on irregular earnings until his only son, Sam, quit school and took over the operations of their small wholesale fruit firm. Although the profits were low, it was nevertheless possible—with the Allans' frugal standard of living—to amass a small store of capital during the depression.

Meanwhile in Cherbourg Morris Ostroff collected junk with a horse and cart and slowly accumulated his own store of capital. In the late nineteen-thirties, Fred Kass—a non-relative—married Morris Ostroff's eldest daughter and Fred was virtually adopted into the Ostroff family.[7] Soon after this, Sam Allan married Morris's daughter Louise and moved to Cherbourg. At this time the Second World War appeared imminent, and to avoid conscription (farmers were exempt) the Ostroffs and Allans bought and settled on a small farm near Cherbourg. On the farm the families congealed into a working composite descent group: they shared a common house; they worked together on the farm as well as in the city selling junk; male work duties were apportioned by Morris Ostroff; the family shared income and expenditure; disputes were settled by Morris Ostroff; and they participated together in all religious festivals. During the war the primary occupations of the group—farming and junk-collecting—were excellent sources of income, and under Morris Ostroff's leadership a considerable store of capital was accumulated by the end of the war.

As soon as the war ended the family sold the farm, set up a similar communal residence in the city, and purchased a small retail furniture shop in downtown Cherbourg. Morris Ostroff, with his son George and his virtually adopted son-in-law Fred,

[6] Two sisters of Harry Allan were definitely left behind in Russia. It was not possible to determine why these two were left behind, nor if others were in fact left behind. This procedure of recruitment by emigration does, however, effectively limit—for a few generations at least—the size of the kin group.

[7] Morris always referred to Fred—as distinguished from his other sons-in-law—as "my son".

each assumed full partnerships in the newly formed Avon Furniture Co., Ltd. The younger sons-in-law, Sam Allan and Pete Gross, were high-salaried employees. In addition, all other adult members of the family assisted in the enterprise, the men acting as salesmen and delivery men, the women acting as book-keepers, secretaries, and cleaners. On the basis of this pool of labour and capital, sufficient resources were available to operate the store without hiring non-kin employees. The firm prospered and by the late nineteen-forties they were sufficiently affluent to provide individual housing for the nuclear families: a single apartment block housed the full partners, and the younger sons-in-law purchased two adjacent homes nearby.

However, a major power struggle had been developing within the corporation. The two younger sons-in-law—Sam Allan and Pete Gross—were dissatisfied with their salaried positions and demanded full partnerships. The full partners were not willing to make this concession and the conflict was at its height when Morris Ostroff died suddenly in 1955, leaving his estate in the hands of his full partners. The full partners sold the stores to the younger sons-in-law and left for the U.S.A., taking most of the Ostroffs with them.

In the new Cherbourg enterprise, Sam Allan, his wife and Pete Gross were full partners (Sam was older and had more capital than Pete, consequently Sam's wife received an equal share), and the remaining cognates and affines were either salesmen or "directors" (a directorship is a business post with virtually no restrictions on the qualifications, duties and salaries of its holders).

By 1963, both Cherbourg and U.S. corporations were multi-million dollar enterprises, based primarily in downtown property and residential apartments. The residence pattern is maintained in Cherbourg, two elaborate adjacent homes now housing the full partners, and one apartment block—owned by the corporation—housing three generations of cognates and affines. In the U.S. city, the pattern is similar.

At present, while personal feuds temporarily disrupt relations between the segmented composite descent groups, relations are in general still close. However, while relations between the groups are exclusively social, relations *within* each group are as much economic as social. Social relations between the groups take the form of frequent visits across the border; economic relations within each group continue as in the original single corporation, consisting of a nucleus of full partners utilizing cognates and affines as salesmen and directors.

While the Ostroffs and the Allans refer to themselves as "the family", there are restrictions on the range of kin permitted membership in the group. While cognates and affines of cognates of full partners are members, relationships are not normally traced further. However, the families have not been in North America long enough for large numbers to have been born and matured, and it has not yet been necessary for strict lines to be drawn. Ranges of kin can be divided into two broad categories: (*a*) The full partners: a group of brothers or brothers-in-law who control the business enterprise and who are obliged to contribute substantially to the support of (*b*) the salesmen and directors: all cognates and affines of cognates of the full partners can claim membership in the enterprise, but are obliged to participate fully in the social activities of the group, and affirm the generosity of the partners to the rest of the Jewish community. Relations between parents and children are rigidly authoritarian, while relations between grandparents and grandchildren are of a highly sentimental nature (as are relations between great-grandparents and great-grandchildren). Within a single generation, all members are at least theoretically peers, although some deference is paid by directors and salesmen to the full partners. In instances where an individual beolngs to two generations (for example, Pete Gross is Sam Allan's nephew and brother-in-law) the individual is placed according to his age and abilities (Pete Gross's brother-in-law, a man of limited business acumen, was considered more a child than a man).

One of the major problems facing the Ostroff and Allan families is that they do not produce a proportionate amount of males. Consequently, the suitability of the in-marrying male is of great importance. It is not surprising then that elaborate mechanisms exist to regulate marriage, *i.e.* to ensure that only suitable males are incorporated by marriage into the group. The suitable in-marrying male must be willing to accept the values and to immerse himself completely in the social and economic activities of the group (he is in fact encouraged to neglect if not sever relations with his own cognates). In the case of an unsuitable suitor, which has occurred twice in the past decade, the suitor is discouraged and the female is sent away to kin in the other city where considerable pressure is brought to bear (including appeals to family solidarity and warnings that a bad marriage would ruin the health of the parents).

This leads to an additional question: how is the unity of the group maintained today? Since the primary economic aim of the group, the accumulation of large sums of money, is already fulfilled what devices exist to ensure that the younger generation will continue to participate in the activities of the group? Basically there are two devices: first, each adult is a potential negotiator and in times of crisis can be called upon to persuade any deviate of his error. Second, and more important, is the economic dependence of all members of the kin group on the full partners. This dependence is maintained by ensuring that any director or salesman enjoys and becomes accustomed to a standard of living out of reach of his own earning power. For example, in 1958, after great conflict, Sam Allan's eldest daughter married a literature student who had academic ambitions and therefore little potential earning power. After his marriage, this student found himself living in a penthouse, with two cars, charge accounts at major stores, and a low-salaried directorship.

If an individual attempts to sever relations with the composite descent group, considerable pressure is also brought to bear. The student mentioned above attempted this in 1962: in the twelve-month period following his attempt he received weekly phone calls and visits from family negotiators and censure and persuasion from friends of the family.

Religious ceremonies, both private and public, were also

approached co-operatively. Before Morris Ostroff's death, most of the "family" gathered for Sabbath dinners; after his death the regular Sabbath dinners were discontinued, but the family continued to sit together in a block in the synagogue.

CONCLUSION

Maintenance of this composite descent group offered costs and benefits, rights and obligations to all members of the group. In Jewish immigrant culture the family is considered a unit of fundamental importance, and much more prestige is gained from being the head of a large and wealthy composite descent group than from being simply the head of a rich nuclear family. Full partners, while obliged to contribute heavily to the support of the directors, could legally write the bulk of the cost off on the income tax; in return they received the esteem of their family and of the entire Jewish community. Directors and salesmen, while obliged to participate in the social and economic activities of the group, received security, a high standard of living, and shared in the Jewish community's esteem for the entire family.

The character of the furniture business and the prevailing state of the market were also important in determining the structure of the group. The furniture business requires a large number of employees with varied, but not necessarily highly developed, abilities: a family group makes available cheap and trustworthy labour for the initial stage of expansion of the business. Further, the state of the market during this period was in general one of expansion, and this made possible the inclusion of a large number of relatives in the enterprise. Finally the Provincial Corporation Law consolidated and maintained the group, providing as it did a legal mechanism for including large numbers at low cost.

One additional point should be stressed—the significance of the "leader" in this type of composite descent group. The personal characteristics of the leader would seem to have considerable bearing on the functions of the group. Without Morris Ostroff's charismatic leadership it seems doubtful whether the composite

---

---

descent group in question would have attained its level of complexity and rigidity.

In sum then, we have a situation in which the composite descent group was the discrete units in residence, property holding, income control and in social affairs; in which occupational roles were closely associated with kinship roles; and in which relations between kin tended to be obligatory rather than permissive. Membership in the group was obtained exclusively on the basis of kinship ties—consangiuneal and affinal—and corresponding rights and duties were allocated to all members of the group. The coincidence of sentiment, economics and law allowed the formation of a composite descent group with important social and economic functions.[8]

REFERENCES

DAVIS, KINGSLEY (1956) *Human Society*, New York, Macmillan.

FIRTH, RAYMOND (1956) *Two Studies of Kinship in London*, L.S.E., Monographs on Social Anthropology, No. 15 London, Athlone Press.

FIRTH, RAYMOND (1956) Bilateral descent groups: an operational viewpoint, in I. Schapera (Ed.) *Studies in Kinship and Marriage*, Royal Anthropological Institute Occasional Paper No. 16, London, 1963.

MITCHEL, W. E. (1961) Descent groups among New York City Jews, *Jewish J. of Social.* **3,** 121–8.

WILLIAMS, W. M. (1963) *A West Country Village*, Routledge.

---

[8] In regard to the future of the groups: the youngest generation is insufficiently mature to have decided its career or social affiliation, and no definitive statements can yet be made. However, menial tasks in the business are now being performed by non-kin employees; and the daughters are marrying professional men (against the objections of their parents) with little interest in the economic activities of the corporations. On the other hand, the eldest Ostroff son has completed his training as a lawyer, and now handles the legal arrangements for the U.S. corporation. It seems likely that the structure of the group will alter to form a more optative system, *i.e.* while participation in the social activities of the group may continue to be obligatory, participation in the economic activities of the group will probably be determined by inclination or need. In addition it will become necessary to distinguish ranges or degrees of kin and concomitant obligations. In fact, this process has already begun, the son (not shown in the chart) of one of Sam Allan's sisters having taken up a career outside the family enterprises.

Kinship and Crisis in South Wales*

J. B. LOUDON

I

IN THIS essay I discuss the significance of extra-familial kinship among the inhabitants of a rural area in South Wales known as the Vale of Glamorgan. The discussion is based on field material obtained in the course of anthropological inquiries carried out between 1957 and 1960.[1] As the title indicates, the discussion is focused upon certain functions of extra-familial kin ties in situations of crisis, by which I mean "occasions which are regarded by the participants as among the most important in their personal affairs".[2] Childbirth, marriage, illness, and death are the most common and universal of such situations. In general I use the phrase "extra-familial kin ties" to denote relationships through consanguinity or marriage outside the family of procreation if the individual concerned is married, and outside the family of orientation if the individual is single. In practice this usually means that extra-familial kin ties are links of kinship or affinity other than those between members of a domestic family.

* This essay is a revised version of a paper presented at a conference on "Family and Kin Ties in Britain and their Social Implications", organized by the Association of Social Anthropologists and the British Sociological Association, and held in London in April 1961.

[1] The inquiries were carried out in the course of a joint programme of social and epidemiological investigation undertaken in South Wales by members of the Social Psychiatry Research Unit of the Medical Research Council. I am grateful to the Director of the Unit, Professor Sir Aubrey Lewis, for permission to present and publish this paper.

[2] Firth, Raymond (Ed.) *Two Studies of Kinship in London*, L.S.E. Monographs on Social Anthropology, No. 15, London, Athlone Press (1956), p. 29.

The Vale of Glamorgan[3] consists of about 150 square miles of fertile agricultural land between the city of Cardiff and the town of Bridgend, bounded on the south by the sea and on the north by the southern edge of the South Wales coalfield. The Vale has a population of about 13,000 people. Most of them live in scattered farms, hamlets, and villages. There are also two small market towns in the area, each with about 1500 inhabitants. Most of my detailed inquiries have been carried out in one of these towns and in three adjoining rural parishes, in one of which I live with my family. A certain number of my informants live in other parts of the area. In addition, a private census of the whole Vale population, carried out in 1960, has provided a good deal of basic information about each individual inhabitant and the composition of each household.

Although a rural and predominantly agricultural area, no part of the Vale is more than 12 miles from major industrial and urban centres. Many of the people who live in the Vale work outside it and travel to and fro each day to earn their livings in adjacent urban areas. Most Vale people also have kin ties with people who live in these areas and in other parts of South Wales with whom they maintain effective social relations. A larger number of Vale people who do not work in the urban areas nevertheless visit them fairly regularly to see friends and relatives who live there or who are in hospital there, to shop or go to the cinema, and for such recreational purposes as to attend football matches and greyhound races. About 40 per cent of the adult population of the Vale consists of people who were born outside it and have lived in it for less than 15 years. The majority of such comparative newcomers were born in other parts of South Wales, mostly in places in the counties of Glamorgan and Monmouthshire which lie within 25 miles of the borders of the Vale. Many of them have close relatives still living at their places of birth or

[3] My definition of the Vale of Glamorgan is primarily an operational one, determined by the need for epidemiological purposes of a predominantly rural defined population for comparison with urban populations elsewhere in the County. Few local historians and geographers agree about the exact boundaries of the Vale.

previous residence with whom they maintain frequent and intimate contact.

The most important sources of employment for those Vale people who earn their livings within its borders are agriculture and forestry, stone quarries and cement works, and the building industry. A large number of men and women are employed in different capacities by public bodies such as the County and Rural District Councils, the Fire Service, and local electricity and water undertakings. There is also a large Royal Air Force station in the Vale which provides employment for a number of locally resident civilians. Further sources of employment are public and private transport and communication services, the distributive trades, and a number of small industrial concerns in the two Vale market towns, among which are an asbestos factory, a printing works, and three firms of agricultural engineers.

II

Most of the material concerning kinship in the Vale was obtained by standard anthropological procedures: the collection of genealogies, unstructured interviews with individual informants, and participant observation. Certain data on particular aspects of kinship behaviour were provided in the course of a study of the attitudes to mental disorder of the relatives of psychiatric patients. I have also had access to a wealth of documentary material, most of it unpublished.[4] After a time, however, I found myself able to make increasing use of direct observation to supplement verbal information. Participation in the life of the locality and growing familiarity with the details of kinship connections made it possible to observe social relations between kin taking place in a wide variety of contexts and to compare behaviour between kin with behaviour between non-kin in similar situations.

[4] Including diaries, letters, Christmas cards, family bibles, photograph and scrap albums, lists of wedding presents, lists of guests at weddings, christenings and the like, parish registers, court and hospital records, newspaper reports, and other published sources.

In collecting materials from informants I have tried as far as possible to relate statements regarding kin ties to the individuals concerned rather than to married couples, elementary families or households. In the field situation this is not, of course, as easy as it sounds. Data on kinship are often obtained from two or more informants simultaneously. The discussions and arguments between them which such inquiries tend to provoke often compensate for the resultant difficulty in comparing knowledge of kin and quality of relationship with them revealed by individual members of the same domestic unit. This emphasis on the kinship universe of the individual rather than the domestic unit arose from certain apparent differences between men and women, between spouses, and between parents and children in degree of recognition of extra-familial kin ties and in their functions in various contexts.

I have also attempted to collect material on the interconnectedness of kin ties by interviewing and observing different members of the kinship universe of individual informants. The difficulties of doing so seem often to be directly related to the degree to which an individual's kinship network is what Bott describes as "close-knit", in which there are many relationships, independent of the individual concerned, among the component units of his kin universe.[5] In many "families" there is generally at least one person who is acknowledged by most other family members to be the expert on genealogical connections. The existence of such recognized experts is particularly common among "families" long settled in the area, other members of which tend to rely on them for details of genealogical connections and to refer the investigator to them when approached for kinship information.

Firth refers to such experts as pivotal kin, "relatives who act as linking points in the kinship structure" and who "hold more threads of genealogical connections in their heads than anyone else".[6] I prefer to differentiate between experts and pivotal kin,

[5] Bott, Elizabeth, *Family and Social Network*, London, Tavistock Publications (1957), p. 59.

[6] Firth, *op cit.*, p. 39.

and to reserve the latter term for those individuals who act as connecting relatives, irrespective of whether they are also experts. The significance of pivotal kin as connecting links is usually greater if they are also experts, as is often the case. But many pivotal kin are elderly men, who, in general, know less about kinship connections than their daughters or nieces; and it is often found that individuals remain pivotal kin after their death. Not only do their graves sometimes form the pivot round which kin ties tenuously revolve, but the dead are often used by living informants as foci from which genealogical connections stem. This is particularly the case when the dead person lived to a great age or had high prestige for some reason among his kindred or in the locality.

Most pivotal kin who are also experts are elderly women who, from their personal knowledge of dead kin of previous generations, maintain links of information and social contact between their own and their siblings' descendants and the descendants of their parents' and grandparents' siblings. In theory, and often in practice, this means that such women carry in their heads kinship knowledge of six generations depth and extending laterally among consanguineal kin as far as the grandchildren of second cousins. When economic and other social factors reinforce relatively remote kinship connections, the lateral extension among consanguineal kin may go further: the grandchildren of pivotal kin may recognize as cousins of unspecified degree the descendants of the pivotal kin's second or third cousins. The same factors often lead to knowledge of, and contact with, affines being very extensive.

There are many individuals in the Vale who are able to identify between 200 and 500 living and dead relatives, about the majority of whom they can provide at least such information as sex, marital state, place of residence, and occupation. Most of these individuals are people long settled in the area, but which I mean people who, in the main, were born in the Vale and one or both of whose parents, and often whose grandparents, were also born there. By contrast, there are other individuals who show a very much more restricted range of kin recognition of the order of about 50 relatives in all. Some of these individuals have always lived in the area but most of them are relatively recent immigrants, that is, adults who were born outside the Vale, often in urban areas, and who have only moved into the locality since 1945. In both instances, in spite of the great differences in size of the average kinship universe, it is rare for the depth of generations over which kin are recognized to exceed seven or to be less than four. Again, while the number of kin with whom an individual may have some kind of periodic contact tends to vary with the size of the kinship universe, the number of kin with whom an individual has frequent and intimate contact is usually little different from those with large kinship networks from those with small.

Degree of physical mobility is only one of a number of interdependent social factors which act directly or indirectly to influence the size of an individual's kinship universe. These factors are also related to the amount of contact the individual has with extra-familial kin and to the differentiations he makes among them; the most important are occupation, economic resources, ownership of property, and degree of social mobility. In some cases religious affiliations and level of education also seem significant. The decisions which an individual makes in choosing how far to observe or disregard in any particular set of circumstances the sentiments, obligations and expectations which are involved in the recognition of extra-familial kin ties appear to be influenced by the interplay of such factors as these. It is within the framework provided by them that idiosyncratic preferences operate.

The same factors also tend to affect the degree to which marriages reinforce already existing ties of kinship and affinity and, among certain sections of the population, the scarcely less significant ties between kith, that is, between friends and neighbours of approximately the same perceived social status. Indeed, kith may be described as consisting of those who are an individual's potential affines.

The multiplicity of roles which every individual fills both successively in his lifetime and simultaneously at any given time is a sociological truism which needs no labouring. In any attempt to study the functions of kinship in a highly complex society it is nevertheless all too easy to lose sight of the importance for social behaviour of role-relationships other than those based on kin ties. Any analysis of a system of social relations necessarily involves the overemphasis, for heuristic purposes, of lines of demarcation between particular aspects of behaviour. In fact it is often very difficult for the observer to disentangle the kinship network of an individual from the wider social network of which it forms a part. This is most clearly seen in the case of farmers and their families who, together with those whose occupations are largely dependent on agriculture and who come, in many cases, of local farming stock, form one of the significant sections of Vale society. At the same time it is possible to demonstrate the importance of the social factors mentioned earlier in relation to the structure and functions of extra-familial kin ties.

Among farmers the degree of physical mobility is relatively low. Although most farmers in the Vale are tenants, holdings relatively rarely become vacant other than through the death or retirement of the tenant, when it is the traditional policy among landowners and their agents to give preference among applicants for the new tenancy to the sons of the previous tenant. The vast majority of farmers are the sons and grandsons of farmers and most farmers' wives are the daughters of farmers. Those children of farmers who are socially mobile tend to maintain close links with their relatives who are still farming. There is a high degree of interconnectedness in the kinship and social networks of farmers; there is also considerable variation between individual farmers in the recognition of extra-familial kin ties, according to the age of the individuals concerned, the stage of development in its life-cycle reached by the elementary family to which they belong and the social context of contacts between them. The result is that it is often almost impossible to know whether social relations between individuals in particular instances should be classified as taking place between kin or between non-kin. Not only do most farmers see each other constantly in a wide variety of circumstances but the role-relationships between them, and between members of their families, are diverse, numerous, interlocking and constantly changing, at particular times and at different periods of their lives. There is often no sharp division made between extra-familial kinship roles and non-kinship roles; rather they form a continuum, with emphasis on different role-relationships in different social situations.

The number of interconnected roles played in particular contexts by each individual actor, and the degree to which the same actors are linked with one another through a network of role-relationships are referred to by Nadel as "summation of roles" and "congruence of roles" respectively. When "a series of diverse relationships (domestic or kin, economic, religious, political) . . . come to link the same sets of persons, constituting a congruent set of linkages",[7] one is able to identify more or less homogeneous groupings or sections of a society or population. Some measure of the homogeneity of a society, or of a section of a society, is thus provided by the extent to which interconnectedness is found within the networks of individual actors. The term "network" is used here to indicate the set of relatively enduring relationships which any one person has with several other persons.[8] To my mind the idea of network in this sense is more useful as a fieldwork tool and as a descriptive device than as an analytical concept. It is convenient, as others have pointed out, because it emphasizes the open-ended nature of sets of relationships and because it may be used to draw attention to the other links between persons in a particular network which are independent of those between them and the individual at its centre. The interdependence of all links in an individual's network of role-relationships is directly related to their interconnectedness; in other words, the qualities of the relationships between persons in a network are affected by the number of persons who have direct

[7] Nadel, S. F., *The Theory of Social Structure*, London, Cohen & West (1957), p. 66.
[8] For recent usages of the idea of networks see Bott, *op. cit.*, Nadel, *op. cit.*, and Barnes, J. A., Class and committees in a Norwegian island parish, *Hum. Rel.* **7** (1), (1954), 39–58.

links with one another and by the number of role-relationships which those links represent.

It is possible to divide the population of the Vale into a number of sections or categories on the basis of demonstrable summation and congruence of roles, that is, according to the degree of inter-connectedness found in the social networks of individual members. These sections may then be ranged, as it were, along a graduated scale of homogeneity. At one end of the scale are those sections with a high degree of homogeneity. Many of them are relatively large and consist of people most of whom are long settled in the area, as previously defined. Most members of such sections live in close physical proximity[9] to numerous kith and kin with many of whom they have close economic, political and religious ties and upon whom they depend for many of their informal social activities. At the other extreme are those sections with a low degree of homogeneity, most of them relatively small but forming larger aggregates of a less cohesive kind. These sections consist of people who are relatively recent immigrants lacking extensive local networks of kith and kin. In addition to being newcomers and outsiders, many of them are socially as well as physically mobile. Between these two extremes are a number of moderately homogeneous sections, showing a relative lack of one or other of those features mentioned as particularly character-istic of highly homogeneous sections. Most persons having highly interconnected networks maintain relatively few social relation-ships with persons living elsewhere than in or near the Vale. Those sections which have a low degree of homogeneity include many people who look to friends and relatives living some distance from the Vale for most of their close relationships outside the elementary family; such sections often consist of a number of fragments of similar sections centred in other localities.[10]

[9] The definition of "close physical proximity" in a rural area obviously varies according to availability of means of transport, possession of telephone, and other factors apart from physical distance between houses.

[10] An ambitious attempt has been made to divide the population into sec-tions according to a number of simple variables which field-work had shown to be among the most important correlates of homogeneity. This operation,

III

This model of Vale society should be borne in mind in the ensuing examination of certain functions of extra-familial kin ties in situations of crisis. Three main kinds of function can be distinguished. My main concern is with what may be termed the ceremonial and evaluative functions. The third or supportive function is, for lack of space, scarcely considered in this paper. Needless to say, all three functions frequently operate simultaneously or merge into one another in particular instances. The way in which the interplay of different factors affects the significance of extra-familial kin ties according to the context may be seen in the case of the funeral of one of my informants.

> J. M., a widower, and a farmer of high standing in the Vale, died in the autumn of 1959 at Ty mawr, the farm at which he had been born in 1887. His body was buried a few days later in his wife's grave in the parish churchyard. About 400 people attended the funeral. Only about twenty of the mourners were women, most of them having kin ties with the dead man. The remainder of those present were men.
>
> J.M. spent the whole of his life in the area and in his time filled a number of public offices, including those of magistrate, rural district councillor, and churchwarden. Until he was about 60 he was a keen rider to hounds and he was generally considered a good judge of cattle and horses. He served for many years in the local Agricultural Society in various capacities, including one year as President, and his entries in the cattle and sheep sections of the Society's annual show generally won several prizes. In short, he was known in the locality as a good farmer and a prominent public figure. He was exceptional among Vale farmers in being the owner rather than the tenant of his land. He inherited Ty mawr and its 280 acres from his father, who had in turn inherited it from J.M.'s grandfather, who came to the farm as a tenant in 1846 and was born in another part of South Wales. J.M.'s grandfather was able to buy the farm after he had been a tenant for about 20 years, partly because his wife, J.M.'s grandmother, inherited from an uncle land in the mountains of north Glamorgan which was found to cover a rich seam of steam coal.

---

based on data from the private census of the Vale carried out in 1960, was intended to provide a means of obtaining sociological samples of the population for epidemiological and attitude studies. The following variables were used: occupation; occupation of father, of husband and of wife's father; place of birth; place of birth of father, of mother and of spouse. On this basis roughly 70 per cent of the population can be said to be members of sections with a high or moderate degree of homogeneity.

Both J.M. and his father were only sons. The genealogically closest patrilateral kin with whom J.M. maintained contact were two second cousins, the sons of his father's father's sister's daughter, who live in southern England. He occasionally called on them when he was in that part of the country attending cattle sales, but the relationship was not an intimate one and neither of these cousins attended or were represented at his funeral. Both, however, wrote letters of condolence to J.M.'s sister, who is my chief source of information on her family's genealogical connections and who is represented by the initials G.D. in the kinship diagram (Fig. 1) in which all those who were present at the funeral of J.M.

Funeral of J.M. (1887-1959)

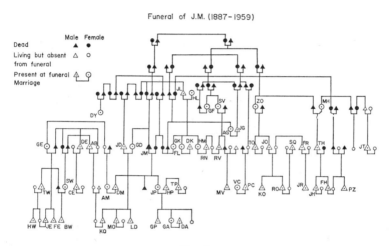

Fig. 1

are indicated by notation and by initials for ease of reference in the text. J.M. and his sister have other patrilateral second cousins in America, but G.D. knows little of them except through the son of one female second cousin who occasionally visited Ty mawr while he was serving in the American forces in Britain during the 1939–45 war and with whom G.D. has since then exchanged Christmas cards.

There are, however, living in the Vale and elsewhere in South Wales, a number of genealogically more remote patrilateral kin with most of whom G.D. maintains (and J.M. until his death maintained) more or less intimate social relations. A large number of these kin attended J.M.'s funeral. All of them are the descendants of a sister of J.M.'s father's father's father. This aunt of J.M.'s grandfather married a farmer, with whom she went out to South Africa in 1820 to settle in the eastern part of what is now the Cape Province, and had a large number of children. The youngest daughter came to Britain in the 1860s to visit her relatives and spent most of her time stay-ing at Ty mawr with her first cousin, J.M.'s grandfather. While there she met and married a local clergyman, the vicar of a Vale parish, and in due course had two children, a son and a daughter, both of whom later married members of local families. The daughter, a second cousin of J.M.'s father, now a widow of over 90 and referred to by G.D. as her aunt, was the oldest patrilateral kin at J.M.'s funeral. She is represented in Fig. 1 by the initials Z.O.

Three other elderly women at the funeral have patrilateral kin ties with J.M. and his sister. One is M.H., the widow of Z.O.'s dead brother. The others are two widowed sisters, S.V. and G.F., the daughters of Z.O.'s mother's eldest sister's daughter, who were born and brought up in South Africa and who, following forty years later in the footsteps of their great-aunt, Z.O.'s mother, came to stay with her in her husband's vicarage in the early 1900s and married local men, both of them members of well-known Vale farming families and both of them, through separate genealogical connections, distant cousins of M.H., the wife of Z.O.'s brother.

These four elderly women—Z.O., her sister-in-law M.H., and her first cousins once removed, S.V. and G.F.—were accompanied to the funeral by a number of male kin and affines. Z.O. was brought to the funeral by her elder son, T.O., a farmer, with whom she lives. Her younger son, J.O., an auctioneer, was there with his two sons K.O. and R.O., his wife's brother and nephew, F.R. and J.R., and his son R.O.'s wife's father, S.Q.

M.H. lives with her niece, the unmarried daughter of her dead brother, who did not come to the funeral; and although her son, T.H., was there, M.H. was brought to the funeral and accompanied by J.T., the son of her dead brother's wife's brother, whose father, one of J.M.'s closest friends, was too ill to attend himself. T.H., like his first cousins T.O. and J.O. a third cousin of J.M., came with his two sons, J.H. and F.H., and with the latter's wife's brother P.Z. P.Z. and his sister, the children of their mother's second marriage, refer to themselves as connections of J.M.'s matrilateral kin because their mother's dead first husband was the son of a sister of the wife of J.M.'s mother's brother. It seems clear, however, that the principal reason for this claim is related to the fact that J.M.'s mother's brother's wife and her sister, the mother of P.Z.'s mother's first husband, had kin ties with a member of the peerage whose name was a household word in the latter part of the 19th century, and a portrait of whom hangs on the wall in P.Z.'s mother's house.

The two widows S.V. and G.F. live together in a small house in one of the Vale villages. They were brought to the funeral by S.V.'s son R.V., a farmer in Herefordshire, accompanied by M.V. her grandson by another son who died a few years ago. R.V.'s wife's brother R.N. is a business-man living in the Vale and married to H.N., one of the three daughters of J.M.'s mother's brother J.L. Unlike her sister, G.F. had no children, but her dead husband's first cousin, J.G. (who was best man at G.F.'s wedding) and his wife, A.G., a matrilateral cross-cousin of J.M., were at the funeral, together with P.C., the son of J.G.'s father's brother's daughter, and his wife, V.C. J.G. is a farmer and a small landowner in the Vale and P.C., though the son of a farmer and living in the Vale, is an architect; V.C., herself the daughter of a farmer, runs a smallholding at their home to which P.C. looks forward to retiring.

P.C. was genealogically the most remote matrilateral consanguineal kin of J.M. to be present at the funeral. His mother, who did not attend, is J.M.'s second cousin, her father's mother being the sister of his mother's mother. G.D. has knowledge of a number of matrilateral second cousins, but none of them attended the funeral and very few of them maintain effective contact with her. Those who are descended from her mother's mother's siblings are resident in East Anglia and, according to G.D., have "never had much to do with us because the family didn't approve of my grandmother marrying my grandfather". G.D. and J.M.'s mother's father was the son of a labourer who rose from being a clerk to being the head of a prosperous firm of land and estate agents. G.D. knows virtually nothing of the descendants of her mother's father's siblings. Her grandfather was the youngest of a large family and married relatively late in life, so that all her mother's patrilateral first cousins were very much older than she was; furthermore, as G.D. says, "they were a very rough lot; some of them used to come to my grandfather for money and try and sponge on him but my mother used to say he never got a thankyou for what he did for them and after a bit he gave up trying".

J.L., the maternal uncle of J.M. and G.D., is the sole survivor of their mother's siblings. Until retirement he was the head of the firm founded by his father. Among the partners in the firm was his eldest sister's husband, whose brother's son, J.D., the husband of G.D., is the present head of the firm. The eldest sister had no children and J.L. himself had three daughters but no son. One of these daughters, H.N., has already been mentioned as the wife of R.N., a business-man living in the Vale whose sister is the wife of R.V., a patrilateral third cousin once removed of J.M. and G.D. A second daughter, G.K., is the wife of a solicitor, D.K., living in the Vale. The third daughter, F.L., married, as his second wife, her first cousin, whose first wife was a sister of J.M.'s wife.

J.M.'s wife and her sister were the daughters of a clergyman. Their parents both died when the daughters were still schoolchildren, and they were brought up by their father's brother and his wife, who had no children of their own. This uncle was a bank manager, whose wife was the sister of a farmer in the Vale with a daughter, D.Y., who grew up as a "cousin" of the two girls, and in due course became the godmother of J.M.'s daughter J.P., whose husband H.P. is a farmer in the Vale, though born in Monmouthshire where his brother T.P. is the present owner of the P. family farm. J.P. and her husband have three children, G.P., who works on his father's farm, G.A., who is married to a young R.A.F. officer, and a second daughter who is still at school.

J.M. had two sons. The elder son, who was his father's favourite and worked with him on the farm, died in a road accident some years ago.

The younger son, D.M., is the proprietor of an antique shop in London, and according to his aunt, G.D., never got on well with his father and takes no interest in farming or in his relatives in the Vale.

M.D., the eldest of G.D.'s three sons, is part owner of a stud farm in the Vale and a well known amateur jockey. The second son, K.D., is the director of a number of companies in Cardiff, travelling to his office each day from his home in the Vale. The youngest son, L.D., who is unmarried, lives at home with his parents in a large house in a village not far from Ty mawr, and works in his father's firm.

K.D. and his mother's brother's son, D.M., married wives from what may be called the E-B-W complex, shown on the left hand side of Fig. 1. The senior members of these three "families", together with some of the junior members and their affines, are directors of a number of engineering and allied concerns in the industrial areas outside the Vale. Thus, 18 members of the E-B-W complex and their affines, among them K.D. and his father, hold directorships in 38 companies. By no means all these individuals are indicated in Fig. 1, though all but four of those who appear there live in the Vale.

Certain other features which are some indication of the highly interconnected nature of J.M.'s kinship network may be summarized as follows. There are 81 living adult individuals shown in Fig. 1, of which 39 are men and 42 are women. Thirty-seven of them (25 men ,12 women) are individual subscribing members of the local Agricultural Society and 55 (27 men, 28 women) are past or present members of the local hunt or of neighbouring hunts. Twelve of them (10 men, 2 women) are members of the local bench of magistrates and 17 (10 men, 7 women) are past or present members of various Church of Wales bodies at the Ruridecanal or Diocesan level. About 50 of them (roughly 20 men and 30 women) are members of local branches of a major political party and the majority play an active part in local branches of one or other of such bodies as the Red Cross, the Order of St. John, the National Society for the Prevention of Cruelty to Children, the Women's Institute and the Mother's Union. Finally, 12 men are members of local lodges of Freemasons.

It has already been suggested that marriages reinforce the many-stranded informal links between kith and kin, and that kith may be described as potential affines. This is well illustrated in the kinship network of J.M. A man who lived in the Vale throughout his life, and died at the age of over 70 in 1918, kept a diary for many years in which he made careful note of all the children living in the locality who were invited to an annual party which he gave each Christmas for his grandchildren. Among those who attended regularly during the period from 1895 to 1910 were 17 of those individuals shown in Fig. 1 who are members of the same generation as J.M., including J.M. himself and his wife; in fact no fewer than 12 of those individuals subsequently married one another.

It may be seen from this account of the kin ties between J.M. and 54 of those who attended his funeral that the dead man's kinship universe consisted of his immediate family, comprising his son and daughter with their spouses and children, and his sister with her husband and three sons; his patrilateral and matrilateral kin, the closest genealogically among the former being his father's second cousin, Z.O., and among the latter his mother's brother, J.L.; and the affines of his son and of one of his sister's sons. The remainder of those at the funeral, numbering about 350 people, included most adult males resident in the parish and many of those from adjoining parishes, together with a large number of farmers from the area, tradesmen and business proprietors, and members and representatives of various bodies with which J.M. had been associated. Some of these people are linked through marriage with individuals on the periphery of the dead man's kinship universe. I have omitted them from the diagram, however, because the chain of links between them and J.M. is not regarded by those concerned as having any social significance.

The people at the funeral may be divided into a number of more or less well defined categories according to the ways in which individuals grouped themselves together during the ceremony. This process is largely spontaneous, is expected by the participants, and, although particularly characteristic of funerals, may of course be observed in any large gathering in the Vale where the aggregation of individuals takes place informally. In this instance the process was influenced by the small size of the parish church. Seats in the church were reserved for close relatives, for female mourners, and for such dignitaries as the Lord Lieutenant and High Sheriff of the County, the chairman of the local magistrates, and the Mayor of the nearby market town.

The remainder of those present formed themselves into clusters in the churchyard and in the road outside. Some clusters consisted of only three or four men, others of a dozen or more. Before the coffin arrived, and while the funeral service was being conducted inside the church, the members of each cluster conversed together in subdued voices and took up positions near the grave and alongside the path from the churchyard gate to the church porch. Standing near the gate, both outside and inside the churchyard, was a large crowd of men, most of them parishioners or employees of local firms with whom J.M. had had business connections, such as the foreman of a local firm of plumbers, two of the lorry drivers working for an agricultural merchant in the local market town, men employed by local building contractors and workers from a quarry in which J.M. had a financial interest. Inside the churchyard and not far from the gate were a number of clusters of men talking together, mostly shopkeepers from the market town, clerical workers from the local council offices, bank employees and some farmers. Farmers and certain business men made up the largest clusters on both sides of the path. One such cluster consisted entirely of certain members of what I have called the E-B-W complex, namely, the following individuals indicated in Fig. 1: D.E.; his sister's husband, A.B.; his son, C.E.; another sister's grandson, B.W.; and his brother's son, J.E., together with the latter's wife's father, T.W., and brother, H.W., respectively the uncle and first cousin of B.W. This cluster was joined by T.P. and J.R., the latter being a close friend of B.W. Other members of J.M.'s kinship network who remained in the churchyard with clusters of non-kin were M.V., K.O., R.O., S.Q., F.R., T.H., J.H., F.H., and P.Z. The last mentioned was stationed at the church porch with two other men, both farmer neighbours of J.M., to superintend the admission to the church of those for whom seats had been reserved.

When the hearse arrived at the churchyard gate the coffin was lifted out and carried to the church by eight bearers, all young men, the sons of neighbours of the dead man, but none of them his kin. Preceded by the parish priest, it was followed by seven chief mourners, who walked behind it along the path to the church door in the following order: J.P. with her brother D.M.; their spouses, A.M. and H.P.; G.A., with her brother, G.P., and husband, D.A., on each side of her. When the service in the church was over the coffin was carried out again for burial in the churchyard. The order in which some of those who were in the church followed it to the grave is indicated in Fig. 2. At some funerals the order of precedence in which mourners walk behind the coffin is laid down beforehand by one or more close relatives of the dead person, usually by women. On this occasion, however, there was no such organized prearrangement; nevertheless, one or two comments may be made.

The fourth rank consisted of the dead man's sister, G.D., and her husband, and D.Y. It appeared from inquiries I made afterwards that D.Y., who is a near neighbour of G.D. and J.D., was encouraged by the latter to join them because she came to the funeral by herself and was the only

Priest

Coffin, with eight bearers

	J.P.(d)		D.M.(s)	
	A.M.(sw)		H.P.(dh)	
G.P.(ds)		G.A.(dd)		D.A.(ddh)
J.D.(th)		G.D.(t)		D.Y.(wfbwbd)
K.D.(ts)		L.D.(ts)		M.D.(ts)
T.O.(ffftdds)		Z.O.(ffftdd)		J.O.(ffftdds)
	M.H.(ffftdsw)		J.T.(ffftdswbwbs)	
F.L.(mbd or wthw)		J.L.(mb)		H.L.(mbw)
G.K.(mbd)		D.K.(mbdh)	H.N.(mbd)	R.N.(mbdh)
R.V.(ffftdddds)		S.V.(ffftddd)		G.F.(ffftddd)
	A.G.(mbd or wtht)		J.G.(mbdh) or mmtss)	
	G.E.(swmt)		F.E.(swmts or tswmmbs)	
S.W.(tswmfbd or tswmmtd)		V.C.(mmtsdsw)		P.C.(mmtsds)

f = father	s = son
m = mother	d = daughter
b = brother	h = husband
t = sister	w = wife

Note that certain individuals have alternative kinship roles.

FIG. 2. Order of kin in procession at funeral of J.M., showing the kinship role of individuals in relation to the dead man.

elderly woman there without a male supporter. It should, however, be noted that, in the absence of any other kin of J.M.'s wife, her position in the procession was one which might otherwise have been filled by a wife's brother or wife's sister; the personal relationship which existed between D.Y. and J.M.'s wife is described as having been "like sisters"; and J.P., who is D.Y.'s god-daughter, calls D.Y. "Auntie D" and is much more intimate with her than she is with G.D., her father's sister. Again, the priority of Z.O. and her two sons over J.M.'s mother's brother seems likely to stem from her sex and great age rather than from her kinship role as the only living patrilateral consanguineal kin of the same generation as J.M.'s father.

At all funerals in the Vale which I have attended it has been possible to divide those present into a number of fairly well defined segments, on the basis of the kinship connections between mourners, the composition of the informal groupings into which they arrange themselves and the degree to which members of different groupings take an active part in the proceedings. At most funerals, especially those attended by a large number of people, four main segments can be described. The first segment, referred to by the participants as "the family", consists of the close relatives of the dead person; at the funeral of J.M. this segment roughly corresponded to what has been called his immediate family. The second segment is also frequently described as "the family" but consists of more distant extra-familial kin. The third segment includes close friends and neighbours of the dead person and his immediate family, most of them non-kin but a few sometimes people who have kin ties with members of the second segment but who, in the particular context concerned, do not consider themselves to be "related" or "belonging" in any real way. The fourth segment includes the remainder of those present.

On any particular occasion the number and relative size of the segments govern the extent to which their members take an active part in the ceremony and seem to depend on the total number of people attending the funeral, which is in turn related to the kind of social roles filled by the dead person and by members of his immediate family. For example, at some funerals attended by a small number of people only two segments are observable, consisting of kin and non-kin respectively, and all those present are expected to attend the funeral tea held after the ceremony at the house of the deceased or of a close relative. At large funerals, on the other hand, where there are four segments each consisting of a considerable number of people, only members of the first segment together with a few particular individuals from the second segment may be expected to go back to the house afterwards.

IV

The most extensive mobilization of extra-familial kin commonly occurs on ceremonial occasions. The evaluative function of kinship is well illustrated by the process of informal grouping which takes place, especially at funerals; ties of kinship play a most important part in the evaluation of people's social position relative to one another, as is shown by the way they place themselves at the ceremony and by their expectations of the behaviour of members of different segments. But this does not necessarily mean that there are clear moral obligations on extra-familial kin to lend more than passive support to those who are actively involved in a situation of crisis. When the number of kin available and living nearby is large, and ties between them other than that of kinship are numerous, the failure of particular individuals to fulfil their obligations to attend funerals may be tolerated more readily than in cases where the number of available kin is small and where the main link between many of them is genealogical connection pure and simple. In such cases people often say that they only meet distant relatives and old acquaintances at funerals. Although they usually explain their presence primarily in terms of the fulfilment of kinship obligations, it is clear that attendance provides many of them with a variety of other satisfactions, including that of creating reciprocal obligations. It is often remarked in jest of those who habitually attend many funerals in the locality that they are "making sure there will be a good turn out when their time comes".

It is on ceremonial occasions that people reveal the extent to which they are aware not only of the details of their own kin ties but of those of members of other "families". One of the chief difficulties facing newcomers is their lack of knowledge of the key kinship connections between their long-settled neighbours. This is not only or chiefly because they are liable in their ignorance to ally themselves irrevocably with the wrong people when they arrive, or with members of one or other faction in a longstanding local feud. The real point is that without some knowledge of kin ties they can take little part in local gossip.[11]

Gossip is undoubtedly the most important channel for constant reaffirmation of shared values about behaviour. Those who cannot join in gossip about their neighbours, friends and relatives, especially gossip which requires that kind of intricate map-reading of kinship connections which comes as second nature to those with lifelong familiarity with the local genealogical landscape, soon find themselves excluded from the conversations at local gatherings. Nuances of expression escape them when discussion turns on the relevance to the speakers' long held opinion of a particular family of the latest example of the behaviour of one of its members. Even where the individual under discussion is referred to by more than his Christian name, more often than not it is by one of half a dozen common Welsh surnames or by the name of a house or farm; and his behaviour may well be related to that of members of earlier generations of his family, now all dead.

Conversely, the newcomer tends to be treated by his neighbours with that reserve which is appropriate towards people who have no easy way of expressing, in relation to particular individuals and instances familiar to their audience, their general ideas about what is right and wrong, still less of showing that they share the expectations of their neighbours regarding customary behaviour in specific contexts. It should not be thought that kinship as a means of evaluating behaviour and placing

[11] Gossip is defined in the Concise Oxford Dictionary (3rd edn.) both as "idle talk, groundless rumours, tittle-tattle" and as "easy unconstrained talk ... especially about persons or social incidents". My use of the term is in accordance with the second definition.

people is primarily employed by women. It is true that, in general, women appear to have a more detailed and systematic knowledge of kin ties than men do, in the Vale as elsewhere in Britain. Men's knowledge of genealogical connections, while usually pragmatic, is often no less extensive than that of women. They themselves deny that this is so; they generally regard "family connections" as women's business. But both men and women use kinship connections in gossip as the most unambiguous way of saying who people are and as a yardstick by which to evaluate their behaviour. People who live in small rural neighbourhoods in the Vale and who cannot be identified in terms of local kin ties are often regarded with latent suspicion by their neighbours.

The importance of this process is obviously dependent on the proportion of the inhabitants who have local kinship connections. In one typical village in the Vale there are 112 people living in 31 households. Only 5 households, comprising 21 individuals, lack kin ties with people living less than 10 miles away. A further 5 households, comprising 19 individuals, are linked through kinship with people living in neighbouring parishes. Each of the remaining 21 households, comprising 72 individuals, have kin ties with other households in the village as well as with other people living elsewhere in the Vale. These 72 individuals live in three sets of interconnected domestic families, numbering 11, 6, and 4 households respectively. In many cases, of course, the links between households are affinal; and it is sometimes said by informants that people who have moved into the Vale never "belong" until at least one of their children has married a member of a local family. In general, informants have no clear definition of what they mean by a local family, though those who consider themselves to be members of one often differentiate between what they call "real Vale people" and others in discussing marriage preferences. Such preferences, colloquially expressed in a variety of ways, oblique, derisive or simply practical, are often best identified by reference to informants' evaluation of exceptions rather than in looking for statements of rules. A woman is said by her husband's kin and neighbours to be a successful farmer's wife in spite of the fact that she is not a farmer's daughter and was born and brought up in a town. A rich member of a long-established gentry family marries, as his second wife, a woman who was originally a servant in his household and his relatives say: "But she's really a decent little woman and Freddy has never been looked after so well in his life", or the envious say, with a sigh, of a marriage between people much better off than themselves, "Well, money marries money, doesn't it?"

Impressions gained from such items of gossip may be confirmed by survey material. The vast majority of farmers' wives are, in fact, the daughters of farmers. Most members of the upper class, however defined, marry members of the upper class. Affinal ties tend to reinforce business connections between entrepreneurs.

The evaluative function of kinship is of particular importance in any study of the ways in which members of a local community identify and deal with unusual behaviour. The social roles, including kinship roles, filled by an individual actor are related to the readiness with which his family, friends, and neighbours regard certain kinds of behaviour on his part as unusual. Further-more, the readiness with which some kinds of unusual behaviour are recognized as evidence of mental disorder, by doctors as well as by others, is related to the perceived social status of the individual. In relatively small communities, especially among what has been described as the highly homogeneous sections of the local population, kin ties are often more important than factors such as occupation, education and economic resources in the perception of social status in certain contexts. Where an individual has no extensive local network of kin ties, evaluation of unusual behaviour is often in terms of general or "national" norms of expectation regarding the performance, for example, of occupational or "social class" roles. Unusual behaviour on the part of those with "close-knit" networks is more likely to be assessed in terms of flexible local norms which are adaptable to particular circumstances.

In conclusion, brief mention must be made of the relevance of this discussion of the ceremonial and evaluative functions of extra-familial kin ties to any study of their supportive function in crisis situations. The mobilization of extra-familial kin to fill supportive roles is usually restricted to those who were once members of the same elementary family, together with their affines. It is here that the elementary family, in Firth's phrase, "juts out in a prominence which has been recognized by the overwhelming attention paid to it by social scientists".[12] Even where genealogically more remote extra-familial kin support individual relatives in times of crisis they commonly express their feelings of obligation to do so not in terms of a larger kin unit but in terms of their role as deputies for pivotal kin. Thus, one woman in speaking of a first cousin of her dead mother whom she visited in hospital regularly and to whom she referred as an "aunt", said: "I owe it to Mam to go and see her, poor thing; it's not because I've ever seen much of that lot myself; but Auntie's mother was Mam's favourite aunt and was always special". On the whole, because of the prominence of the elementary family, the supportive function of extra-familial kinship does not seem to depend directly on the size and degree of interconnectedness of the kinship networks of individuals concerned. Indirectly, however, the existence of a large number of extra-familial kin living locally has a very considerable effect on the performance by immediate relatives of supportive roles. What I have tried to show in this paper is that any study of the part played by kinship in the social life of local populations in Britain cannot ignore the non-supportive functions of extra-familial kin ties.

[12] Firth, *op. cit.*, p. 13.

Mobility and the Middle Class Extended Family

SUMMARY—The paper reports the findings of intensive research on 120 middle class families. The geographical distribution of the members of the extended family was wider, and contact between them was less frequent than among the middle class families sampled by previous authors. In these seemingly adverse conditions the middle class extended family was nevertheless a functioning social entity. The relationship between the head of a household and his father or father-in-law was found to be frequently of great importance. It is by means of this link that the elder middle class generation channels financial aid to the next generation. This aid enhances the living standard of the recipients. It is an aspect of social mobility overlooked by studies concentrating upon occupational mobility.

THIS paper examines some functions of the middle class extended family, and in so doing, analyses the structural supports for those functions. For although Litwak and others in the United States, and those at the Institute of Community Studies, together with Rosser and Harris, have qualified the extremer statements about the effects of social and geographical mobility on the extended family, there still remains the belief that the wider family is relatively unimportant for the elementary family (at least in what Solon Kimball has alliteratively called "its mobile metropolitan, middle class manifestation") when compared with (a) the working class or (b) those who have been immobile both socially and geographically. Or put the other way: it is believed that those for whom the extended family is least important are those members of modern industrial society who are middle class and who have been geographically and socially mobile.

The data utilized for this present discussion were collected as part of a wider study of social mobility among middle class families.[1] The 120 families studied lived on two private housing developments and will be referred to collectively as the "West Side Families". All of the families were middle class by any of the definitions customarily used by sociologists.[2]

GEOGRAPHICAL DISTRIBUTION AND CONTACT

Table 1 shows the geographical distribution of close kin of the West Side families: wives' and husbands' parents, siblings, uncles and aunts. It shows that there are two main distributions, those living in western Swansea and within 25 miles, and those living beyond 100 miles. It also shows that there are scarcely any relatives living in eastern Swansea, emphasizing that very few of these families have been socially or geographically mobile locally. It also demonstrates that there was little difference in the geographical distribution of husband's parents compared with wives' parents. This basic distribution of close kin was very important to the major conclusions of the research as a whole because it shows that there were two types of middle class families; those with the core of their kin-group living within 25 miles of those whose kin live more than 100 miles away.

[1] This study is reported fully in *Middle Class Families* (published 1968). I must acknowledge the assistance given with earlier versions of the paper by Professor W. M. Williams, Dr. J. B. Loudon, Mr. C. C. Harris, and Mrs. M. Stacey.

[2] All but three of the West Side families were already or were becoming owners of their houses. The mean school leaving age of the husbands was 16.92. All were in non-manual occupations; the husbands occupations were classified by the Registrar-General's Socio-Economic Groups in the following way:

Socio-economic group	Number
1	57
2	13
3	15
4	26
5	2
6	5
Unclassified	2
	120

TABLE 1. GEOGRAPHICAL DISTRIBUTION OF THE CLOSE KIN OF 120 WEST SIDE FAMILIES

	Dead	In household	Swansea W	Swansea E	Within 25 miles	Within 50 miles	Within 100 miles	Plus 100 miles	Abroad	Don't know	Total
Wife's mother	43	5	12	4	19	4	4	28	1		120
Wife's father	57	2	9	2	11	5	3	29	2		120
Husband's mother	39	1	17	4	18	4	4	30	3		120
Husband's father	50	1	15	3	17	5	3	23	3		120
Wife's siblings	31	1	34	14	45	14	15	67	10		231
Husband's siblings	40		41	17	40	13	17	62	20		250
Wife's parents siblings	171		59	32	71	40	24	174	17	15	603
Husband's parents siblings	181		50	24	74	44	34	153	14	8	582
Totals	612	10	237	100	295	129	104	566	70	23	2146
Per cent	28.8	0.5	11.1	4.7	13.7	6.0	4.8	26.3	3.3	1.1	100

If the West Side families are compared with figures for families representative of Swansea as a whole it is found that the West Side extended families have a greater geographical spread and that contact between their members was less than that for the Middle Class in the sample drawn by Rosser and Harris. For Swansea it was found that only 20 per cent of all married sons and 15 per cent of all married daughters with at least one parent alive, were living more than 12 miles from this parent. By social class these figures dropped to 17 per cent and 10 per cent for the working class, and rose to 28 per cent and 32 per cent for the middle class (Rosser and Harris, 1965; pp. 212–13). The figures for the West Side families were 56 per cent and 67 per cent for sons and daughters respectively, which is almost double that for the middle class in Swansea. Both the figures for the West Side families and for Swansea show a tendency for middle class sons to live closer to their parents than do their wives. This is not as marked as the opposite tendency among the working class: that for wives to live closer to their parents than to their husband's parents; but it is nevertheless noticeable. Twenty-three per cent of the married sons of the West Side families lived in the same locality as their parents as opposed to 14 per cent of their daughters. And as mentioned above, 67 per cent of married daughters' parents lived beyond 12 miles as opposed to 56 per cent of married sons' parents.

The West Side families had been more geographically mobile than those living in Swansea as a whole. Rosser and Harris found that 74 per cent of their sample were brought up in Swansea and 26 per cent outside, of whom 20 per cent were brought up further than 12 miles from Swansea. On the other hand, in the West Side families 24 per cent of the husbands were brought up in Swansea compared with 21 per cent of the wives; 76 per cent of the husbands and 79 per cent of the wives were brought up outside the borough, while of this number 67 per cent and 72 per cent respectively were brought up further than 12 miles from Swansea.

Most of the West Side families were living at some distance from their parents and had been brought up away from Swansea.

There was a smaller group who have always lived in the borough, in the more select parts of western Swansea, and whose parents are living in the same locality. These variations in the geographical distribution of members of the extended family, need to be remembered when considering measures of contact between members. It is also necessary to bear in mind the arbitrariness involved in deciding what is to constitute "contact"—especially when definitions of the extended family require "daily or almost daily contact"—(Townsend, 1964, p. 92). Very few of West Side groupings would have met Townsend's specification. It is such variations in the form of the extended family which oblige the research worker to widen the definition of the extended family. The definition that is followed in this paper: "any persistent kinship grouping of persons related by descent, marriage or adoption, which is wider than the elementary family, in that it characteristically spans three generations from grandparents to grandchildren" (Rosser and Harris, 1965, p. 32), concentrates attention on the extended family as a social entity and leaves its actual form under varying conditions to be determined by analysis.

TABLE 2. FREQUENCY OF CONTACT WITH PARENTS (MARRIED PERSONS ONLY WITH PARENT CONCERNED ALIVE)

	Percentages							
	Swansea				West Side families			
	Mothers		Fathers		Mothers		Fathers	
Last seen	Marr. sons	Marr. daus.	Marr. sons	Marr. daus.	Marr. sons	Marr. daus.	Marr. sons	Marr. daus.
Within last 24 hr	31	54	29	47	12	13	10	5
Within last week	40	27	41	30	24	29	18	27
Week–month ago	14	7	15	9	27	24	28	32
Less frequently	15	12	15	14	37	34	44	36
Total	100	100	100	100	100	100	100	100
Numbers	345	348	237	254	78	77	70	63

Table 2 shows the frequency of contact with parents. The most important point is that whilst in Swansea 54 per cent of married daughters had seen their mothers in the last 24 hours only 13 per cent of the West End wives had. Nineteen per cent of married daughters in Swansea had *not* seen their mothers in the last week whereas 58 per cent of those discussed here had not. Table 3 emphasizes this contrast. The really relevant comparison here is with the Swansea middle class: 74 per cent of the sons and 76 per cent of the daughters had seen their mothers in the last week whereas the figures for the West Side families were 36 per cent and 42 per cent respectively. The striking thing about the figures for Swansea as a whole is the similarity between the middle class and the working class contact rates, although the middle class figures tend to be slightly lower. But the contact rates between the West Side families and their parents was in most cases less than half that for Swansea.

Similarly the West Side families had a lower contact rate with siblings than the rest of Swansea, where it was found that just over half the men interviewed and two-thirds of the women had seen a brother or a sister living apart in the last week (Rosser and Harris, 1965, p. 222), whereas less than one-third of the men and just over one-fifth of the women in the West Side families had seen a sibling in the last week. Though the frequencies are slightly lower for the middle classes in Swansea, within the West Side families they are much lower than the overall picture given by Rosser and Harris.

An indication of the inadequacy of direct frequency of contact as a measure and indicator of the structure and function of the extended family can be shown for example by the use of the telephone. Just over a quarter ($n = 33$) had telephoned a wife's parent in the last week and a fifth ($n = 22$) had rung a husband's parent in the same period. A similar proportion had rung siblings. Similarly 48 households had written to the wife's parents in the last month and 46 to the husband's parents. With the increasing frequency of car ownership, sheer physical distance becomes less of an obstacle to contact between relatives. All but four of the

TABLE 3. FREQUENCY OF CONTACT WITH PARENTS BY SOCIAL CLASS OF SUBJECT-PERCENTAGES

	Swansea								West Side families			
	Mothers				Fathers				Mothers		Fathers	
	Middle classes		Working classes		Middle classes		Working classes					
	Sons	Daus.	Sons	Daus.	Sons	Daus.	Sons	Daus.	Sons	Daus.	Sons	Daus.
Within 24 hours	39	44	27	56	37	39	26	48	12	13	10	5
24–1 week	35	32	43	27	26	28	45	31	24	29	18	27
Total within 1 week	74	76	70	83	63	67	71	79	36	42	28	32
Numbers	97	91	248	256	57	64	180	190	78	77	70	63

West Side families had at least one car and all but nine had a telephone.

The West Side families were characterized by a wide geographical dispersion together with a lack of day-to-day contact when compared with the population of Swansea as a whole or even with the middle class within the borough. Yet in these seemingly adverse conditions the extended family was a functioning institution even amongst the most mobile. It would be possible to argue from much of the evidence assembled above that these are relatively isolated elementary families. But actual physical distance seems unimportant for the middle class; families are free to live where they choose and their relationship with their kin does not depend on frequency of contact. Geographical mobility may affect the type of interaction pattern (e.g. rates of contact as discussed above) but there seems to be no reason why it should result in a lessening of ideological and emotional commitment to kin or should disrupt relations between kin altogether. Despite, and in some cases because of the distance between members, the middle class extended family does have functional importance. In an analysis of some of its functions, aspects of its structure will be emphasized that have hitherto been somewhat overshadowed by the emphasis in a mother–married daughter link.[3]

STRUCTURE AND FUNCTION

On the basis of the American evidence it has been argued that the middle class extended family is used as "a principal source of aid and service when member families are in personal difficulties or in times of disaster and crisis and on ceremonial occasions" (Sussman and Burchinal, 1962, p. 234). Although data were

[3] It is interesting to compare the 120 West Side families with the results of the L.S.E. Highgate study as far as is possible from published material (Firth 1964, Crozier 1965, Hubert 1965). The major difference between the two studies is that among the L.S.E. families there were no "locals"—this is a reflection of the metropolitan nature of their sample. And Hubert (1965) found that "Contact" rates were inflated by their sample being in London and suggests that they would be lower in a more provincial town. The final report of this study is now published: Firth, et al. (1969).

collected about crisis situations and ceremonial occasions, in this paper the ordinary is emphasized rather than the unusual. Middle class extended family aid is not dependent upon crisis and ceremonial; and it is not only on these occasions that the middle class extended family is a functioning social entity. It works continually, to maintain and/or advance the status of its members.

Mutual aid between members of an extended family flows in several directions depending upon phase in the family cycle. Most of the West Side families were in the first two phases: that of "home-making" and "child-rearing".[4] These two phases are the time of greatest expenditure and, because of the nature of the middle class career-pattern the time of lowest income. Whereas the large literature of gerontology (see Townsend, 1964) has added to our knowledge of the structure and function of the family through the study of support and aid flowing towards people in the final phase of the family cycle, there is no systematic study of support and aid flowing towards people in the first two phases. Table 4 shows the distribution of the West Side families through the family cycle. These figures demonstrate that most of these families were passing through the phases in the family cycle of greatest need.

TABLE 4

Phase in family cycle	No.	Per cent
Home-making	31	26
Child-bearing	80	67
Dispersal	7	6
Final	2	1
	120	100

[4] Definition used of phases in the family cycle.
1. Home making: from marriage to the birth of first child.
2. Child rearing: from birth of first child until marriage of first child.
3. Dispersal: from marriage of first child until marriage of last child.
4. Final: from marriage of last child until death of orig nal partners.

The kind of aid discussed is not exceptional aid in exceptional times. Shaw, writing about a predominantly working class London suburb, gives a very fine example: one of the very few professional families she studied reported that the husband's mother and father had bought a new winter outfit for the first child when the expense of the second left them short of money (Shaw, 1954, p. 185). This was an example of the middle class extended family providing important and significant increments of aid for the idiosyncratic needs of the elementary family. There was no need for geographical proximity.

The ability, although not the desire to provide this type of aid will vary with social class. Middle class family networks may have fewer day-to-day demands but there is little evidence to suggest that they necessarily show any different affective quality. Townsend has suggested that there is only a small variation in function and frequency of contact between middle and working class extended families (Townsend, 1963, pp. 240–1). Measures of contact are, however, very dubious for families that are geographically scattered and the middle class extended family can perform functions that the working class extended family cannot, through financial inability rather than difference in sentiment.

An "apt illustration" (Gluckman, 1961) will be used to demonstrate this point. The speaker is a 37-year-old geographically mobile but socially immobile architect, (defined occupationally and intergenerationally).

> I wanted to leave the firm I was working for and buy into a practice as a partner. I had had a very attractive offer. But I wanted a couple of hundred more than I had. When we went home [to a town in the midlands which both husband and wife came from and returned to visit parents about four times a year] I went to the local with my father-in-law [his father is dead] and told him I was considering changing my job like I said. I didn't ask but to tell the truth I hoped. He said "How much?" and I told him and he said that he would see. Eventually he gave it to me, called it a loan but said I needn't pay it back. But I am though—£5 a month so I don't feel obligated to him. I didn't ask my bank because they were also the firm's bank and you know Rotary and that. It was easier to ask him.

He would have approached his father had he been alive. As Rosser and Harris have pointed out in their paper on relationships through marriage, one function of affinal relationships under certain circumstances is for them to be utilized as substitutes for missing consanguineal kin (Rosser and Harris, 1961, p. 318). This has been well documented for the working class mother–daughter link (Young and Willmott, 1959; Townsend, 1963). It would seem that substitution (in the sense of role adoption) can also be found in the middle class father–son link.

This illustration also shows that because the recipient had not asked for aid, he did not feel that his acceptance of it had put him under so great an obligation: moreover it illustrates a recurrent mechanism. The money was not asked for: the case was stated and the action was left up to the parent. In this way, there seems to be at least a partial resolution of the conflict between the stress on independence and actual dependence. Physical distance allows the recipients to maintain an appearance of independence and the ubiquity of financial institutions means that distance is irrelevant to aid of this kind. Jane Hubert has written "It is not the done thing to be on the receiving end of kin help and influence but to use one's influence is quite acceptable. Though they do not necessarily see it in these terms, status is conferred by giving not receiving" (Hubert, 1965, p. 68). As the majority of the West Side families are in the first two stages of the family cycle and at the beginning of a middle class career, they are disproportionately on the receiving end of extended family aid.

In contrast to the first example is a 35-year-old geographically mobile but socially immobile insurance man. He borrowed from the bank to buy a new car rather than from his father to avoid the obligation of going to his parents for his holidays. By going to an institution rather than his father he thought he avoided obligations and kept his independence. In another case the need was stated to siblings, but the parents were not told directly. The siblings however were quite expected to tell their parents who were expected to act on this information.

Another mechanism was secrecy or quasi-secrecy. When the

wife of a 34-year-old geographically mobile but socially immobile engineer had a baby her father-in-law paid for a home-help secretly because his wife thought her son and daughter-in-law should be independent. The "independence" here referred to monetary independence. It also illustrates the invasion of the sphere usually dominated by the mother–daughter relationship by that of the father and son. Another mechanism frequently utilized is the giving of aid on socially approved occasions: this is acceptable and can be accepted without any loss of independence. It may begin at the wedding: the house may be given outright or at least a substantial deposit put down on it, arrangements were made through the bank but it was the father or father-in-law that made them. Other socially approved occasions are Christmas and birthdays; there was a case of central heating being given as a Christmas present from the husband's parents. Indirect aid may be given through the children, i.e. from grandparents to grandchildren, when for example £100 was given to "buy things for the baby" it was grandfather who signed the cheque.

This is, of course, a way of raising the standard of living of the recipients, because it releases money to be spent on other things. In the words of one informant extended family aid "makes things that much easier". Extended family aid is often used to provide important status props and helps in the purchase of status signs. Central heating has already been mentioned which, apart from its obvious utilitarian value, was an important indicator of status amongst the families studied, as was having regular help in the home. This is emphasized by the wife of a geographically mobile but socially immobile chemist who used the money for a carpet that she no longer needed (because it had been bought by her father-in-law) to get her son a new bicycle: she remarked, "without little bits like that I don't know how we could live here". The giving of status props to children: the expensive "toys" like the bicycle mentioned above or a trampoline by members of the extended family was quite frequent. Great pressure was being put on several parents by their young daughters to be allowed to have riding lessons. This expensive and status conferring pastime was initiated by one girl whose grandfather was paying for her.

It is not coincidence that all these examples are taken from informants who have not been socially mobile, i.e. have middle class parents. Working class parents would very rarely be in a position to give aid of the proportions described above. If no geographical mobility had been experienced mothers could still give aid to their daughters of the kind described by Willmott and Young and others for the working class. But none of the West Side families had been socially mobile *and* geographically immobile. Consequently there was a readjustment in emphasis in the structure of the extended family away from the mother–daughter relationship towards the father–son relationship.

It is very difficult to determine the exact effects of extended family aid from father to son especially because of the obstacles to the collection of systematic information. As a rough guide the ages of husbands who had been socially mobile, i.e. had come from manual homes, were compared with those who had come from middle class backgrounds. The hypothesis was that the estates could represent a certain status level, and that those who were in the theoretical positions to receive extended family aid would reach this status level sooner than others. A striking case was that of a 25-year-old bank clerk who could only have been classified as "junior non-manual"; he was the recipient of a great deal of financial assistance from both his father and father-in-law. The 31 socially mobile husbands were on average 2.1 years older than those from middle class backgrounds. This 2.1 years advantage cannot be attributed completely to extended family aid, but, as a socially mobile informant said, "there's a lot of what I call real money here, you know, family money. We lived in a two roomed flat when we started, but look at them". She was referring to a family who had moved to the estate on marriage. The variable of social mobility was much more important to the function of the middle class extended family than was geographical mobility. Amongst the West Side families the amount of aid received from their extended families by those with middle class backgrounds was far in excess of that received by those who had been socially mobile out of the working class.[5]

CONCLUSIONS

The first concern of the research was to study the effect of social mobility on the family. The data and arguments assembled above cast some doubt on the conclusions of Lipset and Bendix who from behind great ramparts of documentation, declare that "Many middle class fathers in salaried positions have little to give their children except a good education and motivation to obtain a high status position" (Lipset and Bendix, 1959, p. 59). This theme runs throughout most studies of social mobility. However, a particularistic kinship ideology may be of great importance for the individual's emotional needs in an industrial society, though in his behaviour he may be completely committed to a universalistic pattern of relationships. Indeed Raymond Firth has gone so far as to suggest that physical separation between kin increases the possibility of selecting relationships; and that this "is one of the ways in which urban industrial influences towards individuation and impersonal isolation are counteracted" (Firth, 1964, p. 85). Extended family ties become theoretically possible when universalistic and particularistic value systems are not seen as a continuum pervading all social systems, but as applicable to different systems of society independently of each other. Extended family aid in the middle class context has to do with standard of living and only in unusual circumstances with occupational appointments. Extended family aid rarely operates in the occupational dimension but this is usually the only dimension of

[5] Österreich (1965) compared 45 English speaking middle class Canadians who were homogeneous in all other respects and compared those who had been geographically mobile with those who had not. She found that the greatest difference between the mobile and the non-mobile was in caring for children, help during illness, taking care of the house and advice on personal matters. In other words the greatest differences were in those actions that depended on availability at short notice and/or physical presence. She found that she could support Litwak's findings. However, she completely ignores the factor of social mobility which seriously detracts from her findings.

social mobility that sociologists study. The standard works on social mobility, by their concentration on the occupation/status dimension to the exclusion of all others, e.g. property—where extended family aid is more important, have missed important variables.[6]

A major conclusion of recent works on the British extended family has been that the key sequence of relationships within it is that of wife's mother–wife–husband–husband's mother (see Willmott and Young, 1960, pp. 126–7; Rosser and Harris, 1965, p. 289). However the analysis of aid amongst members of the middle class has demonstrated the importance of the relationship between father or father-in-law and son or son-in-law. Amongst the middle-class who have been geographically mobile, frequent contact between mother and married daughter is not possible. Within the middle class many wives have been independent before marriage (31 of the West Side wives had lived away from home for at least 2 years before marriage), and so are not so dependent on their mothers at least for day-to-day emotional needs. Aberle and Naegele, in a paper on the socialization of middle class children in the United States, wrote that "one reason we are stressing the father is that he is forgotten or recedes into the background in the face of the over-whelming focus on the mother in recent work" (Aberle and Naegele, 1952, p. 367). There is a similar need to stress the father–married son link in the face of the over-whelming focus on the mother–married daughter link in recent work. It is by means of the male link that the elder middle class generation channels financial aid to the next generation.

BIBLIOGRAPHY

ABERLE, DAVID F. and NAEGELE, KASPAR D. (1952) Middle class fathers' occupational role and attitudes towards children, *Amer. J. Orthopsychiatry* **22,** 366–78.

---

[6] S. Thernstrom (1964) has shown in his historical study of "Yankee City" that the concentration on the occupational/status dimension of social mobility totally obscures the property mobility that was taking place. Manual workers begat manual workers but meanwhile they bought houses.

BELL, COLIN (1966) A study of social mobility among middle class families living in Swansea, unpublished M.Sc.Econ. thesis, University of Wales.

BELL, COLIN (1968) *Middle Class Families*, London, Routledge and Kegan Paul.

CROZIER, DOROTHY (1965) Kinship and occupational succession, *Sociol. Rev.* **13**, 14–43.

FIRTH, RAYMOND (1964) Family and Kinship in Industrial Society, in Paul Halmos (Ed.) 1964, *The Development of Industrial Societies, Sociol. Rev.* Monograph **8**, 65–87.

FIRTH, R. *et. al.* (1969) *Families and their Relatives*. Routledge.

GLUCKMAN, MAX (1961) Ethnographic data in British social anthropology, *Sociol. Rev.* **9**, 5–18.

HUBERT, JANE (1965) Kinship and geographical mobility in a sample from London middle class area, *Int. J. of Comp. Soc.* **6**, 61–80.

LIPSET, SEYMOUR MARTIN and BENDIX, REINHARD (1959) *Social Mobility in Industrial Society*, Berkeley, University of California Press.

LITWAK, EUGENE (1960a) The use of extended family groups in the achievement of social goals, *Social Problems* **7**, 177–87.

LITWAK, E. (1960b) Geographic mobility and extended family cohesion *Amer. Soc. Rev.* **25**, 385–95.

LITWAK, E. (1960c) Occupational mobility and extended family cohesion, *Amer. Soc. Rev.* **25**, 9–21.

OSTERREICH, H. (1965) Geographic mobility and kinship: a Canadian example, *Int. J. Comp. Sociol.*, **6**.

ROSSER, C. and HARRIS, C. C. (1961) Relationships through marriage in a Welsh urban area, *Sociol. Rev.* **9**, 293–321.

ROSSER, C. and HARRIS, C. C. (1965) *The Family and Social Change*, Routledge and Kegan Paul, London.

SHAW, L. A. (1954) Impressions of family life in a London suburb, *Sociol. Rev.* **2**, 179–94.

SUSSMAN, MARVIN B. and BURCHINAL, LEE G. (1962) Kin family network. Unheralded structure in current conceptualization of family functioning, *Marriage and Family Living* **24**, 231–40.

THERNSTROM, STEPHAN (1964) *Poverty and Progress, Social Mobility in a Nineteenth Century City*, Cambridge, Mass, Harvard University Press.

TOWNSEND, PETER (1963) *The Family Life of Old People*, Harmondsworth Pelican Books.

TOWNSEND, PETER (1964) as discussant to Firth in Halmos, *op. cit.*

WILLMOTT, PETER and YOUNG, MICHAEL (1960) *Family and Social Class in a London Suburb*, London, Routledge and Kegan Paul.

YOUNG, MICHAEL and WILLMOTT, PETER (1957) *Family and Kinship in East London*, London, Routledge and Kegan Paul.

Marriage

Mate Selection in Various Ethnic Groups in France

A. MICHEL

THE present study deals with mate selection in two populations living in France, the French group and the foreign group, primarily composed of natives of Southern Europe (Spaniards and Italians) and of Moslem immigrants from North Africa.

We have precise statistical data on the former group, whereas the data relative to the latter have been the object of qualitative studies only.

MATE SELECTION IN THE FRENCH GROUP

It is a commonplace to say that in our industrial and urban cultures the patriarchal family has disintegrated in such a way that parents no longer select their children's mate; the children have a free choice. However, far from being complete, this freedom is still subject to the influence of several factors the pressure of which the individual is unaware. In his choice of a spouse, the individual in France is still influenced by factors related to geographical proximity, identical social and occupational category and existing norms relative to mate selection. Homogamy within the kin-group is nevertheless disappearing.

MARRIAGE BETWEEN BLOOD RELATIONS

Whereas endogamy still subsists in underdeveloped populations, marriage between blood relations is diminishing in France.[1]

[1] Jean Sutter and J. M. Goux (1962), Evolution de la consanguinité en France de 1926 à 1958 avec des données récentes détaillées, *Population* **17** (4).

In Sutter's study, all marriages contracted between blood relations in the period 1946–58 were recorded. This study was made possible thanks to the dispensations granted by the Catholic Church for endogamous marriages contracted between uncle and niece, aunt and nephew (category 3 D), between first cousins (category 4 D), cousins differently removed (category 5 D), children of first cousins (category 6 D), or double cousins. The percentage of blood relation marriages within the categories of dispensation was established in relation to the corresponding number of religious marriages per year for every department, that is for a total of 3,450,000 Catholic marriages during the period 1946–58. The following facts may then be stated: During this period and for this area, the absolute number of blood relation marriages classified according to the categories defined above, as well as the percentage of such marriages of the total number of Catholic marriages contracted, decreased rapidly in 83 French departments. Stability was observed in only 7 departments where the rate of such marriages was already very low. As an example Table 1 shows this decrease for the Seine department.

From this decline, the authors may conclude, as far as marriage is concerned, that the breaking up of isolated groups allowed partial populations to mix up into larger unities. Furthermore, according to the authors, this breaking up "has actively

TABLE 1. NUMBER OF BLOOD RELATION MARRIAGES ACCORDING TO DEGREE OF KINSHIP BETWEEN SPOUSES; AND PERCENTAGE OF THESE MARRIAGES IN RELATION TO THE TOTAL NUMBER OF MARRIAGES IN THE SEINE DEPARTMENT IN THE PERIOD 1946–58

Years	Number of blood-relation marriages in relation to degree of kinship					% of blood-relation marriages in relation to the total number of Catholic marriages
	3 D	4 D	5 D	6 D	Doubles	
1946–50	11	561	137	405	1	% 0.82
1951–5	8	435	93	316	2	0.72
1955–8	4	205	73	173	1	0.68

continued during the recent years". The fact that blood relation marriages are disappearing does not however suppress homogamy. Although homogamy is declining on the family level it persists on the geographical, ethnical, social, and occupational levels.

GEOGRAPHICAL HOMOGAMY

Jean Sutter already pointed out how in two French departments—Loir et Cher and Finistère—the dying out of blood relation marriages was accompanied by an increase in the distance between the spouses' residences at the moment of the wedding. In these two departments, during the period 1870–1954, the dying out of blood relation marriages occurred in proportion to the decrease in the number of marriages between spouses residing in the same locality and was proportional to the increase in the number of marriages between spouses residing in two different departments.[2] These changes do not, however, impede a certain homogamy on the geographical level. In France, everything looks as though geographical mobility was not yet sufficient to secure a distribution of marriages totally independent from the proximity of the residence at the moment of the marriage. This was indicated by a study on mate selection based on a sample of 1646 French couples interviewed at the end of 1959, stratified according to the geographical distribution of the localities and to the economic and social category of married men.[3] The husbands had to be less than 65 years of age and to have been married since 1920 at the earliest. It was established that a majority of French couples are still characterized by geographical homogamy: in 7 couples out of 10, the spouses are of the same geographical origin (same "commune", "canton", "arrondissement",

[2] Jean Sutter (1958), Evolution de la distance séparant le domicile des futurs époux, (Loir-et-Cher 1870–1954, Finistère 1911–1953), *Population* **13** (2), 227–58.

[3] Alain Girard (1964), *Le choix du conjoint*, P.U.F. The results given here were mostly communicated by Alain Girard in 1961 at the *International Population Union Conference*, paper no. 16, New York, 1961, pp. 3 and 4.

"département" or "région."[4] Whereas 2 out of 10 are born in the same "commune", 6 out of 10 were living in the same "commune" at the moment of the wedding because of previous movements.

Table 2 illustrates homogamy among French couples:

TABLE 2. GEOGRAPHICAL HOMOGAMY IN FRANCE

	Place of birth of the two spouses		Residence of the two spouses at the moment of the marriage	
	%	Cumulative %	%	Cumulative %
Same commune	21.6	21.6	57.4	57.4
Same canton	10.6	32.2	11.5	68.9
Same arrondissement	19.8	52.0	12.1	81.0
Same department	11.3	63.3	6.9	87.9
Same region	8.9	72.2	3.3	91.2
Other cases	27.8	100	8.8	100
	100.0		100.0	

The study also gives information about the factors affecting the degree of geographical homogamy:

(a) *Age group:* whereas 72 per cent of the couples studied are natives of the same region, this proportion increases to 81 per cent when their parents are considered.

(b) *Regional level:* whereas in some regions (Flanders, Artois), geographical homogamy reaches percentages superior to the mean score (up to 84 per cent of the couples), this percentage decreases to 60 per cent in some other parts of the country and to 40 per cent in the Paris district.

(c) *Occupational and social categories:* the higher in the occupa-

[4] Administrative divisions of the French territory from the smallest to the largest.

tional and social category, the less marked is geographical homogamy. Thus, among farmers and workers, only 10 per cent of the spouses are not born in the same department, while in the middle and upper class and in the professions the corresponding percentage is 20 per cent.

Nevertheless, the coming of industry to farming regions of strong homogamous traditions brought new habits. Some local studies in Haute–Maurienne show that during a period of 90 years (1872 to 1959) new occupational structures produced by the recent coming of an electrical steel industry have caused an increase in marriages between spouses from distant places.[5] Whereas the majority of the men living at Saint Jean de Maurienne still marry girls from the surrounding rural region, the workers from the suburbs frequently marry girls from remote parts of the country. Industrialization of a rural area brings about the formation of a new working class, less bound to geographical homogamy than the traditional peasant class.[6]

Another important study dealing with 13,431 French families recorded between 1919 and 1944, measured homogamy from a geographical point of view (here called "homochtonie") by taking the *distance* measured in kilometers between the spouses' birthplaces into account instead of the localization (identical "commune" or regions.[7])

This distribution is illustrated by Table 3.

Thus, geographical homogamy remains an important phenomenon in France (even though the author finds differences related to social classes[8]) and to the various regions of the country.[9]

[5] Monique Vincienne, Immigration rurale et vie urbaine, *Revue Française de Sociologie* **2** (4), (1961).

[6] Placide Rambaud, Eléments pour une sociologie de la montagne, *Revue Française de Sociologie* **2** (4), 274.

[7] Paul Vincent (1961), *Recherches sur la fécondité biologique. Etude d'un groupe de familles nombreuses*, Paris, PUF, Collection "Travaux et Documents", cahier no. 37, p. 93.

[8] Five per cent of farmers marry a mate whose birth-place is more than a 100 km away, whereas the proportion is 15 per cent in the other social and occupational categories.   [9] *Ibid.*, p. 101.

TABLE 3. DISTRIBUTION OF 13,431 FRENCH FAMILIES IN RELATION TO THE SPOUSES' DISTANCE OF BIRTH-PLACE

Distance between the spouses' birth-places	Number of families	
	Abs.	%
Less than 30 km	10,093	75
From 30 to 100 km	1,843	14
More than 100 km	1,495	11
Total	13,431	100

Table 4 shows the distribution of couples other than cultivators in relation to the size of the town or city.

Homogamy decreases with the size of the locality for the first four categories of localities, but slightly. However, this decrease no longer exists for larger centers, either because the number of very large centers is very small in France, or because of the "personality" of some large centers. The only marked exception

TABLE 4. DISTRIBUTION OF COUPLES ACCORDING TO THE DISTANCE BETWEEN THE SPOUSES' BIRTH-PLACES AND IN RELATION TO THE HUSBAND'S HOME-TOWN (CULTIVATORS NOT INCLUDED)[10]

Size of the husband's home-town	% of couples whose birth-places are less than 30 km away from one another
Less than 5,000 inhabitants	72
From 5 to 10,000 inhabitants	65
From 10 to 20,000 inhabitants	62
From 20 to 50,000 inhabitants	60
From 50 to 100,000 inhabitants	63
From 100 to 200,000 inhabitants	50
From 200 to 1,000,000 inhabitants	67
Paris district	34
Total mean	69

[10] *Ibid.*, p. 99.

concerns Paris and its urban area, where homogamy concerns only a third of the couples, whereas 59 per cent of Parisian men select their wives among provincial girls born more than 100 km away from Paris.

One may say that Paul Vincent's study confirms Girard's as to the importance of geographical homogamy. Furthermore, Paul Vincent shows how geographical mobility tends to decrease homogamy.[11]

Finally, if we take the changes under way into account, we can say that proximity of residence, which is linked to common geographical origins, still constitutes a privileged factor in the union of individuals for a large majority of French people, except for the Paris urban area which constitutes a pre-eminently important melting-pot.

SOCIAL AND OCCUPATIONAL HOMOGAMY

The occupational and social category to which the individual belongs exerts an indirect pressure on mate selection. This pressure goes towards homogamy within the same occupations: that is, an individual has more chance to marry within his own group. This fact is demonstrated in Alain Girard's above-mentioned study.[12] The degree of occupational homogamy may be evaluated either by comparing the husband's father's and the wife's father's respective occupations or by comparing the wife's father's and her husband's occupation. In the first case, the distribution of the couples in intervals of 7 social and occupational categories (the intervals go from 0 for complete homogamy to 6 for a maximum deviation between two occupations) is illustrated by Table 5.

This table shows how occupational homogamy (interval 0 between wife's father's and husband's father's occupation) is shown by 45 per cent of French couples, and even 69 per cent, if we include the unions contracted in the next closest group. This

[11] *Ibid.*, p. 101.
[12] A. Girard, *op. cit.*

TABLE 5. SOCIAL AND OCCUPATIONAL HOMOGAMY MEASURED BY A
DISTRIBUTION OF COUPLES IN RELATION TO THE INTERVALS BETWEEN
WIFE'S FATHER'S OCCUPATION AND HUSBAND'S FATHER'S OCCUPATION[13]

Distribution of intervals	Observed distribution of the couples in %	Random distribution of couples in %
6	0.0	0.3
5	0.8	2.1
4	1.4	3.3
3	3.6	6.3
2	8.3	10.6
1	11.4 ⎤	16.7 ⎤
0(homogamy)	45.1 ⎬ 69	21.4 ⎬ 54.8
1	12.5 ⎦	16.7 ⎦
2	10.2	10.6
3	4.1	6.3
4	1.8	3.3
5	0.7	2.1
6	0.1	0.3
Total	100.0	100.0

percentage is more than twice that expected if couples married at random (45 per cent vs. 21.4 per cent).

If we now compare the wife's father's occupation with her husband's occupation (and not occupational groups at a given time, as was done above), we see that homogamy still holds for 39 per cent of the couples, and for 65 per cent if we include the unions contracted in the next closest group. So, the pressure exerted by the social and occupational group on mate selection is confirmed. Besides, social and occupational homogamy varies also in relation to social classes. This phenomenon is strongest in the socially less mobile classes; that is, among cultivators and workers, and less strong in the middle class, which is the most mobile one. Below and above the middle class, mixed unions remain exceptional.

[13] Occupations are divided into 7 categories: Agricultural workers, cultivators, workers, craftsmen and tradesmen, middle-class white-collars, upper-class white collars, and the professions. (1960.)

A remarkable exception to the low homogamy of the middle class is worth mentioning: male teachers in the Seine department marry within the same occupation at a very high rate of homogamy,[14] about 80.9 per cent in 1954–5, compared to about 47 per cent among the female teachers.[15] (The discrepancy between the two rates is probably due partly to the high sex ratio among school-teachers of the primary schools in the Paris region, and partly due to differential social status aspirations.[16])

Girard's study will probably give data on the relationship between social and occupational homogamy on the one hand and age group and industrialization on the other.[17] Anyhow, public opinion approves of social and occupational homogamy: it is considered to be better if the spouses belong to the same occupational group and the first advice given to a youth of marriageable age is to choose someone from the same class.[18]

ETHNIC HOMOGAMY

(a) Mixed Marriages between a French and a North African or African

The family, as well as work and leisure groups, holds city youth under a social control which is negatively directed in the case of mixed marriages with a Moslem from North Africa or an African. However, this particular social control is only exerted on women, since the immigrants from Africa are essentially men. Almost all the 400,000 Africans in France are men. But whereas all Moslem women in France are married to other Moslems, only 50 per cent of Moslem men living in France married in North Africa and left their wives there to come and work in France. Therefore, 150,000 North Africans remain bachelors although they are marriageable. Since these men work in factories,

[14] Ida Berger, Instituteurs et Institutrices, *Revue Française de Sociologie*, **1** (2), 181–3, (1960).
[15] *Ibid.*
[16] *Ibid.*
[17] A. Girard, *op. cit.*
[18] A. Girard, *ibid.*

it is mostly among young factory girls that they might find a wife. Consequently, the working classes express hostility towards mixed marriages between French girls and North Africans.

In short, only 8850 European wives and concubines living with Algerian men are recorded, although more than a million Algerians stayed in France between 1946 and 1960. The study of mixed couples composed of a European woman and a North African or an African enabled us to analyse the motives set forth to oppose the mixed marriage by the family and the social group to which the young woman belongs.[19] Racial prejudice is primarily expressed as: "I don't like this race". When, in second resort, they put forward the difference of religion and mores, it is to justify a latent racial prejudice. Therefore a certain number of mixed couples live semi-clandestinly to escape hostility from the group. Some other young women prefer to break with their relatives in order to escape reproach. Various degrees of intolerance are found. Tenants of residential hotels from the Seine department are less intolerant than renters of ordinary lodgings, for, as they live in those hotels, they came to know the Africans and North Africans better. The young women coming from very poor rural families (Britanny, Oise) and living in Paris do not encounter the same hostility from their parents as those whose parents live in Paris. Parents who are employees or civil servants are more hostile to mixed marriages than workers are. Mothers accept mixed marriages for their daughters better than fathers do. Lastly, foreign women living in France who want to marry a North African or an African do not encounter the same resistance from their parents as French girls do.

We can say that a mixed marriage between a French woman and a North African or an African constitutes a threat to the feeling of superiority of the French community towards Africans and North Africans. Mixed marriages constitute the greatest threat to superior racial status. Hence the very strong resistance

[19] Andrée Michel (1959), *Famille, Industrialisation, Logement,* Paris, Centre National de la Recherche Scientifique (Collection Centre d'Etudes sociologiques), 3e partie, ch. III.

with which the French group opposes such mixed marriages. The French group's behaviour towards mixed marriages with foreigners is related to the *social distance* between the French group and each of the ethnic groups. Thus, among the foreigners, North Africans come next to last (before the Germans) in the feelings of liking of French people.[20] Consequently the strongest resistance is against mixed marriages with North Africans. However, the degree of dislike weakens when the level of affluence of the interviewed person decreases, as Table 6 demonstrates.[21]

TABLE 6. FEELINGS OF LIKING TOWARDS NORTH AFRICANS ACCORDING TO THE ECONOMICS OF THE INTERVIEWED

Ranking of North Africans in the feelings of liking towards ten nationalities	Among people belonging to:			
	Well-off class %	Well-off middle class %	Poor middle class %	Poor class %
Among the three first	9	11	11	18
Among the four intermediate	34	45	41	46
Among the three last	57	44	48	36
Total	100	100	100	100

But even 70 per cent of those who consider North Africans to be the most likeable of all still say that it would be most unpleasant if their daughter married a man from North Africa.[22] And the Algerian war strengthened these feelings of hostility.[23]

[20] A. Girard and J. Stoetzel, *Français et immigrés, l'attitude française. L'adaption des Italiens et des Polonais,* Paris, PUF, Cahier no. 19 de l' INED (collection Travaux et Documents), p. 144.

[21] *Ibid.,* p. 152.

[22] *Ibid.,* p. 41.

[23] A. Michel, *op. cit.,* p. 178.

(b) Mixed Marriages between French People and Foreigners, not including Africans and North Africans

Although the resistance of the French group is less strong when the foreigner is neither a North African nor an African, public opinion remains nevertheless hostile to mixed marriages.[24]

A majority of the persons interviewed (52 per cent) think that it is a good thing (22 per cent) or that it makes no difference (30 per cent) if a French man marries a foreign girl. Only 31 per cent say it is a bad thing. But in the case of a marriage between a French girl and a foreigner, the majority of those who express an opinion (47 per cent) are hostile to mixed marriages. Only 15 per cent say it is a good thing.

Statistical data indicate that the least hostility and the highest level of indifference towards mixed marriages between a French woman and a foreigner are developed by workers, whereas cultivators express the strongest feelings of hostility towards this type of marriage (54 per cent).[25]

The actual behaviour in the population conforms to the expressed opinions. Whereas the percentage of mixed marriages slightly increased after the Second World War this percentage started to decrease in 1951. In 1920, 3.7 per cent of all marriages were mixed. From 1945 to 1951, the percentage was about 6. (6.2 per cent in 1948, 5.7 per cent in 1951.) In 1952, the percentage was 5.3 per cent.[26]

As for the nationality of the foreigner who married a French girl between 1945 and 1952, there were many Americans after the war (24 per cent) but already few in 1948 (3.5 per cent). Similarly, marriages between French and German (particularly prisoners of war) suddenly increased between 1945 and 1948 (from 1 per cent to 13.2 per cent), to decrease as soon as 1950

[24] A. Girard and J. Stoetzel, *op. cit.*
[25] *Ibid.*, p. 149.
[26] *Statistiques du Mouvement de la Population, année 1952*, INSEE, Paris, PUF, 1959, n.s., tome XXVI.

(10.7 per cent). From 1952, mixed marriages between French girls and Italians, Spaniards and Poles outnumbered the others with a percentage of 57.1 per cent of all mixed marriages, as these nationalities are the most numerous and the oldest immigrants. We lack data to say whether the massive introduction of foreign workers since 1952 contributed to an increase in mixed marriages.

MATE SELECTION
IN THE FOREIGN GROUPS IN FRANCE

Although we lack comprehensive data, various studies allow us to recall the norms and values which guide mate selection in the different foreign groups living in France.

MATE SELECTION
IN THE NORTH AFRICAN GROUP IN FRANCE

Even if the main impediments to marriage between North African men and French women come from the French group's racial prejudice, mate selection in the North African group is influenced also by moral pressures, norms and values from within their own group.

Mate selection in the North African group primarily obeys ethnic homogamy. Only 5 per cent of the Algerians said they would rather marry a French than an Algerian girl.[27] This preference is not the result of a racial prejudice, for marrying a French girl is often considered by the foreigners residing in France as a sign of individual promotion. This preference for ethnic homogamy merely reveals that Algerians in France are attached to the customs, the religion, and the political views of their community in France.

In the first place come the pressures from the relatives of the Algerian bachelor who fear that a French daughter-in-law might

[27] A. Michel (1956), *Les travailleurs algériens en France*, Paris CNRS, p. 203 (collection Centre d'Etudes Sociologiques).

induce her husband to neglect his duties of assistance to the old people of the family—these duties being traditional in the North African family group.[28] Resistances against mixed marriages also came from the Algerian boy's compatriots who feared that marrying a European girl might drive him away from his duties of human and political solidarity towards his native community, and consequently, some Algerians used to hide their union with a French girl from their compatriots.[29]

It might also be pointed out that even nowadays Algerian parents select their children's mate, particularly in the Kabyle peasant families, who form an important part of the Algerian emigration in France.

It may also be noted that one of the mate selection norms respected by the North African parents consists in a *preferential marriage* with a cousin.[30] How widely this norm is followed among North Africans in France we don't know, but it may be ascertained that the custom has survived until now, effective mostly among people who are more than 40 years old.

MATE SELECTION IN THE FOREIGN IMMIGRANT GROUP RESIDING IN FRANCE
(OTHER THAN AFRICANS AND NORTH AFRICANS)

There are few statistical data on the problem, but several documents enable us to characterize the behaviour also of the Italian, Polish and Spanish groups in France.

Among these, marriages between blood relations are not recorded and seem to be exceptional cases, as they are in the French group. Social and occupational homogamy remains high. However, the geographical and occupational mobility of the foreign immigrant—whether Spanish, Italian, or Polish—does not con-

---

[28] A. Michel, *Famille, Industrialisation, Logement, loc. cit.*, p. 176.

[29] The former "Movement for the Triumph of democratic freedoms", an Algerian nationalist party, organized in 1952–3 a campaign for tolerance of mixed marriages and improvement in this line actually developed among the members of the Algerian group. A. Michel, *ibid.*, p. 176.

[30] *Ibid.*, p. 173.

fine him, as it confines the autochtons, in a particular social class where social and occupational homogamy is the rule.

As for ethnical homogamy, it seems to be less strong in the Italian immigrant group than in the other immigrant groups. The Italians constitute an immigration of older origin than that of the other groups. Moreover, the above mentioned statistical data show that after the fluctuations due to the Second World War, Italian men and women come first among the nationalities in the percentage of mixed marriages with the French (27.8 per cent of the total number of this type of mixed marriages in 1952).

The statistical data indicate that the factors which foster the disintegration of ethnic homogamy are not only the proximity of ethnic groups but also the geographical location, occupation, density of foreigners in a given region, etc. The data also allow us to establish that, whereas ethnic homogamy does not diminish in the French group, it decreases noticeably with the second generation in the Polish or Italian group living in France.

In the Spanish group, the disintegration of ethnic homogamy is not so rapid, perhaps because this immigration is more recent. They prefer to marry compatriots. The pressures exerted by the Spanish group against mixed marriages of its members, the fact that the group fears loss of traditional values and norms must be added to the resistance of the individuals to the adoption of other roles by the marital couple after marriage. This resistance was pointed out by Spanish women during an interview. They fear that marrying a Frenchman might deprive them of the traditional image of the Spanish husband, the undisputed head of the family whose status permits him to avoid household chores.[31]

Besides, we must note that the opposite resistance is manifested by French girls about to marry a Spaniard or an Armenian. They fear that they might lose the prerogatives French women have acquired in the working class marriage: equal rights and the husband's co-operation in the household chores.[32]

[31] *Ibid.*, p. 179.
[32] *Ibid.*, p. 179.

The study of the resistances to mixed marriages among foreigners in France reveals that the ethnic group tends to reject any threat directed against its national values and norms; and at the same time the individuals hesitate to break away from the image they have of the role distribution of the sexes in the marital group of their native country. However, these resistances noticeably weaken with the second generation of immigrants.

SUMMARY

The study of mate selection in the various ethnic groups in France makes it clear that in spite of a progressive dying out of marriages between blood relations in all the ethnic groups (except in the North African group), homogamy subsists on other levels: geographical, social, occupational, ethnic, etc. Moreover, some values and norms respected in each ethnic group or social class determine the acceptance or rejection of other choices.

In most ethnic groups, a marriage with a mate belonging to another ethnic community is met with very strong resistances. This is particularly true in the French and the North African groups living in France, whereas Italians and Poles residing in France seem to adjust themselves better to mixed marriages in the second generation.

Ethnic homogamy does not always mean the same thing for each ethnic group. For French girls' parents, the refusal of the mixed marriage with an African or a North African arises from the superiority feelings towards the group of the former colonized peoples. In the North African and African groups, the resistances against mixed marriages stem from a different origin: attachment to old norms and values regulating the family status of the sexes and generations; and fear of seeing alteration in the political views and the religion of the native community. Although the foreign group—Africans and North Africans not included—considers a marriage with a French girl to be a sign of success and a hope for a better integration into French life, the fact remains that resistances against mixed marriages persist.

These resistances are formulated both by the group which tries to defend its national norms and values and by the individuals who fear an alteration in their personal status in a union with a person of a different nationality. However, these resistances diminish in the second generation.

It seems that continuous urbanization, the diffusion of mass culture, industrialization and geographical and occupational mobility progressively corrode what geographical homogamy persists. On the other hand, social and occupational homogamy seems to disappear more slowly in a country such as France, where social classes have definite historic origins and precise limits. As for ethnic homogamy, it stubbornly resists the impact of urbanization and industrialization when the ethnic groups are separated by great social distance. And the less the social distance, the less resistance to mixed marriages.

The resistance to mixed marriages between the various ethnic groups—with the remarkable exception of the Italians in France—indicate that these groups remain strongly attached to the integrity of the values, norms, status and traditions which characterize them.

From this point of view, we can say that homogamy is only the translation into the rules regulating marriage of the tendency each human group has to cling to its ethnic and cultural characteristics, and to protect its norms and values. It appears somehow like a challenge to the universalization of values, inevitable in this second half of the twentieth century thanks to the facility of transport, the development of the mass media and the interpenetration of cultures.

Conjugal Roles and Social Networks
A Re-examination of an Hypothesis*

C. Turner

BOTT concentrated on two main aspects of family organization in an intensive study of twenty families in the Greater London area (Bott, 1955, 1956, 1957). On the one hand she carried out a thorough analysis of the patterns of conjugal role relationship, on the other she examined the network of kinfolk, friends, and neighbours of each family. A major hypothesis advanced as a result of this exploratory study is that "*The degree of segregation in the role-relationship of husband and wife varies directly with the connectedness of the family's social network.*" (Bott, 1957, p. 60). Two recent American studies by Udry and Hall (1965) and Aldous and Straus (1966) question the general validity of the hypothesis. Although both of these pieces of research purport to test Bott's hypothesis, it can be argued on methodological grounds that neither of them constitutes a reasonable test.

This paper is an attempt to re-examine Bott's hypothesis in the light of information from a somewhat different social setting. The data upon which this report is based was collected as part of a much wider study of the social structure of a Pennine parish, which will be referred to by the pseudonym of Leadgill. The study was not specifically oriented towards a test of the Bott hypothesis. Nevertheless an *ex post facto* analysis seems justifiable in this instance, since it sheds some light on the original hypothesis and suggests certain potentially fruitful ideas for future research.

* I am indebted to Professor R. Frankenberg for the initial suggestion that my data could be used to throw further light on this hypothesis, and for his subsequent encouragement and comments.

Both Bott (1957) and Udry and Hall (1965) base their findings on married couples drawn from large urban areas. Aldous and Straus (1966) drew approximately half of their married female informants from small town backgrounds and half from rural farm backgrounds. The Leadgill data is drawn from the married couples living in a small relatively isolated rural community, at a given point in time. Twenty couples formed the "sample" for Bott's analysis, forty-three for the Udry and Hall study, and 115 for the Leadgill research. Aldous and Straus "sampled" 391 people, but confined their attention to wives only, which may possibly have biased their results. A further distinction is provided by the fact that Bott concentrated on couples in the early child rearing phase of the developmental cycle of the family as a domestic group, Udry and Hall upon middle-aged couples with at least one child at college, and Aldous and Straus upon married women with at least one child at home. The Leadgill data includes couples at all major phases of the developmental cycle.

PROBLEMS OF OPERATIONAL DEFINITION

A recurrent problem in contemporary sociology is that of operational definition. Bott's work on degree of conjugal role segregation and interconnectedness of social networks provides an interesting illustration of intuitive definition based on considerable empirical evidence (Bott, 1957, pp. 58–9 and 238–40). The use of this type of definition renders an accurate replication of the study almost impossible. In contrast, Udry and Hall (1965) and Aldous and Straus (1966) developed relatively simple, though differing, operational definitions of degree of network interconnectedness and type of conjugal role segregation, and incorporate reference to them in their respective papers. A distinct advantage of the questionnaire method is that the study can easily be replicated, but an associated criticism is that their narrow operationalism hardly does justice to the ideas behind the concepts suggested by Bott.

The procedure adopted with the Leadgill data resembles that of Bott, rather than that of the other writers, although the data were not specifically collected in order to test the Bott hypothesis. The definitions used are unsatisfactory in two main respects. Firstly the data available set certain limits on the definitions. Secondly there is too much reliance on the judgement of the researcher. Nevertheless it is hoped that the present discussion will help to clarify at least some of the issues and problems raised by Bott's initial insightful analysis.

The Interconnectedness of Social Networks

The basic unit used by Bott in the analysis of the social network is somewhat ambiguously referred to as "the family". This term is used variably to denote (1) the household groups comprising parents and their dependent children, which were the basic units studied; (2) the married couples in the household groups defined under the first heading; (3) the other household groups, or possibly just their adult members, with whom the married couples under examination regularly interacted. A social network as defined by Bott is a network of households rather than of individuals, but the criterion by which inter-household linkages are judged is the interaction of individuals (presumably adults). A particular household is conceptualized as the central focus of a social network, thus each network is "closed", in the sense that the focal household is directly connected to a finite number of other households. Bott defined the "interconnectedness" of each social network in terms of the extent to which households other than focal households are linked directly by regular interaction between members.

The maximum possible number of *interconnecting* linkages of this type is given by the formula:

$$\frac{n\,(n-1)}{2} - (n-1),$$

where n equals the total number of households in the network (see

Kephart, 1950, for further elaboration). These interconnecting linkages range from a fixed minimum of zero to a variable maximum, which is a function of n for any particular network. The point which should be noted is that the potential of interconnecting linkages increases at a much faster rate than the number of households in the group, as the following series indicate:

No. of households	3	4	5	6	7	8	9 ...
Maximum no. of interconnecting linkages	1	3	6	10	15	21	28 ...

Thus the number of households in a particular network is an important factor to take into account when attempting to calculate degree of interconnectedness.

Both American studies set out to examine the interconnectedness of partial social networks. Udry and Hall (1965) defined the network of each husband and wife in terms of *the four persons with whom each spouse claimed to have had most frequent social contact* in the year prior to the interview. Aldus and Straus (1966) defined the network of each married woman in terms of *the eight women whom she most often visited socially*. It seems quite possible that such predetermination of network closure might seriously bias the results, insofar as they purport to relate to Bott's original hypothesis. It is also necessary to note that the original hypothesis refers to interconnections between households, not to networks of the individual spouse. This represents a further potential source of discrepancy.

An attempt has been made to analyse the Leadgill data in terms of the social networks of married couples both at the individual level and at the household level. The main focus, however, is upon inter-household connexions, following Bott. An important point which requires consideration is the method of identifying households or individuals, who are to be included in each closed social network. This problem was first approached in terms of individual rather than household networks. Members of a focal individual's network were defined as persons (1) to whom the focal individual was bound by positive affectional ties (i.e. kinfolk and friends), and (2) with whom the focal individual had regular social contact (in this instance "regular" is defined as at least once per fortnight on average throughout the year). The same criteria were used for assessing interconnecting links between the non-focal individuals in each specific network. It must be admitted that these two indicators taken in combination provide a fairly arbitrary and subjective basis for the reckoning of network membership. The individual networks of each married couple were aggregated and expressed in terms of inter-household connexions. Similarly the data on non-focal individuals was aggregated and expressed in terms of inter-household connexions for each network. It should be noted that this method of calculating inter-household linkages only takes account of a selection of the possible universe of household connexions.

On the basis of these calculations three degrees of network connectedness can be distinguished at the inter-household level: (1) loose-knit, (2) medium-knit, and (3) close-knit. A *loose-knit* network is characterized by the existence of interconnecting linkages between less than one-third of the non-focal households in a particular network. The equivalent proportions of interconnecting linkages for a *medium-knit* network is between one-third and two-thirds, and for a *close-knit* network more than two-thirds. A minimum number of five households, i.e. the focal household and four others, was arbitrarily set for inclusion in the analysis. As a result the networks of five couples in Leadgill were excluded. The maximum number of households in any network was twelve, and the median was seven.

Conjugal Role Relationships

It is obvious from a reading of available literature on the husband–wife relationship that "degree of conjugal role segregation" is not an unidimensional concept (see, for example, Blood and Wolfe, 1960). Varying degrees and forms of co-operation and independence are found in each of the major spheres of marital organization. The time which a married couple have available to devote to their husband–wife relationship is partially controlled by many factors, including occupation, place of work, hours of work, the presence of children, relatives or unrelated persons in the home, and by the various extra-family commitments of each spouse. Even a crude classification of marital role relationships, therefore, involves an extremely complex set of problems. The three areas of marital organization, for which there is adequate information on Leadgill couples, are (1) leisure activities outside the home, (2) domestic tasks, and (3) child rearing.

Leadgill couples were classified according to whether their activities in each of the first two spheres, and where applicable in the third sphere as well, were predominantly joint or predominantly segregated. As far as leisure activities outside the home are concerned, a couple was counted as having a joint relationship if they predominantly went out together, and as having a segregated relationship if they predominantly went out separately. (It is perhaps worth noting at this point that there was no significant correlation between amount of time spent in leisure activities outside the home and a given type of marital relationship.) As far as domestic tasks are concerned, the criteria used to distinguish a couple with a joint role relationship were, (1) the regular participation of the husband in domestic duties, and (2) the interchangeability of at least certain domestic tasks between husband and wife. If a husband did not regularly carry out domestic duties, or if there was a rigid division of labour in respect of domestic work, the conjugal relationship was recorded as segregated. As far as child rearing is concerned, a joint relationship was defined as one in which father and mother, (1) usually discussed methods of discipline and/or child rearing, and (2) shared certain of the tasks of child rearing: a segregated relationship was defined as one in which they did not.

An overall classification of the marital role relationship was derived from a combination of the classifications for the applicable sub-areas. A joint conjugal role relationship was characterized by joint relationships in all applicable sub-areas. Correspondingly a segregated conjugal role relationship was one in which segregated relationships were found in all applicable sub-areas. If there was any discrepancy between sub-area classifications, the conjugal role relationship was counted as intermediate. This gives a crude threefold classification of types of conjugal role relationship. Four couples have been excluded from the analysis because of the difficulty of classifying them in this manner.

LEADGILL RESULTS

The Leadgill results are presented in Table 1, with Bott's figures listed in brackets for purposes of comparison.

TABLE 1. CONJUGAL ROLES AND SOCIAL NETWORKS IN LEADGILL[a]

Conjugal role relationship	Interconnectedness of social networks		
	Close-knit	Medium-knit	Loose-knit
Segregated	42 (1)	10 (0)	4 (0)
Intermediate	13 (0)	0 (9)	7 (0)
Joint	8 (0)	8 (0)	14 (5)

Total number of married couples = 115 (20); Not classified 9 (5).
[a] Bott's figures in brackets for comparative purposes.

An initial visual inspection of the data suggests that the Bott hypothesis is not fully supported, although a general statistical test does indicate that the observed values differ significantly from those expected by chance ($\chi^2 = 26.92$: significant at the 0.01 level).

Leadgill can fairly accurately be described as a face-to-face community. It is not surprising, therefore, that the proportion of couples with close-knit networks is substantially higher than in the other studies. There tends to be a high degree of inter-connectedness in the role networks because the majority of individuals in most networks were drawn from within the community. This had the additional advantage of allowing for cross-checking on network membership, and on interconnecting linkages.

When the individual networks of Leadgill husbands and wives are analysed separately an interesting set of facts emerges. Firstly both husband and wife tend to include the same kinfolk in their respective social networks. Secondly, when kinfolk are excluded, thirty-two couples could be unambiguously identified for whom the husband's friends constituted a close-knit *male* network, and the wife's friends a close-knit *female* network. These thirty-two couples also demonstrated a high degree of conjugal role segregation. In each instance a strict division of labour within the home was accompanied by a sharp division of leisure interests. Even when kinfolk and friends were entertained in the home, the males and females showed a marked proclivity for splitting into separate groups. It must be noted, however, that the husbands spent much of their leisure time outside the home with their male companions (cf. Dennis, *et al.*, 1956). It is not altogether surprising that the segregation of the sexes within the total social network of a couple is accompanied by marital role segregation, but it does appear to constitute something of a special case. When the networks of husband and wife show considerable overlap, no distinctive pattern of conjugal role relationship appears to be associated with them.

The degree of network interconnectedness seems to provide only a partial prediction of the form of conjugal role relationship developed between husband and wife. Therefore it is pertinent to investigate further factors which might be directly related either to network interconnectedness or to marital relationships, and possibly to both. Bott found type of neighbourhood to be an important factor underlying network connectedness. This variable is regarded as "controlled" for the Leadgill data, since all the married couples from one single community have been used as the subjects. One other major variable which Bott investigated, personality characteristics, is not reported on here because it was beyond the scope of the Leadgill study. Five further factors seem to merit attention on both theoretical and empirical grounds:

(1) occupation, (2) geographic mobility, (3) education level, (4) stage of developmental cycle, and (5) cosmopolitan or local orientations.

1. Occupation

Perhaps the most striking difference in the Leadgill data is between farm and non-farm families, as shown in Table 2. Membership of a farm family seems conducive to the development of both a close-knit social network, and a segregated conjugal role relationship.

Leadgill farms are for the most part small. The farmer himself usually runs the farm, with the help of his family. In a few cases the "farmer" has a second job in order to make a better living. The farmer works in and around the homestead most of the time.

TABLE 2. CONJUGAL ROLES AND SOCIAL NETWORKS OF FARM AND NON-FARM COUPLES

Conjugal role relationship		Interconnectedness of social networks		
		Close-knit	Medium-knit	Loose-knit
Segregated	Farm	27	3	0
	Non-farm	15	7	4
Intermediate	Farm	3	0	1
	Non-farm	10	0	6
Joint	Farm	0	1	0
	Non-farm	8	7	14

Total number of (i) farm couples = 35; (ii) non-farm couples = 71.

There is a strict division of labour between husband and wife concerning farm tasks and duties. A similar division of labour is also to be found in household activities—the farmer clearly does not expect to be asked to do "women's work", such as cooking, sewing, mending, ironing, or putting the baby to bed. Most farmers like to spend at least some of their leisure time away from the home, and they usually choose to be with male friends who have a definite interest in farming. A favourite pastime is discussion of the *minutiae* of farm affairs.

The whole family is organized around the running of the farm and it seems reasonable to advance the hypothesis that when both husband and wife work in and around the home, the form of the work relationship will exert a strong influence upon the form of other aspects of the conjugal role relationship. Evidence from five non-farm couples in Leadgill lends support to this hypothesis. In these five instances, husband and wife share the running of the business and organize their work activities so that they are to some extent interchangeable. There is a similar interchangeability in the extra-occupational activities of these couples. Nevertheless it must be emphasized that this new hypothesis is only tentatively advanced and requires rigorous testing. It should be also noted that this hypothesis may be complementary to Bott's hypothesis. Among farm couples, for example, there is not a single case of segregated conjugal role relationship occurring with a loose-knit network, nor is there any case of a joint conjugal role relationship occurring with a close-knit network among the business couples cited.

Other non-farm families in which home and workplace are clearly separated do not show any distinctive pattern of marital or network interconnectedness. Nor does the fact that a wife goes out to work (6 cases) seem to produce any specific pattern of conjugal role relationship.

2. Geographic Mobility

Bott found that geographic mobility tended to correlate with a loose-knit network structure. Leadgill couples were categorized into *dalesfolk* (both spouses born and bred in the area), *mixed* (one spouse only born and bred in the area), and *incomers* (neither spouse born and bred in the area). The conjugal role relationships and network interconnectedness for couples in each of these three categories are given in Table 3.

TABLE 3. CONJUGAL ROLES AND SOCIAL NETWORKS OF DALESFOLK AND INCOMERS AND MIXED COUPLES

Conjugal role relationship		Connectedness of social networks		
		Close-knit	Medium-knit	Loose-knit
Segregated	Dalesfolk	24	5	1
	Mixed	16	4	2
	Incomers	2	1	1
Intermediate	Dalesfolk	8	0	1
	Mixed	5	0	4
	Incomers	0	0	2
Joint	Dalesfolk	6	2	1
	Mixed	2	4	2
	Incomers	0	2	11

Total number of (i) Dalesfolk = 48; (ii) Mixed = 39; (iii) Incomers 19.

In Leadgill, married couples in which *both* husband and wife were not born in the area showed a marked tendency to develop loose-knit networks. This was undoubtedly due in many cases to the fact that incomers were able to maintain contacts with kinfolk and friends outside the community, and were in some instances not able to establish close friendships with many dalesfolk. These same couples were also likely to have joint conjugal role relationships. Unfortunately data are not available to demonstrate the types of social network and conjugal role relationships which they had developed before migrating to the community, although such a longitudinal analysis could possibly throw important light on processes involved in the development of social networks. It is interesting to note that the two incoming couples with close-knit social networks and segregated conjugal role relationships both belonged to farm families.

In instances where one spouse is a dalesfolk and the other an incomer there is a comparatively wide spread of both conjugal role segregation and network interconnectedness. The relatively high number with segregated conjugal role relationships and close-knit networks can possibly be accounted for by the fact that twelve of these sixteen couples are from farm families.

When both spouses are dalesfolk they are much more likely to have a close-knit social network (twenty-three couples) than a medium-knit (four couples), or a loose-knit one (three couples). The conjugal role relationships of these couples, however, do not show such a clear pattern: there are only fourteen couples with marital role segregation compared with seven with an intermediate, and nine with a joint conjugal role relationship. Geographic mobility, therefore, seems to be an important variable related more to network connectedness than marital role relationship.

3. Educational Level

The Leadgill evidence with regard to educational level is fairly inconclusive. The overwhelming majority of spouses, especially dalesfolk, left school at the minimum leaving age. If both spouses had spent the minimum statutory time in formal education this seemed to have little influence either upon network interconnectedness, or upon conjugal roles. Amongst the few couples in which one or both had received some form of higher education, there were no instances of a segregated marital role relationship. There is a high positive correlation between receipt of higher education and following a professional or business occupation, however, which may possibly account for this finding.

4. Stage of Developmental Cycle

The stage a family has reached in the developmental cycle appears to have no significant influence upon either conjugal relationships or network interconnectedness amongst farm families. Similarly when the effect of geographic mobility is controlled there is no significant influence in the case of non-farm families. Bott's married couples were all in the first part of the child-rearing stage of the family cycle (i.e. they had one or more children under 10 years of age). Non-farm couples from Leadgill at the same stage provide an interesting comparison group (Table 4).

TABLE 4. CONJUGAL ROLES AND SOCIAL NETWORKS OF NON-FARM COUPLES WITH CHILDREN UNDER TEN YEARS OF AGE[a]

Conjugal role relationship	Interconnectedness of social networks		
	Close-knit	Medium-knit	Loose-knit
Segregated	3 (1)	4 (0)	2 (0)
Intermediate	4 (0)	0 (9)	2 (0)
Joint	4 (0)	1 (0)	2 (5)

Total number of couples = 22 (15).
[a] Bott's figures in brackets for comparative purposes.

Differences between London data (Bott) and Leadgill data obviously cannot be explained in terms of differences in the stage of the developmental cycle.

5. Cosmopolitan or Local Orientations

Finally, an analysis of the nine couples with a cosmopolitan orientation failed to reveal any single pattern of marital role relationships or network interconnectedness. There was not one case in which both a close-knit network and a segregated conjugal role relationship coincided, but the pattern of marital role relationships, (two segregated, two intermediate, five joint) and the degree of network interconnectedness, (two close-knit, three medium-knit, four loose-knit) of these cosmopolitan couples did appear to be influenced to a certain extent by occupation and geographic mobility.

SUMMARY AND CONCLUSION

This paper, unlike the work of Udry and Hall (1965) and of Aldous and Straus (1966), is not claimed as a test of the Bott hypothesis. Rather, the Leadgill data have been explored in order to see whether any useful suggestions can be made for future research. The general approach has been to examine a number of variables in addition to network connectedness and degree of conjugal role segregation. These variables, occupation, geographic mobility, educational level, local and cosmopolitan orientation, and phase in the developmental cycle of the domestic group, were ones upon which at least some data were available, and also ones which at an intuitive level seemed relevant to the analysis.

In line with Bott's hypothesis it was found that a marked segregation of the sexes in activities involving network members was invariably accompanied by marital role segregation. In other cases, however, network connectedness was not a good predictor of degree of conjugal role segregation. Occupation appeared to be an important variable, and a tentative hypothesis was advanced that when husbands and wives both work in and around the home the form of the work relationship exerts a strong influence on the form of other aspects of the conjugal role relationship. This hypothesis may or may not prove to be complementary to Bott's hypothesis. A second variable, geographic mobility, appears to be related more closely to network connectedness than to a degree of conjugal role segregation, and on this ground alone merits attention in future research. The evidence with regard to educational level, cosmopolitan local orientations, and stage of the developmental cycle was fairly inconclusive, but more systematic investigation is probably warranted.

The difference between Bott's results, the Leadgill results, and the two sets of American results may arise from (1) methodological differences in respect of the operational definition of the key variables, (2) differences in sampling techniques—the "sample" was not drawn so as to be representative of a general population in any of the studies, (3) genuine differences in the local social structure and styles of family life—i.e. the hypothesis may not hold in every community–neighbourhood context.

One general conclusion which clearly emerges, is that there has not yet been any satisfactory test of the original Bott hypothesis. A second conclusion which can be drawn from the examination of the Leadgill data is that several variables other than degree of network connectedness and degree of conjugal role segregation might profitably be taken into account in any rigorous attempt to test the Bott hypothesis. In other words a multi-variate rather than a bi-variate research design is desirable.

In a multi-variate research design the set of dependent variables would concern the marital relationship. The independent variables would include connectedness of social networks, size and composition of social networks, selected aspects of occupation, degree of geographic mobility, stage of the developmental cycle, educational level, and cosmopolitan and local orientation, besides any additional variables which the researcher might consider relevant. The systematic measurement and analysis of the relationship between the variables outlined in the research design might also be accompanied by an investigation into the mechanisms and processes by which the variables are linked one to another. This is a challenging research problem.

REFERENCES

ALDOUS, J. and STRAUS, M. A. (1966) Social networks and conjugal roles: a test of Bott's hypothesis, *Social Forces* **44,** 576–80.

BLOOD, R. O. and WOLFE, D. M. (1960) *Husbands and Wives,* Glencoe Free Press.

BOTT, E. (1955) Urban families: conjugal roles and social networks, *Hum. Rel.* **8,** 345–83.

BOTT, E. (1956) Urban families: the norms of conjugal roles, *Hum. Rel.* **9,** 325–41.

BOTT, E. (1957) *Family and Social Network,* London, Tavistock.

DENNIS, N., HENRIQUES, F. and SLAUGHTER, C. (1956) *Coal is our Life,* London, Eyre and Spottiswoode.

KEPHART, W. M. (1950) A quantitative analysis of intragroup relationships, *Amer. J. Sociol.* **55,** 544–9.

UDRY, J. R. and HALL, M. (1965) Marital role segregation and social networks in middle-class, middle-aged couples, *Journal of Marriage and the Family* **27,** 392–5.

Urbanization and the Family

Traditional Household and Neighbourhood Group: Survivals of the Genealogical-Territorial Societal Pattern in Eastern Parts of the Netherlands

E. W. Hofstee and G. A. Kooy

"It does not matter whether marital relations are permanent or temporary; whether there is polygyny or polyandry or sexual license; whether conditions are complicated by the addition of members not included in our own family cycle: the one fact stands out beyond all others that everywhere the husband, wife, and immature children constitute a unit apart from the remainder of the community." This is the conclusion of R. H. Lowie, the well-known and outstanding American cultural anthropologist. So the group consisting of husband, wife, and immature (unmarried) children—with a living Dutch term called "gezin" and with an Anglosaxon artificial term called "nuclear family"—is, according to Lowie, a social unity in every society. This unity, however, has often been integrated in a larger familial group sometimes with such a functional importance that the "gezin" is totally over-shadowed by it. In the non-Western world, we generally find not only such an integration, but also such an over-shadowing. A "gezin" autonomy hardly exists there. The "gezin" has to respect and to obey the norms and decisions of the larger kin group and it also has to comply with the rules of the local community. (It hardly needs mentioning that the larger kin group and the local community in many cases are wholly or for the greater part identical.) This societal type, in which the individual is more a member of its extended family and the neighbourhood than of its "gezin", can be defined as a type with a genealogical–territorial pattern.

Where the spirit of individualism and the social–economic process of differentiation go together, this pattern grows weaker and gives way at last to interpersonal relations which for a considerable part are based on individual, revocable choice. If one only has a superficial idea of Western history and of the acculturation in those regions, where whites and non-whites meet each other, one knows that this is true. As to the Western world, here we find in the early Middle Ages—at least in the country—the genealogical-territorial pattern. Today the individual family typically determines its destination itself. The group consisting of husband, wife, and unmarried children liberated itself from the formerly extended family and neighbourhood. Ideological, social, and economic factors caused the loss of the most important functions of these larger units and at the same time a decrease of their power over the smallest kin group, which —becoming a more autonomous unity in a society, characterized by increasing individuation—acquired a unique meaning. Modern Western "gezin" life does not deviate from that of previous generations, only because the "gezin" underwent a very important functional and structural change; it also deviates from it, because the relation between the "gezin" and the other institutions changed fundamentally.

As in other Western countries, the process of "gezin" individualization in Holland did not start at the same time and did not show the same pace everywhere. In general the city led the way and the country followed; the bourgeois class was more progressive in this respect than the nobility and the labourers. The rural regions along the Dutch coast, already taken up in the world economy for many centuries and relatively prosperous, showed clear indications of "gezin" individualization in the middle of the nineteenth century; in the rural regions along the German boundary, long isolated and poor, one can still discover vestiges of the genealogical–territorial pattern. As such may be considered the *traditional household* and the *neighbourhood group*.

We define the traditional household as that type of household which embraces more related individuals than a "gezin" household and this not by incidental individual circumstances, but as a result of an old locally or regionally rooted cultural view. A "gezin" household can embrace only three categories of related persons (father, mother, and children), a traditional household can include many more categories. In a traditional household may live together a "gezin" and the parents of the husband, but also a "gezin" and the widowed mother of the wife, plus the unmarried brother of her mother. The traditional household can contain; (a) several nuclear families, (b) a nuclear family and one or more individuals, who are not members of a "gezin", (c) two, possibly more, nuclear families and one or more individuals, (d) two or more individuals. These four sub-types are all present in those parts of the Netherlands, where the traditional household exists. Are they primarily a consequence of poverty? This question has to be answered in the negative. For in those Western regions, where the agrarian population has the same standard of living as that near the German boundary, the traditional household does not exist any longer as it does in the Eastern regions. It is clear that the continuance of the traditional household finds its most important reason in a familistic spirit, which belongs to a phase of culture in which the process of social differentiation has not yet reached the modern stage and in which the individual does not yet know the same longing to follow his own ways as contemporary urbanized man.

The neighbourhood group is a group arising from and conforming to rules in the minds of the members of a local or regional society. As contrasted with many other neighbourhood groups this neighbourhood group has its sharp limit; one belongs to it or one does not. One joins it according to a certain rule and one likewise leaves it. The rights and duties of the neighbour are fixed and everyone knows them. One can possess a special status in the neighbourhood group, which gives rights and duties not shared by the other group-members. In short, this neighbourhood group is not at all an amorphous group with a vague limit, but on the contrary a social unit with a specific structure, specific functions, and a clear outline. Beyond the special rights which the individual can derive from his membership of the neighbour-hood group (help during child-birth, wedding, death, harvest, etc.), he also gains a place in local society through this member-ship. If the newcomer does not take the step necessary to become the neighbour of a number of surrounding people, he will stay an outsider. He cannot be "one of us" if he fails to ask for the neighbour-bond. From the social point of view he stands isolated from those who are geographically his neighbours and this implies that he is a stranger in the community. Therefore it is not surprising that hardly any newcomer dares to settle down in the agrarian community, where the neighbourhood group still exists, without asking for neighbourhood according to the rules in force.

It was not before August 1955 that we were really confronted with the two phenomena which form the subject of this paper. During a study among the agrarian population of the munici-pality of Winterswijk, situated near the German border, we also had the opportunity to consider the traditional household and the neighbourhood group. The situation at Winterswijk is perhaps not representative in all respects of the part of the Netherlands where these phenomena stemming from an earlier phase of culture are still perceptible. On the other hand it is probable that the problems for the individual, caused by the collision of old norms and new individualism, are the same at Winterswijk as in other places where the genealogical–territorial pattern still exists as an influential "survival". Therefore we can take Winterswijk as an example.

Winterswijk has about 21,000 inhabitants, of whom 10,000 are living in the 9 predominantly agrarian hamlets, situated in a circle around the town (which everyone calls "the village"). In the town agriculture has not yet disappeared; even along the main street one can find farm houses. But the important source of livelihood is the textile-industry. The largest of the 7 textile mills has a labour force of 1000. The agrarian population is predominantly Protestant. Only in the hamlet of Meddo near the Roman Catholic municipality of Grol we find a strong minority of Catholics. Type and size of the farms in Winterswijk are rather representative for agriculture on the Dutch sandy soils. The small family farm prevails, and the farm is a so-called mixed farm on which the products of agriculture are used for animal husbandry. There are 1514 farms of which 589 are smaller than 5 ha., of which 638 are larger than 5 but smaller than 10 ha., of which 187 lie between 10 and 15 ha., and of which 100 are over 15 ha.

It was possible to obtain data about the structure of the household on 497 farms at Winterswijk. These 497 farms may be considered as representative for all agrarian enterprises larger than 2 ha. It appeared that a "gezin" household occurs in 252 cases, so this type of household is somewhat more represented in the total sample than the traditional household. It is *not* so, that, if one comes nearer to the "village", one finds fewer traditional households. Nor do we find a decrease of traditional households in connection with an increase in farm size. If we join together all farms, smaller than 15 ha., and we compare them with those over 15 ha., the percentage of traditional households in the first group is 46.5 and in the second one 53.5. From the data obtained at Winterswijk, one cannot state that increasing farm size (and so probably increasing material prosperity) causes decrease of traditional households. The data suggest a connection between traditional household and religious denomination, but the members of the Dutch Reformed Church form such a majority, that it is dangerous to suppose a stronger inclination among the Dutch Reformed to accept the old type of household than among other groups. Moreover the Dutch Reformed Church is a dwelling with many compartments.

An exact knowledge of the structure of the traditional household is important, because every structure causes its own psychological difficulties. It appeared then, that in 125 cases a married couple lives together with the parents-in-law and that in 100 cases a couple lives together with the father or mother of one of the partners. It rather seldom happens, that a "gezin" lives together with an individual of the husband's and wife's generation. A "gezin" and an "uncle" (wife's or husband's brother) were found together 14 times, a "gezin" and an "aunt" only 6 times. Probably the relatively high frequency of the three-generation household must be explained by the old rule of primogeniture. Although modern Dutch law gives every child a similar portion of the legacy, the old idea of primogeniture is not dead at Winterswijk. If possible, the eldest son inherits the farm and the other children, compensated by money, leave it. But the successor accepts the duty "to bring his parents to their end".

The type of traditional household, so frequently found at Winterswijk, has the following consequences:

(a) the child is educated by its parents, its grandparents, and possibly by their still unmarried children (the child's uncles and aunts),

(b) if the younger pair lives together with the parents of the husband, the young woman has to adapt herself to the mother of her husband, who is, in her opinion, the master of the house,

(c) if the younger pair lives together with the parents of the wife, the young man has to adapt himself to his wife's father, who will claim to be the "farmer" until his last gasp of breath,

(d) the partner who lives with his or her parents, is in danger of remaining in the position of a "child" until his old age.

It is impossible here to consider these consequences more thoroughly but it is clear that there is an interesting psychological and sociological problem in the structure of the traditional household. It depends on the sort of structure which problems will arise. If the household consists of a "gezin" and a brother or sister of one of the partners, one may mainly expect difficulties between brother and sister-in-law, whereby the unmarried one of these two is in the weakest position.

Nearly every agrarian family at Winterswijk has accepted the neighbour bond, from which it derives rights on the one hand, but from which arise duties on the other hand. Rights form an agreeable side of human existence, but man is inclined to under-estimate them. The duties, which man has, are not seldom experi-enced by him as a heavy restraint. When a child is born in one of the neighbouring families, it may be experienced as very pleasant to visit mother and child with 10 or 11 other near-by women; but when one has a baby herself and she is obliged to see 11 or 12 ladies, the situation has a fundamentally other character. When one of the members of a person's family dies and his neigh-bours pay (in accordance with their neighbour duty) the death announcements, then this is hardly noticed by him, for it is a matter of course; but when someone dies in a neighbouring family and he is obliged to pay the death announcements, then this is not always a task which he fulfils with all his heart. Especi-ally younger people feel it as a burden, but they do not dare to throw it off, for the norm lies deeply anchored.

The traditional household and the neighbourhood group are acceptable to the individual as long as he considers himself primarily a member of the larger genealogical unit and the local unit. They are acceptable for man in "primitive" society, in societies geographically and socially isolated, little differentiated, and lacking a money-economy. When the "primitivism" of society is broken through, however, there grow tensions in and between members of this society, which may be hidden from the eyes of outsiders, but which are intensive. Traditional house-hold and neighbourhood groups are today considered by many younger people in the eastern parts of the Netherlands as serious restraints. Modern culture has awakened wishes and desires which do not reconcile with the old norms and forms. There are indica-tions that those old norms and forms give way to entirely other ones, but it seems that many and long-lasting tensions are reserved for the agricultural population in the Eastern parts of the Netherlands, for the power of the old norms is great.

Qualitative Changes in Family Life in the Netherlands

J. PONSIOEN

1. EXTERNAL AND INTERNAL FACTORS OF CHANGE IN FAMILY LIFE

Recent literature on family life in all countries strongly stresses the influences of total society, so that one might easily get the impression that family life is merely a function of culture and society. Experience in the Netherlands with various types of families under similar social and cultural circumstances has shown that today we are apt to overrate the social and cultural determination somewhat, while underestimating the originality of the family as an institution. The originality of every family, appears most clearly perhaps in family care, within the limits of a social welfare policy. The assistance given by the social worker is digested by each family in a non-predictable way. This originality arises from the two great social facts determing the development of Dutch society, namely the rapid industrialization and urbanization of the last 50 years.

Both these factors are a result of the growth of the population. (In 1897 it passed 5 million and in 1950 10 million.) This is a factor which in its turn is based on the behaviour pattern of family life. Although this pattern has the semblance of remaining unchanged it appears on closer inspection that there is after all a change in the different groups of the population. As a general trend, which does not hold good for each group separately, a tendency may be observed in the various provinces and among the various religious denominations towards a greater similarity, and as regards the grouping based on income a tendency towards adjusting the number of children to the economic possibilities.

Now these changes have sometimes been explained as a result of the industrialization process, and this may be partly true; the curious reaction to the war shows that the psychological attitude of the population is much more important in explaining the number of children born, and that industry only has an influence on it via its psychological consequences. Family life in itself has quite as important an effect as industrial life, at least in some types of families.

Helmut Schelsky has shown how the family reacted in Germany to the insecurity of the outside world, by shutting itself off and retiring into itself.[1] Such a study is lacking for Holland, but there also two factors attract attention, namely the rise of the closed family in an open society in the beginning of the industrialization process in the first half of the nineteenth century, and the greater consolidation of the family during the war and especially the tightening of bonds with the circle of acquaintance. These facts derived from common observation are in keeping with Schelsky's conclusions. The very low percentage of married women in occupational life round about 1920 probably shows that the zenith of the isolated family is to be found at about that time.

Of greater importance is the fact that six types of families may be distinguished in Holland today. A number of them may be found in areas of a similar degree of industrialization and urbanization, so they cannot be directly related to degrees of industrialization. Perhaps this can be explained by a tendency to have the pattern of family life of the previous generations as one's ideal and to make that the standard to live by.[2] Nevertheless the entire originality of family life cannot very well consist in remaining a few paces behind in social development, because today we see new, better-adjusted patterns of family life developing. But we must not only record the adjustment of the family to external factors, but also the development of what Burgess and Locke[3]

[1] Helmut Schelsky, *Wandlungen der deutschen Familie in der Gegenwart*, Dortmund, 1953.
[2] René König, *Materialen zur Soziologie der Familie*, Bern, 1946.
[3] Ernest Burgess and Harvey Locke, *The Family*, N.Y., 1950.

called "from institution to companionship", in other words the emancipation of women and their increasing share in public life, as well as the longer period of youthfulness in the parents and the more rapid maturing of the children. All these are factors in present day families, and they are not wholly to be explained as the results of industrialization and urbanization. They are autonomous trends in development that may be observed in the whole of our Western culture, and they manifest themselves both in the industrialization process and in family life.

2. TYPES OF FAMILY LIFE

Systematic research into Dutch family life, the nature of family relations, the extent of integration and the norms of diverse groups is entirely lacking, let alone systematic field research into the changes that have taken place during the last 50 years. Partial data may be gathered here and there from reports on investigations, but these usually relate to problem areas or problem groups, so that they easily give rise to a lop-sided view. It is possible to get some information all the same. For instance it is amply clear that the young people in all the various social groups, especially those from 14 to 18 years of age, have become a social problem group of their own during the last decades, and every one is convinced that the family as such is no longer capable of solving it. Initiation into adulthood, has escaped from family guidance. It has passed into the hands of institutions for the young (youth organizations and especially secondary schools) or alternatively it does not take place at all, a thing which has lately caused a great deal of anxiety.

By the side of these clearly observable facts the intuition of the sociologist is perhaps also of value, even without its being tested by a formal investigation (although that of course remains the ideal). This leads me to believe that in our Dutch society six types of family may be distinguished.

(a) The Patriarchal Type

Under this heading I would not include the joint family under the supreme authority of a grandparent. This no longer occurs in Holland.[4] But the patriarchal conjugal family, in which the children have no rights as against the father until their majority, whilst he has the disposal of his children as if they were his property, can still be found sporadically in rural districts. From this it does not necessarily follow that the woman is subject to the man; she may be his partner. The children, however, are not free to choose their own vocation and their choice of a matrimonial partner is strictly limited by the authority of the father. This patriarchal type, however, is disappearing and seems to be pre-industrial.

(b) The Open Family within a Closed Village or Neighbourhood

In this type the local community prevails over the individual family. This community has its male society which gathers in the evening to discuss the day's events over a drink and its female society whose members solve household problems in neighbourhood chats during the day. The children are fed, clothed, and sent to school under the watchful eye of the community. The children from about their twelfth year to the time of steady courtship often form a communal group of their own, with the boys and girls segregated, which forms a strong check on the behaviour of its members and thus develops a powerful character-shaping influence. Neighbourhood and family life intermingle freely. This type of family with its small inward concentration is mostly found in small rural hamlets or in the so-called slum areas of the towns.[5] This seems to be another pre-industrial type, and displays a resemblance to the conjugal family within the joint family. The milieu in which this type of family occurs has consequently

[4] A few remains of this type still appear to exist in Drente, see the (strictly confidential) report Zuid-Oost Drente of the Ministry of Social Welfare.

[5] Dr. I. Haveman, *De ongeschoolde arbeider*, Assen, 1952.

been called the proletarian rearguard by van Doorn.[6] The suggestion which this term implies is that as the proletariat advances this type of family life will disappear. The resistance these areas in the towns put up against the process of individualization of industry and urbanization is so strong, however, that this assumption is rather dangerous.

(c) The Closed Family in an Open Society

This type of family lives in a certain amount of isolation in an industrialized and urbanized society, and as an institution it displays a certain amount of enmity towards that society. It attempts to safeguard its members from the dangers threatening it from without. Those dangers are especially considered to lie in the system of standards which industry and the town together have built up as social ties which threaten to disturb the traditional system of standards of the family. This antithetic attitude also often reveals itself in regard to the school youth organizations and societies for grown-ups, because all these make calls on the time which the family considers its own. But just because this type of family does not provide any social training, the school, the youth organization and the societies for grown-ups are starting to demand more time, because they are taking over this social education. Thus the conflict, in which the family is converted into a bastion, is increasing. The function of this type of family is perhaps to maintain traditional values in times of rapid change. But the family only exercises a function of sociability without making its members do something in common. Few outsiders enter such a family. In spite of the idea of wishing to be pleasantly together the result as often as not is pure boredom. This closed type of family undoubtedly has a fertile breeding-ground in Dutch culture, which is of the typically domestic sort. In this connection one should note the curious pattern in which Catholics, Protestants, Liberals, Socialists all have their own party, their own press, radio corporations, television com-

[6] Jac. A. A. van Doorn, soc. drs., *De proletarische achterhoede*, Meppel, 1954.

panies, and trade unions. Most schools are denominational, as well as many sports clubs and recreation centres.

The number of families of this closed type cannot be established without an accurate investigation. Perhaps the figures for the percentage of married women in employment show that this type reached its zenith in the years round about 1920 since when there was a decline.

(d) The Counterfeit Family in an Open Society

Included in this type is the family whose avowed ideal is the closed family and which pretends to be one to the outside world, but which cannot really realize this ideal of integration within the home on account of the pull society has on it. This kind of family lives in a situation of conflict because it accepts the system of standards of the closed family whilst its members have already unconsciously accepted the system of standards of society, i.e. working milieu, recreation milieux, and urban ways of life The emancipation of women and the right of self-determination on the part of the children where work and the choice of their friends is concerned, has made its entry in such families without their altering their system of standards. It then becomes an inner conflict of a neurotic nature. In addition a large number of the children receive an education which is higher than that of the parents, with the result that the milieux of the parents and the children grow apart so that they have difficulty in understanding each other. Moreover the new society gives ample opportunity of rising in the social scale, in which rise the man often takes part but not the woman. Notwithstanding all this there is a persistent effort to appear a "decent" family to the outside world by which is meant the closed, firmly integrated family. Here again we cannot fix the number of these families, without closer investigation. My personal impression is that this type occurs mostly in families whose religious denominations have identified their system of standards too much with a type of family in which this system of standards was safe.

(c) The Boarding-house Type

This is a type of family that sociologically speaking is hardly a family, a social unit, at all. There are still affective ties between the blood relations but there is no or very little integration. There is only the house in common, but joint meals are not regularly taken, nor is leisure time spent together, nor do the members of such a family do any work in conjunction. They eat and sleep at home as it happens to be convenient to them. They do not know of the others where they are or what they are doing. This does not happen between husband and wife and seldom between the mother and the children under 12, but it does happen between the parents and the children over 14 and among brothers and sisters.

This type of family is restricted to the town, especially large towns. It is to be found in working class milieux, especially of the unskilled type; sometimes in the new lower middle classes as well, but not in the older type of middle class. It seems that when the slum areas of the towns lose their closed character it is the open families who are the first to be ready to sink into the boarding-house type.

(f) The Open Family in an Open Society

A new type of family is developing which seems to be succeeding in combining family life with participation of all its members in social functions such as work environment, the school as social institution and community on its own, recreation and games, trade unions, and social and charitable activities.

Family life is then no longer looked upon as a natural self-evident fact, but as a definite task for which time should be found or set aside and for which trouble should be taken. It is a task for all the members, the father and the mother as well as the older children. The housework is done by all, whilst in the older types of families it fell to the mother and/or the eldest daughter. In the new type there is much more comradeship, also between the parents and the children, in fact more democracy than in the older types. They often make an appointment with each other for the whole family to be together, setting aside the time for it. But this does not prevent each separate member from moving in his own social milieu as well. On the contrary it is considered an enrichment that each makes a contribution from his own milieu.

With the rise and growth of this type of family one also often finds that the circle of acquaintance is of increasing importance: similar families which call upon each other, go out together, where the children can be brought when a set of parents wishes to go on holidays, a circle in fact that helps each other in word and deed. It is as if the joint family, after having fallen apart in autonomous families, has risen again in the circle of acquaintance, which often means more to these families than their relatives do. This open type of family, which has succeeded in its integration, seems to be increasing. Perhaps one may look upon it as a family that is matured, that has overcome industrialization and urbanization and that is a new form in which an equilibrium has again been attained.

It is not necessary to stress the fact that the above types are ideal types in Max Weber's sense of the word. Field research will have to prove their validity and it will very probably discover traits of more than one type in particular cases. Research will finally have to settle whether and how the types also succeeded each other in history.

New Aspects of Rural-Urban Differentials in Family Values and Family Structure

G. Baumert and E. Lupri

INTRODUCTION

The process of urbanization finds its most visible expression in the growth of metropolitan areas—or in other words, in the population shift from country to city. One of the simplest ways to measure urbanization is to calculate the historical trend of the proportion of the population residing in rural areas and in urban centres. Census data for Germany presents a concrete picture of the increasing urbanization of modern society.

During the course of approximately 90 years Germany has changed from a predominately rural society to a predominately urban one. In 1871 almost two out of three of the population lived in rural areas, i.e. in communities of less than 2000 inhabitants. By 1959 less than one out of four persons of Germany's 53 million inhabitants resided in rural areas, and slightly more than three out of four in urban places, i.e. in communities of 2000 inhabitants and above.

Another outstanding fact is the extent to which Germany's inhabitants are increasingly concentrating in and migrating to urban centres of 100,000 inhabitants or more. Whereas only 5 per cent of the German population were living in cities of 100,000 or more in 1871, by 1959 the figure had increased to 30 per cent. The reverse trend can be observed for places under 2000 inhabitants for which the percentages are 64 and 24, respectively. The figures presented in Table 1 are an indication of this trend.

The urbanization index as developed by Kingsley Davis, Table 2,

279

TABLE 1. NUMBER AND PROPORTION OF POPULATION OF
GERMANY RESIDING IN PLACES OF STATED SIZE, 1871 TO 1959
(IN MILLIONS)

Year	Under 2000		2000–19,999		20,000 – 99,999		100,000 +	
	(N)	(%)	(N)	(%)	(N)	(%)	(N)	(%)
1871	26.2	64	9.5	23	3.1	8	1.9	5
1890	26.1	53	12.3	25	4.8	10	5.9	12
1910	25.9	40	16.3	25	8.6	14	13.8	21
1939	11.6	30	9.4	24	5.2	13	12.9	33
1950	13.7	29	14.0	30	6.7	14	13.0	27
1959	12.5	24	15.1	29	8.7	17	16.1	30

SOURCE: Compiled from data given in *Statistisches Jahrbuch* 1960
der Bundesrepublik Deutschland, Stuttgart, 1960.

reveals the contemporary stage of urbanization in Western Germany as compared with some other industrial societies. By this measure, Western Germany is one of the most urbanized countries in the world, interestingly enough, more so than the United States, and is only surpassed in Europe by Great Britain. For Western Germany, the index number is 46 as against indices of 42 for the United States and 31 for France.

TABLE 2. PERCENTAGE OF POPULATION IN CITIES BY SIZE CLASS IN
DIFFERENT COUNTRIES

Country	In cities 5000+	In cities 10,000+	In cities 100,000+	In cities 500,000+	Index
Western Germany	57.4	51.7	43.5	31.8	46.1
France	41.7	37.5	29.8	16.0	31.2
Sweden	37.1	33.4	27.0	17.5	28.7
Great Britain	81.7	73.6	63.1	45.2	65.9
United States	52.7	47.6	40.1	28.8	42.3

SOURCE: Abridged from Kingsley Davis and Anna Casis, Urbanization in Latin America, *Milbank Memorial Fund Quarterly*, 24 April 1956. The index of urbanization represents the arithmetic mean of the previous columns.

THE PROBLEM

The foregoing classification of the German population into rural and urban segments is one of the first steps in the analysis of the urbanization process. Such measures, however, are very limited indicators of urbanization. They cannot take into account the phenomena of social life associated with urban concentration. The concept urbanization implies the spread of a certain mode of life commonly called the "urban way of life".[1]

As most students of urban society state, because of the spread of the urban way of life in the industrial countries the social and cultural differences between rural and urban areas are rapidly disappearing. Data indicate that in Germany also the urban way of life increasingly extends its influence, and that the rural–urban differentials are vanishing.[2] But as far as family life is concerned, the statement of the vanishing rural–urban differentials is based more on general speculation than on empirical evidence. It is the primary objective of our study to investigate some aspects of the relationship between urbanization and the family. We will focus on the question as to whether the high degree of urbanization in Germany as measured by the proportion of rural and urban population and expressed in Davis's index coincides with an equally strong extension of an urban way of life in the sense of homogeneous norms and values. Two aspects of this phenomenon were selected for the investigation: family size values and family structure. We shall make an attempt to follow the trend of urbanization in both urban and rural areas and to test the hypothesis of the vanishing rural–urban differentials.

[1] Urbanism as a way of life is often characterized by rapid social change; by increased mobility of the population; and by a sharp decline in intimate communication. A classic in this respect is the article by Louis Wirth, Urbanism as a way of life, *Amer. J. Sociol.* **44**, 1–24 (July 1938). Howard Becker's concept "Secularization" reflects the same process. See his *Man in Reciprocity* New York, 1956, pp. 169–97.

[2] Compare, for example, Herbert Kötter, *Landbevölkerung und sozialer Wandel*, Düsseldorf-Köln, 1958.

URBANIZATION AND FAMILY SIZE VALUES

The trend in birth-rates in Germany shows a sharp decline in the past hundred years. A persistent reduction could be observed from 40.6 in 1875 to 17.6 in 1930.

After the Second World War and the immediate post-war years no consistent trend was recognizable. The birth-rates again continued to decline from 16.8 in 1949 to 16.5 in 1953, although since then there has been an increase to 17.4 in 1960.

In the long-term development the statistical correlation between birth-rates and urbanization is clear-cut: *birth-rates decline with an increasing degree of urbanization.*

When in the ensuing analysis we attempt to examine the effect of urbanization, our main concern will be with the relationship between fertility measures and community size. We are also interested in the change to be observed between the last and the present generation. Since the data of vital statistics do not meet all the requirements of our analysis, we will also use the material of inquiries into family size and family values in West Germany undertaken by means of sample surveys and personal interviews.[3]

The rates of natural increase of Germany's population serve as a first reference point of the urban–rural differences. In 1959 the increase per 1000 inhabitants was 8.8 for communities under 2000, 6.4 for communities up to 100,000, and 3.6 for communities of 100,000 and over.[4]

Table 3, which gives the mean numbers of children for married couples in rural and urban areas, reveals a similar picture. The table gives also a comparison of the figures for 1933, 1939, and

[3] The inquiries have been undertaken in co-operation with Ronald Freedman, University of Michigan and Martin Bolte, University of Kiel. Field-work and processing were conducted by the DIVO-Institut, Frankfurt am Main. The inquiries altogether encompass three survey waves with more than 5000 interviews based on a multi-stage probability sample representative of the West German population between the ages of 16 and 79. The figures presented here are related to the group of married respondents under 45 with 1850 cases and the group of married respondents over 45 with 1662 cases.

[4] Statistisches Bundesamt. *Statistisches Jahrbuch* 1961 *für die Bundesrepublik Deutschland*, Stuttgart und Mainz, 1961, p. 63.

1950, which will be analysed later. In 1950 the mean number of children was 2.28 for communities under 2000 inhabitants and 1.52 for communities with 100,000 and over. The average for West Germany was 1.90.

TABLE 3. MEAN NUMBERS OF CHILDREN FOR
MARRIED COUPLES IN RURAL AND URBAN
AREAS, WEST GERMANY
1933, 1939, 1950

Size of communities	1933	1939	1950
Under 2000	2.69	2.61	2.28
100,000 and over	1.77	1.69	1.52
Total (West Germany)	2.42	2.28	1.90

SOURCE: *Statistik der Bundesrepublik Deutschland*, vol. 35, Issue 9, p. 50.

The data presented so far show a definite association between fertility as measured by the actual number of children and the size of community of residence.[5]

The question arises whether other measures such as the number of children expected or the number of children desired show a similar association with community size. While birth-rates and means of actual number of children can be used as indices for the more biological aspects of fertility, the other measures mentioned here more clearly represent a picture of the values and norms prevailing in the society. We know that sometimes values and norms lag behind the actual performance. On the other hand sometimes social values and norms anticipate later performance, and for this reason studying values and norms can be important for purposes of prediction.[6]

[5] For a further compilation of data consistent with this statement see Dudley Kirk, Economic and demographic development in Western Germany, *Population Index*, vol. XXIV, No. 1, January 1958.

[6] Sociologists who have made use of the concept of value for predictive purposes include among others: Robin M. Williams, *American Society: A Sociological Interpretation*, New York, 1960; Howard Becker, *Through Values to Social Interpretation*, Durham, 1950; Talcott Parsons and Edward A. Shils (Eds.) *Toward a General Theory of Action*, Cambridge 1951; Eugene A. Wilkening, Techniques of assessing farm family values, *Rural Sociology*, **19** (March 1954).

On the average, the West German family now expects to have two or three children. In our survey, of the married respondents under 45 years, 45 per cent expected to have two children, 22 per cent expected to have three children, and 18 per cent to have one child only. The mean number of children expected was 2.2. This figure is roughly equivalent to the number of children required for replacement of the West German population estimated by the West German Statistical Office at 2.24.[7]

A confrontation of the expected family size with the number of children considered ideal for the average German family and with the number desired by the couples shows significant differences. On the average, married respondents would like to have more children than they actually expect to have: the mean number considered ideal for an average German family is 2.6; the mean number desired under favourable circumstances is 2.7.[8]

We will now compare the rural–urban differentials for the various measures mentioned here, with the mean number of children ever born of respondents under 45 (Table 4). We again find a clear indication of the tendency towards the smaller family with the increasing size of the community. With increasing community size there is not only a decline in the number of children families really have, but also a decline in the number of expected children and in the ideal and desired family size. The

[7] See Ronald Freedman, Gerhard Baumert and Martin Bolte, Expected family size and family size values in West Germany, *Population Studies*, **13** (2) (November 1959), 140.

[8] The following questions were asked:

For "expected number": "As you know, a family plans for the future—questions like the size of the apartment, purchases and others are related to the family size they expect to have. How many children do you think you will have altogether?" If the respondent said: "Don't know" or "Depends" he was asked: "As you think things will turn out for your family, how many children do you think you will have altogether?"

For "ideal number": "Now thinking of family generally, what do you feel is the ideal size for an average German family—husband, wife and how many children?" If the respondent said "Don't know" or "Depends" he was asked: "As things are for the average German family: How many children would you say?"

For desired number: "How many children would you like to have yourself, if the financial and other circumstances would be very good?"

differentials in fertility values are consistent with the differentials in fertility performances.

Comparing these data with those obtained in the United States, we find that in the United States, as in Germany, the birth-rates and the numbers of children per couple continue to

TABLE 4. MEAN NUMBER OF CHILDREN EVER BORN, EXPECTED, CONSIDERED IDEAL, AND DESIRED FOR MARRIED RESPONDENTS UNDER 45 BY SIZE OF COMMUNITY, WEST GERMANY, 1958

Size of community	Mean number ever born	Mean number expected	Mean ideal number	Mean desired number
Under 2000	2.0 (346)	2.6 (460)	2.8 (491)	3.0 (484)
2000–4999	1.8 (179)	2.1 (261)	2.5 (275)	2.7 (265)
5000–19,999	1.9 (193)	2.3 (275)	2.7 (298)	2.8 (294)
20,000–99,999	1.7 (174)	2.1 (251)	2.6 (268)	2.7 (264)
100,000–499,999	1.5 (147)	1.9 (203)	2.5 (212)	2.6 (209)
500,000 and more	1.4 (183)	1.8 (258)	2.3 (267)	2.3 (265)

differ with city size. With regard to the expected number of children, however, the results of the Freedman, Whelpton, Campbell study show no difference with respect to community size in the United States. There are only differences between farm groups on the one hand and non-farm groups on the other. [9]

Thus, in contrast to Germany there is no consistency in fertility values and fertility performance in the United States. While the traditional rural–urban differentials still prevail with respect to fertility performance, the differentials in expected fertility as a measure for the social values and norms (at least in a country with a widespread practice of birth control and family planning) have vanished. We may follow Freedman's speculation that in the United States communities have now been drawn into a single

[9] See Ronald Freedman, Pascal K. Whelpton, Arthur Campbell, *Family Planning, Sterility and Population Growth*, New York, 1959.

urban–metropolitan network in which interaction and inter-dependence are so close that fertility expectation differences become blurred.[10]

We may conclude that with respect to fertility, urbanization first affects the social values before it affects the actual perform-ance. Thus the United States has reached the first stage of the development toward a homogeneous urbanized society with the rural–urban differences in social values vanishing, and it seems to experience the second stage where the differences in the per-formance will vanish, too.[11]

Germany, on the other hand, shows a different picture. We have no data on expectations and ideals in former decades, but we can make an inference by comparing the values of the younger generation with the values of the older generation. In this respect the data seem to indicate diminishing rural–urban differentials as far as fertility values are concerned. There is also a slight decrease in rural–urban differences in fertility performance, as the comparison of the mean number of children for 1943 and 1950 shows: the number in rural communities (under 2000 inhab-itants) decreased by 16 per cent and in cities with more than 100,000 inhabitants by 14 per cent. We can still say, however, that in Germany both the fertility values and the fertility per-formance continue to differ significantly by size of the com-munity.

URBANIZATION AND FAMILY STRUCTURE

We shall now turn to the second part of this paper. In the fol-lowing analysis we will be concerned with the social–psychological structure of the family as it is expressed in the position and role of each family member. The analysis will be based on data which were collected by means of sample survey and personal inter-

[10] R. Freedman, G. Baumert, M. Bolte, *op. cit.*, p. 146.

[11] The average number of births by cohort clearly shows a strong tendency toward a levelling of differences in birth rates. Cf. Freedman, Whelpton, Campbell, *op. cit.*, p. 313.

viewing.[12] For this preliminary paper we selected the data we obtained from questions about the role of family members in the process of decision-making.[13]

In Germany, as in other Western societies, the process of urbanization is accompanied by a shift from a traditional patriarchal type of family to a more equalitarian partnership-type family. The role of the father and husband has changed fundamentally, and with it the conception of his position in the society at large.

Although his former patriarchal nature—a subject of perpetual dispute[14]—is definitely weakening as many recent sociological studies and surveys demonstrate, the father and husband is still predominant.[15] Concomitant with the diminuation of the authori-

[12] The inquiries were part of an international study on the role of the citizens in England, Germany, Italy, Mexico, and U.S.A., and directed by Gabriel Almond, Yale University. The German survey was undertaken by DIVO-Institut, Frankfurt, Germany, in June 1959. Included in the nationwide probability sample were 955 respondents, 18–79 years of age. We are indebted to Professor Almond for permission to use the material for secondary analysis.

[13] The following questions were asked:
1. "We should like to find out how decisions were reached in your family when you were 16 years of age. Here is a list of possibilities how family decisions can be reached. (CARD) In general, how were decisions reached in your family?"
1. By and large, *father* reached the decision.
2. By and large, *mother* reached the decision.
3. By and large, *both* reached the decision jointly.
4. By and large, each parent reached the decision *individually*.
2. Posed to married respondents only: "How would you compare this with your own family today? In general, how are decisions reached in your family?" (CARD) Precode as in question 1.

[14] David Abrahamsen, *Men, Mind, and Power*, New York, 1945; Bertram Schaffner, *Fatherland: A Study of Authoritarianism in the German Family*, New York, 1947; David Rodnick, *Postwar Germans: An Anthropologist's Account*, London, 1948.

[15] Gerhard Baumert, *Jugend der Nachkriegszeit*, Darmstadt, 1952; Gerhard Wurzbacher, *Leitbilder gegenwärtigen deutschen Familienlebens*, Dortmund, 1953; Helmut Schelsky, *Wandlungen der deutschen Familie in der Gegenwart*, Dortmund, 1953; Gerhard Baumert und Edith Hüninger, *Deutsche Familien nach dem Kriege*, Darmstadt, 1954; René König, Family and authority: the German father in 1955, *Sociol. Rev.* **5** (1) (July 1957), 107–27.

While Wurzbacher and Schelsky, who collected data on the German family by means of family monographs, conclude that the German family can be characterized as equalitarian, Baumert and König, relying on sample surveys, maintain that a semi-patriarchal type is still prevailing, especially in the upper classes.

tarian position of the German husband, is the gradual but consistent disappearance of subordination of both wife and children.

The exposition of generational differentials with respect to the role of husband and wife in the process of decision-making shows the well-known pattern.

The classification according to the last and present generations reveals quite clearly the diminution of the father's dominant position as well as the development towards a more equalitarian position with respect to the wife (Table 5).

TABLE 5. GENERATIONAL DIFFERENCES IN PREDOMINANCE OF
HUSBAND AND WIFE, WEST GERMANY, 1959

Predominance	Parent generation		Present generation[a]	
	(%)	(N)	(%)	(N)
Father/husband	30	(283)	17	(117)
Mother/wife	13	(122)	8	(55)
Jointly	49	(472)	63	(438)
Others	8	(78)	12	(81)
	100	(955)	100	(691)

[a] Married respondents only.

While there is evidence of the predominance of the father and husband in 30 per cent of the cases for the parent generation, we find a corresponding figure of 17 per cent for the present generation. The figures equally apply to the earlier indicated modification of the wife's role. The high percentage in the "Joint" category of the present generation is a manifestation of the increasing trend towards a companionship family in the German society.[16]

[16] A brief methodological note with regard to the data under study may be in order. To be sure, statements about decision-making within the family cannot be taken uncritically at face value. (See, for example, W. F. Kenkel and D. F. Hoffman, Real and conceived roles in family decision-making, *Marriage and Family Living*, **18** (November 1956), pp. 311–16.) We know that those statements are subjective evaluations based on societal norms and values, a fact that has to be kept in mind especially in cross-cultural research. On the other hand, there is ample empirical evidence that points to a high correlation between evaluative statements and actual predominance within the family. With the necessary reservations, the data may be taken as indicative for the phenomenon under study.

The association between the process of urbanization and the structural change of the family reflects itself in the processual stages of urbanization such as community size (Table 6).

TABLE 6. PRESENT RURAL-URBAN DIFFERENCES IN PRE-
DOMINANCE OF HUSBAND AND WIFE, WEST GERMANY, 1959

Predominance	Rural area		Town area		City area	
	(%)	(N)	(%)	(N)	(%)	(N)
Husband	20	(49)	18	(42)	12	(26)
Wife	9	(22)	8	(18)	7	(15)
Jointly	59	(145)	64	(146)	68	(147)
Others	12	(30)	10	(23)	13	(28)
	100	(246)	100	(229)	100	(216)

Rural: up to 5000 inhabitants. *Town:* 5000 up to 100,000.
City: 100,000 and over.

The figures show that the authority of the father diminishes with increasing community size. Parallel to this tendency is the notable increase in the category of respondents who state that family decisions are reached jointly by husband and wife.

More central to our focus, however, is the inspection of generational differences within rural and urban areas (Table 7). We find that in each of the categories for the community size,which we have used in our analysis, a change from the parent to the present generation takes place. This may be interpreted not merely as an effect of urbanization in the sense of rural–urban migration, but rather as an effect of the extension of the urban way of life influencing all community sizes.

If we again examine the differentials within each community category, we observe an unanticipated phenomenon: *the changes in the urban areas are greater than the corresponding changes in the rural area.*[17]

[17] The relative high percentage of joint decision-making in the parent generation in the rural area may be accounted for by the involvement of the peasant wife in the economic sphere on the traditional small farm holdings in West Germany.

It should be pointed out that the figures presented here are taken from a rather limited sample. However, the data suggest a reconsideration of the formerly conceived hypothesis with reference to the trend toward diminishing rural–urban differences as far as the social structure of the family is concerned.

TABLE 7. RURAL-URBAN AND GENERATIONAL DIFFERENCES IN PREDOMINANCE OF HUSBAND AND WIFE, WEST GERMANY, 1959

Predominance	Rural area		Town area		City area	
	(%)	(N)	(%)	(N)	(%)	(N)
Parent generation: husband	30	(132)	35	(97)	24	(52)
Present generation: husband	20	(44)	18	(42)	12	(26)
Parent generation: wife	11	(44)	10	(27)	14	(41)
Present generation: wife	9	(22)	8	(18)	7	(15)
Parent generation: jointly	52	(233)	46	(128)	49	(107)
Present generation: jointly	59	(145)	64	(146)	68	(147)

The classification of the Parent Generation is based on the place of birth of the respondents. The classification of Present Generation is based on place of residence of the respondents in the survey.

If the change of norms pertaining to the role structure of the family system is still more dynamic in urban areas than in rural areas—and that is exactly what our data suggest, then the levelling of the difference between country and city is actually not progressing as rapidly as it is commonly assumed. On the contrary, we must assume on the basis of the empirical evidence that with respect to family structure the differences between rural and urban areas have increased during the last decades. Theoretically relevant is the fact, that, while the extension of the urban way of life is not limited to urban areas, the accentuation of this way of life in Germany still seems to develop at a much faster rate in urban than in rural areas.

Comparing the German materials with those obtained in the United States (Table 8 overleaf) we find, first of all, a close correspondence concerning the general long-term trend: the proportion of the American respondents indicating a predominance of the father/husband declines from 23 per cent for the parent generation to 8 per cent for the present generation while the respective percentages for the category "jointly" show an increase from 45 to 81.

The comparative data also tend to support—as far as survey data of this kind can provide such a support—the well-known observation that the emergence of new relationships between spouses, characterized as the development from the traditional-patriarchal type toward a more equalitarian-companionship type, has proceeded farther in the United States than in Germany. While we find a proportion of 17 out of 100 married respondents stating a predominance of the husband in their own family in the German sample, the respective figure for the United States is 8 per cent; and while we find that 63 out of 100 in the German sample indicated joint decision, the figure is 81 for the United States.

The generational comparison for the two countries, in addition, seems to indicate that the American family has changed with a higher rate of acceleration during the last decades as compared with the German family. Table 9 (p. 294) gives the ratios between the proportions in the parent and the present generation stated by the respondents. For the predominance of the father/husband it shows ratios of 0.57 for Germany and 0.39 for the United States, i.e. a considerably higher decrease for the United States; the corresponding increase in the category "jointly" is expressed in the ratios of 1.28 for Germany and 1.82 for the United States. These data are not completely consistent with the notions implicit in a good part of the literature on the German family. However, the results of our analysis are more explorative than definitive and a more rigorous testing of the hypothesis of differential acceleration in family changes must be carried out in connection with other comparative data.

The outstanding feature of Table 8, presenting the data on

TABLE 8. RURAL-URBAN AND GENERATIONAL DIFFERENCES IN PREDOMINANCE OF HUSBAND AND WIFE, UNITED STATES, 1959

Predominance	Rural area		Town area		City area		Total	
	(%)	(N)	(%)	(N)	(%)	(N)	(%)	(N)
Parent generation: husband	25	(132)	24	(55)	18	(34)	23	(221)
Present generation: husband	8	(19)	12	(18)	7	(23)	8	(60)
Parent generation: wife	11	(56)	17	(39)	20	(37)	14	(132)
Present generation: wife	7	(19)	6	(9)	7	(22)	7	(50)
Parent generation: jointly	47	(246)	42	(98)	43	(80)	45	(424)
Present generation: jointly	82	(211)	78	(118)	82	(251)	81	(580)
Parent generation: others	17	(89)	17	(40)	19	(36)	18	(165)
Present generation: others	3	(8)	4	(6)	4	(11)	4	(25)
Parent generation: total	100	(532)	100	(232)	100	(187)	100	(942)[a]
Present generation: total	100	(257)	100	(151)	100	(307)	100	(715)[b]

The classification of the Parent Generation is based on the place of birth of the respondents. The classification of Present Generation is based on place of residence of the respondents. Total sample 970 cases.
[a] No responses to place of birth 28 cases.
[b] Not married 155 cases.

predominance in the United States broken down by community size, is its consistency in showing that there are only slight rural–urban differences with respect to predominance. Another notable aspect is the parallel development between present and parent generation in both rural and urban areas—an aspect which can even be better recognized in Table 9 (overleaf), which presents the date in term of ratios.

Indeed, the data show that the structural changes within the American family developed at the same speed both in rural and urban areas, whereas the ratios indicate marked differences in the development within these areas. This seems to be in congruence with the interpretation of the earlier analysis of the fertility data, suggesting that the two countries Germany and the United States are in different phases in the processual development of urbanization.

SOME FURTHER REFLECTIONS ON URBANIZATION

When we try to summarize our findings, it should be kept in mind that not all the data intended to be included in the analysis were available for the preparation of this first report. This is especially true for the cross-cultural comparison with the data obtained in other countries. It is our impression, however, that already the limited material indicates that the development of rural–urban differentials regarding the family is far from being simple and global.

As a matter of fact, the material suggests the differentiation of distinct phases in the process of urbanization. One of the phases might be characterized by an increase of a close interdependence of values and norms in which, however, the levelling in the performance lags behind. This situation was to be found in the United States during the last decades with respect to fertility. The prevailing conditions in Germany regarding fertility measures, with an only slight tendency to a diminuation of rural–urban differentials even of values and norms, may be recognized as another phase.

TABLE 9. RURAL-URBAN AND GENERATIONAL DIFFERENCES IN PREDOMINANCE OF HUSBAND
AND WIFE, WEST GERMANY AND UNITED STATES, 1959, IN RATIOS[a]

Predominance	Rural area		Town area		City area		Total	
	W.G.	U.S.A.	W.G.	U.S.A.	W.G.	U.S.A.	W.G.	U.S.A.
Father/husband	0.67	0.32	0.51	0.50	0.50	0.39	0.57	0.39
Jointly	1.14	1.72	1.40	1.88	1.42	1.90	1.28	1.82

[a] The ratios express the proportions in the present generation as compared with the proportions in the parent generation. Methodologically this must be considered a very crude measurement, which, however, seems to suffice for the present purposes.

Besides these distinct phases whose occurrence is in line with the presently prevailing theoretical assumptions, there are indications which are at variance with these assumptions. For the United States the findings relative to the family structure— with a parallel development within rural and urban areas—show even more clearly than the analysis of the fertility data how far America has proceeded in the development toward a homogeneous urbanized society as far as the way of life is concerned. However, the fact that with respect to the social–psychological structure of the family the rural–urban differences during the last decades became greater instead of smaller in Germany, gives evidence that there is not necessarily a strong relationship between urbanization as measured by proportions of rural and urban population on the one hand and the extension of the urban way of life in the society at large on the other.

It is mainly this deviation from the commonly accepted theoretical postulates, which stimulates the formulation of a set of hypotheses that takes into account a complex and refined conception of the processual development of urbanization. An attempt to formulate such hypotheses should be made in connection with further analysis of data obtained on an international basis.

Urbanization and Nuclear Family Individualization ; A Causal Connection?

G. A. KOOY

INTRODUCTION

A revolution never causes a complete break with the past. However far-reaching its consequences, there is always some continuity. It is therefore not legitimate to maintain that through the industrial and French revolutions Western history entered a new phase in which nothing remained of the preceding phase. Far from it: in all fields old values, traditional ways of thinking, and usages balanced out in the past are still at work. However, the two revolutions mentioned above did establish a new cultural era despite all the remaining ties with the previous period. In this instance there is much new under the sun.

The present phase in Western history beginning with the industrial and French revolutions is characterized by a dynamism which overshadows that of all preceding dynamic phases. Not only do some states decline rapidly in power and influence while others come to the fore, but there are also frequent and profound changes in the responses of groups and individuals. These changes constantly occur in almost all sectors of human life. While it is extremely difficult to determine all the main currents in our present dynamic times, some four trends certainly play a governing if not a dominating role in the existence of modern man and society in the West. These are *mechanization, secularization, socio-cultural differentiation, and individuation.*

Never before have techniques based on scientific findings acquired a determining role in human life. Social and cultural life is now highly linked with and dependent on the machine.

In the eighteenth century the predominating implements were operated as an extension of the human hand; they were restricted in their action by the human rhythm of work. In the nineteenth century the machine, made independent of the human hand, begins to play a governing role. Although adapted to human needs, and originating from human intervention, the machine itself begins to regulate the patterns of living of individuals and groups. Again, as never before, secularization begins to play a part. In the past, secularization, where it occurred, was the exclusive property of the cynical elites who had lost faith in the religious myths of their ancestors. Now the idea that life on earth is the here-and-now has a meaning independent of the hereafter, is shared by the "masses". In so far as Christianity is followed, secularization works in such a fashion that life is generally "partitioned". Economics, culture, in a narrower sense, and recreation are becoming independent units no longer subject to religion.

Did social and cultural differentiation ever occur to such a degree and at such a rate as in the present Western development? The mental horizon has been expanded and at the same time narrowed with the extremely rapid multiplication of separate domains of work and life, of specific outlooks, and of specific social units. In addition there is do doubt that modern Western man has developed a degree of self-consciousness surpassing that of any previous epoch. Of course, even among primitives there are highly self-conscious individuals, but never before has the ego of the ordinary man so focused upon himself as in the West of the present.[1]

These tendencies must have had a striking influence on the nuclear family life of all classes of society. To specify what this is and how it has occurred is no mean task. The family sociologist

[1] Considering mechanization, secularization, socio-cultural differentiation, and individuation the four main trends in the present West, the author does not consciously follow any particular sociologist, historian, philosopher, or time critic. Probably his evaluation reflects most the ideas and observations of several thinkers whose work he has tried to assimilate critically as an empirical sociologist. Among them are Emile Durkheim, Alexander Ruestow, Ortega y Gasset, Hans Freyer, David Riesman, and Erich Fromm.

faces great difficulties in obtaining accurate information and insights concerning the sociologically typical features of modern Western development in the family, not to mention the task of disentangling the causes of these typical features. The reflections which follow are designed to clarify and sharpen some of these problems and to suggest possible solutions. One typical feature which will receive special attention is the tendency of the nuclear family in the West toward individualization as this is affected by the phenomenon of urbanization within the Western world.

CLARIFICATION OF TERMS

The sociologist studying the nuclear family is especially interested in the following aspects: its structure, its functions, its psychic climate and its hierarchic dependency relations with the surrounding society.[2] Thinking and speaking of nuclear family individualization, the family sociologist is not concerned in the first instance with the structure, the functions or the psychic climate, but with the hierarchic dependency relations of the nuclear family in regard to its environment. It is true, however, that structure, functions, and psychic climate in their particular temporary–local nature often reflect the specific temporary–local "colour" of this relation. What, then, should be understood by nuclear family individualization? Nuclear family individualization develops when the nuclear family's traditional subordination to the objectives of other institutions is replaced by a morally acknowledged autonomy of the smallest kin group; that it creates its own closed world in order to live its own life. If this definition proves correct a danger remains yet of its being misunderstood. Probably it is therefore not completely superfluous to dwell further upon the traits of nuclear family individualization.

---

[2] No doubt approaches differ in family sociology. The article by Reuben Hill and Donald A. Hansen, The identification of conceptual frameworks utilized in family study, *Marriage and Family Living* **22,** 299–311, contains an excellent picture of different preoccupations with the topic. Nevertheless, those who consider the nuclear family as an institution, pay attention more or less explicitly to the four aspects mentioned.

It is definitely not justifiable to say that nuclear family indi-vidualization and nuclear family isolation are identical. A nuclear family with a low degree of individualization may live a highly isolated life, e.g. when after a geographical move it is not accepted in its new social surroundings. On the other hand, a highly individualized nuclear family may maintain frequent and emo-tionally profound contacts with the outside world. The degree of communication and interaction with others is not a criterion for nuclear family individualization. A more suitable criterion is the degree of esteem of the "choice relations", the relationships which ultimately may be broken, and which in their nature require a degree of privacy. Relatives, neighbours, friends, and other acquaintances may meet with a warm reception up to a certain point, in the highly individualized nuclear family, but at this point they are made to understand that they are "strangers" by this family. Their continued presence is seen as a painful intrusion on the family's integrity. Indeed, an index of nuclear family individualization in space and over time might be the ratio of nuclear family households to households containing extended family members. However, one should be most cautious in applying this standard to large populations. Statistical investi-gations concerning nuclear family individualization by determ-ining the relative frequency of the number of nuclear family households, is only justified when it is certain that true nuclear family individualization rather than family isolation is being measured.

Nuclear family individualization as described above is un-doubtedly a typical phenomenon of our modern Western society. Many serious investigators have stated this both implicitly and explicitly.[3] The modern nuclear family as compared with the

[3] The trend is described as typical for the present Western phase by leading American family sociologists, for example, Ernest W. Burgess and Harvey J. Locke, *The Family: From Institution to Companionship* (New York: American Book Company, 1953), by the well-known German sociologists René Koenig, *Materialien zur Soziologie der Familie* (Bern, 1946) and Ferdinand Oeter, *Familie im Umbruch* (Guetersloher Verlaghaus Gerd. Mohn, 1960) as well as by the great French scholar Emile Durkheim in a number of his publications.

family in earlier centuries does not subject itself willingly to the interests and desires of other groups, such as kinship extensions, the neighbourhood, the guild, the church, and/or the State. In its behaviour and judgement it gives evidence that it desires independence and freedom such as was never before demanded in the West.

It is not difficult to find a provisional explanation for nuclear family individualization as a general and continuing process both in the present Western epoch, and in places where the process has not yet come to full term. This process can be understood best by placing it against the background of the four trends already identified: mechanization, secularization, socio-cultural differentiation, and individuation. In their mutual interaction they enable modern man to discover that only in the nuclear family can he hope to find the optimal fulfilment of his most profound desires.

A closed family, that is an independent, nuclear family, appears to meet, as does no other social unit, man's needs for personal freedom and affective protection in a world where these needs are repeatedly ignored. If nuclear family individualization can be ascribed to the interaction of the four trends described above, then it seems clear that nuclear family individualization also has its basis in urbanization. Two reasons may be advanced. The first is that the city far more than the country is the milieu where life is subjected to the depersonalization tendencies alluded to above. The second is that the city has more and more become *the* milieu of modern Western man. Those who consider nuclear family individualization as a predominantly urban phenomenon therefore seem to argue correctly from the impressionistic data at hand. At least we should reckon with the possibility that they are right and see what tests can be devised to confirm or disconfirm their theory. Before proceeding in that direction let us clarify what is meant by urbanization, giving its properties and components.

Urbanization, of course, is the development of typically urban features, that is, the development of those characteristics specific to the city. On analysing its properties in social terms it appears that different sociologists often have different variables in mind.[4] Sometimes the definition of urbanization is restricted to conglomerations of population residing in a relatively limited area of geographical space first occupied by plants and animals and now occupied by men and their houses. This might be called *physical urbanization*. However, this physical urbanization is apparently accompanied by the development of a typical urban mentality. Those who participate in dense conglomerations are subjected to mental influences, which make them distinct from residents of less dense conglomerations such as rural residents. Physical urbanization is thus accompanied by *mental urbanization*. Sociologists talking about urbanization often mean the change in mentality consequent to physical urbanization. That there is a correlation between these two phenomena cannot be denied, but so far few empirical results have been assembled to demonstrate how close the relation is. A number of questions need to be asked: How far are the norms and values of the average inhabitant of an average city less "past bound" than those of the average country-dweller? How much does the "pastboundness" in norms and values decrease as the size of city increases? These are questions about which sociologists have opinions but for which they have no ready answers. Still a third expression of urbanization is that used by rural sociologists who see the transfer of the mentality of the city-dweller to the country-dweller as urbanization, a characteristic development of the modern Western countryside.

Which of these several uses of urbanization is most related to nuclear family individualization? Let us first reject the concept of urbanization as the transfer of urban mentality to the country-dweller. If this were to be the case, comparisons between city

---

[4] It would go too far to quote authors who represent the different views upon urbanization, even names and titles are omitted here. However, in H. P. Fairchild's *Dictionary of Sociology*, New York, Philosophical Library—urbanization: "The process of becoming urban; the movement of people or process to urban areas; the increase of urban areas, population, or processes." It is questionable whether this definition really clarifies the concept.

and countryside would be excluded. Indeed, even if it were true that the countryside is being urbanized, it is not clear whether the city has contributed more to nuclear family individualization than the countryside itself. Using the term urbanization in the sense of mental urbanization also has disadvantages. Notwithstanding the change in mentality as a possible correlate of city growth, no guarantee exists *a priori* that the mentality of all those living in cities will be less "past bound" than of those living in the countryside. There are several indications that rural individuals are more "urban" in thought and action on some issues than the inhabitants of the largest cities.[5] Without necessarily rejecting the notion that physical urbanization has a mental correlate, we would be better served to limit the term "urbanization" to physical urbanization if we wish to test the relationship between urbanization and nuclear family individualization. An objectively circumscribed urban milieu placed against an objectively circumscribed rural milieu, appears indispensable for the reliable measurement of the influence of urbanization upon nuclear family individualization.

Studies of nuclear family individualization have taken place in several different countries. Seven studies have been made by the author himself or under his guidance, in which the phenomenon of nuclear family individualization was considered thoroughly. The most recent of these Wageningen studies throws some light upon the connections between these two phenomena. Because it is impossible to dwell here upon the other six studies, it is stressed, that together they contributed a qualitative basis for the statistical investigation which is described below.[6] These

---

[5] An interesting example of modernization preceding urbanization is that of Het Oldambt, a rural region in the Netherlands. The remarkable development of the region is brilliantly described by E. W. Hofstee, *Het Oldambt— vormende krachten*, Groningen, 1938. It is a pity that this exemplary sociographic analysis of the leading Dutch rural sociologist has not yet been translated.

[6] The six Wageningen studies are:

G. A. Kooy: *Het veranderend gezin in Nederland*, Assen, 1957, pp. 241.

G. A. Kooy: *De oude samenwoning op het nieuwe platteland*, Assen, 1959, pp. 270.

A. F. Bosma: Het contact met buren en familieleden in een Wagenings flat-milieu, mimeographed M.A. thesis, not published, pp. 45.

studies were all undertaken in rural as well as in urban surroundings. As a result of their findings the author ventured to use official statistics for an investigation into nuclear family individualization in all of the Netherlands' 1000 municipalities.

METHODS

In 1940 a new census was planned in the Netherlands, but the war intervened and the census was carried out in 1947. Although many valuable data were obtained, it was considered necessary to hold a second census in order to get a better insight into the shortage of houses caused by the war and the rapid increase in population. This particular census—the General Housing Census —was held on 30 June 1956. In many respects this census, which was intended to be more restricted than a normal one, has provided the sociologist with as much material as that of 1947. The Central Bureau of Statistics at The Hague published two reports which have considerably eased the efforts of the present author to become better informed about the relation between urbanization and nuclear family individualization. These reports are *General Housing Census, 30 June* 1956; *series B. Principal regional data; part I, Dwelling stock and dwelling occupation Typology of the*

D. A. de Vries: Een onderzoek naar de beoordeling van de maisonette als type flatwoning in Den Haag en naar de individualisatie van het daarin wonend gezin, mimeographed M.A. thesis, not published, pp. 115.

A. Hartmans- V. d. Ende: *Het contact met buren en familieleden in een Wageningse arbeidsbuurt*, non-published M.A. thesis, pp. 41.

W. H. Douma: *Het gezinsleven op een verstedelijkend platteland*, bull, no. 20 of Department of Sociology, Wageningen, pp. 129 (English Summary added). The foreign reader will find a brief treatment of the subject dealt with by *De oude samenwoning op het nieuwe platteland* in: E. W. Hofstee and G. A. Kooy: Traditional household and neighbourhood group: survivals of the genealogical-territorial societal pattern in Eastern parts of the Netherlands (Reprinted above, p. 263)

G. A. Kooy: The traditional household in a modernized society, *Recherches sur la famille*, **3**, (1958), Göttingen.

G. A. Kooy: "Sistema sociale e problema dell'invecchiamento" (Longevità, anno IX, pp. 10–22).

Dutch municipalities according to the degree of urbanization, 31 May 1947 and 30 June 1956.[7]

The report containing the principal regional data of the General Housing Census formed the point of departure of the author's method to measure the degree of nuclear family individualization in the different municipalities and regions of the Netherlands. Although completely aware of the desirability of measuring this degree with a "multi-dimensional" yardstick, the author realized the use of such a yardstick would be a practical impossibility. Because of time and money limitations the measurement could only take place on the basis of already collected official statistical data. Contact with the Head of the Bureau's Department for Population Statistics showed that data could be obtained to enable a provisional determination of the degree of nuclear family individualization in each municipality. This unpublished material made it possible to set apart from all private households counted in a municipality in June 1956, those cases in which the author was really interested.

During the General Housing Census the *dwelling* functioned as a starting point for the distinction of households: "A dwelling is regarded as a room or suite of rooms and their accessories, which forms a permanent building, or a structurally separated part of a building, and which by the way it is built, rebuilt, converted, etc., is intended for habitation by one private household. As criterion each dwelling must have a separate access to a street (direct or via/garden or grounds) or to a common space within the building (staircase, passage, gallery, and so on)."[8] The author's objective now was to receive full information about these cases in which, *for reasons other than housing shortage*, a nuclear family lived in a dwelling with one or more relatives.[9] The data

[7] Both reports are written in Dutch, with an English summary.

[8] The quotation has been taken from the English Summary of *General Housing Census*, 30 *June* 1956; *series B, Principal regional data; part I, Dwelling stock and dwelling occupation*. This summary contains the definition of all basic concepts used during the General Housing Census.

[9] Regarding the reason for joint residence (two households in the same dwelling), the Central Bureau of Statistics remarks: "In considering whether joint

were available, in such a form that three categories of cases, occurring in different tables, had to be added to obtain the desired sum total. The first table contained all cases in which two related nuclear families lived in the same dwelling, but formed separate households. The second table included the cases, in which a nuclear family and a related single person shared a dwelling as separate households, while the third gave those cases, in which a nuclear family and one or more related single persons formed one household. The statistical material of the Central Bureau has been assimilated according to the following formula:

$$\frac{\begin{array}{ccc} & \text{nuclear family plus} & \text{nuclear family plus} \\ \text{2 related nuclear} & \text{related single} & \text{one or more single} \\ \text{families, forming} & \text{person forming} & \text{persons in same} \\ \text{separate households} + & \text{separate households} + & \text{household} \end{array}}{\text{multi-person households} + \text{single-person households}} \times 100$$

In this way a percentage for the degree of nuclear family individualization was obtained for each of the 1000 Dutch municipalities on 30 June 1956. This percentage was also calculated for groups of municipalities which either were part of the same region or belonged to the same urbanization category.

As elsewhere in the Netherlands, until recently, municipalities were classified according to number of inhabitants. *A Typology of the Dutch municipalities according to the degree of urbanization* contains the results of an endeavour to reach a sociologically more satisfactory distinction between rural and urban municipalities. In this report the smallest administrative units of the Netherlands are divided into twelve categories, which are supposed to represent the different phases of urbanization visible on 31 May 1947 (date of the first post-war census) and 30 June 1956. The

residence has been caused by housing shortage or not we relied on communications of the occupants, whereby an important indication has been whether the party living in had been registered for an independent dwelling at the housing office. Joint residence based on financial considerations, care of parents, etc., has not been considered as a necessary joint residence caused by housing shortage."

main criteria used for the rural–urban division are the following: (a) the number of inhabitants of the largest cluster within each municipality; (b) the percentage distribution of the economically active male population by branch of industry; (c) the number of salaried employees to 100 wage earners; (d) the density of built-up area based on the ratio of one-family houses to multi-family houses, and (e) the percentage of commuters of the economically active male population. Operating these 5 yardsticks in combination, the Central Bureau of Statistics reached a division of the Dutch municipalities regarding their degree of physical urbanization which has placed all Dutch sociologists in their debt.[10] To be sure, the division is not perfect, but it is greatly improved over its predecessor. The author has not hesitated to adopt this operational classification for testing the validity of the proposition that nuclear family individualization and urbanization are closely connected.

For an understanding of the results of the investigation some further attention is necessary to the components entering into the classification of urbanization devised by the Central Bureau of Statistics. The new typology embraces twelve classes of urbanization of which three may be distinguished as major divisions and the balance as sub-classes. The major divisions are category A: municipalities of a predominantly rural character; category B: municipalities of a transitional character, and category C: municipalities of a predominantly urban character. Each of these major categories are further subdivided into 3, 4, and 5 sub-classes respectively. The characteristics of these several classes and the numbers of municipalities for each in 1946 and 1956 are presented in table form in Table 1, Municipalities by Degree of Urbanization on 31 May 1947 and 30 June 1956. From a comparison of these figures in the third and fourth columns the reader gets

[10] A critical reader will realize that urbanization as measured by the Central Bureau of Statistics is actually more than physical urbanization, because of the socio-economic data employed. The author feels no need to defend himself extensively at this point. Let it suffice here to state that the typology is at least fully independent of the *mentality* of the inhabitants of municipalities with different degrees of urbanization.

TABLE 1. MUNICIPALITIES BY DEGREE OF URBANIZATION ON
31 MAY 1947 AND 30 JUNE 1956

Category	Characteristics	Number of municipalities	
		1947	1956
A1	Rural municipalities with over 50% of total economically active male population in agriculture (including fisheries). Number of inhabitants of largest cluster less than 5000	411	173
A2	Same as A1, except percentage of those working in agriculture is 40–50%	158	181
A3	Differing from A1 and A2 because percentage in agriculture is between 20 and 40%	174	316
B1	Industrialized rural municipalities (over 50% of economically active male population in industry). Largest population cluster less than 5000 inhabitants	73	125
B2	Industrialized rural municipalities with largest cluster having 5000–20,000 inhabitants	43	52
B3	Specific resident municipalities of commuters (over 30% commuters of the economically active male population as well as over 40 salaried employees to 100 wage-earners)	34	32
B4	Municipalities which, because of their heterogeneous composition (partly urban, partly rural) could not easily be included in one of the other sub-categories	15	16
C1	Country towns (2000–10,000)	40	38
C2	Small towns of 10,000–30,000	32	31
C3	Towns of 30,000–50,000	14	10
C4	Towns with 50,000–100,000	12	17
C5	Cities of 100,000 and more	10	12

a quick picture of the rapid development of physical urbanization in post-war Netherlands.

FINDINGS

If the yardstick adopted for the determination of nuclear family individualization in the Dutch municipalities is sufficiently discriminating there should be wide differences in the degree of family individualization in the Netherlands. It is possible to show the distribution of municipalities in the Netherlands by percentage of joint residences to total number of households, the reciprocal of the percentage of nuclear family individualization. Differentiation is most apparent in those municipalities which are at the extremes in joint residence, those above 25 per cent and below 5 per cent. Thirty scored lower than 5 per cent, and eighteen scored higher than 25 per cent. The range is from 40 per cent joint residence in one municipality to as low as 1 per cent joint residence in a municipality in category A3 which is predominantly rural in character. Two short comments seem in order here. It is remarkable that the thirty municipalities with a percentage lower than 5 are for the greater part non-urban. Nuclear family individualization has apparently gone very far in certain parts of the rural Dutch milieu. Indeed, it is very nearly as characteristic of rural areas as built up urban agglomerations. Another discovery is that municipalities with extreme values (less than 5 or more than 25 per cent) are clustered regionally. Their distribution is an affirmation of the proposition that nuclear family individualization in the Netherlands appears to correspond with regional cultural patterns even more than with rural–urban differences.[11]

The correspondence between the character of regional and nuclear family individualization as it was measured by the author can be better expressed by grouping the municipalities into so-called agricultural areas of which the Central Bureau of Statistics distinguishes some 120 for the country as a whole.[12] While it is true that the agricultural areas are not identical with cultural

[11] A common sociological nomenclature not yet having been reached, the author feels obliged to define the concept of "culture pattern" as he uses it. For him a culture pattern is a pattern of value orientations in a group, exercising a thorough influence upon the actions of both the group and its individual members.

[12] The agricultural areas which the Central Bureau of Statistics distinguishes are areas characterized by the type of agriculture practised. For their distinction a number of criteria were used, for instance, farm size and arable farming, versus cattle breeding.

areas, in several instances their boundaries are the same as those of cultural regions, while in several other instances a combination of agricultural areas forms a cultural region. The degree of nuclear family individualization per agricultural area was calculated, through the omission of all the more urbanized municipalities in an area. The calculation was only related to A1, A2, A3, B1, B2, B3, B4, and C1 municipalities as they are described in Table 1 (70 of 1003 municipalities were omitted). The reason for the omission of the more urbanized municipalities can be explained very briefly. Because larger population centres in the Netherlands are often characterized by a high influx of people from outside the region, their insertion into the calculation would probably have upset the individualization picture shown by the original population of a region.

There are differences between agricultural areas in the degree of individualization of the nuclear family. It would be possible to draw a map which would divide the Netherlands into three large zones of nuclear family individualization. There would be an almost closed zone where many, or even most, nuclear families live together with relatives. This zone, although penetrating into the heart of the country, no doubt represented relationships which traditionally existed on either side of the Dutch–German boundary. It expresses the existence of a folk culture grown and maintained in isolation from the dynamic development along the North Sea coast.[13] In this folk culture there was little room for the growth of an individualistic conception of life and thus hardly a need for self expression and privacy as they are expressed in nuclear family individualization. To prevent any misunderstanding: in technical and economic respects this "dark" zone has been rapidly modernized during the last ninety or one hundred years, but in its basic social relationships it is still "lagging behind" the rest of the Netherlands. In the second place

[13] On the partly surviving folk culture of the German–Dutch region which is often, but mistakenly called the Saxonian Region several historical and sociological studies have been published. One of them is the author's *De oude samenwoning op het nieuwe platteland;* another study is John and Dorothy Keur's *The Deeply Rooted*, Assen, 1955, pp. 208.

there is a "grey" zone where only an appreciable minority of the nuclear families share their houses with relatives, on the map designated by those agricultural areas with a percentage between 8 and 14. This zone can be defined as marginal, for it falls between the "dark" zone, and the areas where nuclear family individualization appears to have its focus, viz. the North-Western Netherlands. As can be shown easily, this marginal zone has been longer under the impact of modern trends than the Eastern part of the country.

Honesty, however, compels the author to confess his difficulty in giving a satisfactory explanation for the shape of this zone. According to his theory the picture should have been different in at least two areas, the Veluwe and North Bravant. Instead of being "grey", they should have been "dark" on the map. Provisional explanations for their "deviant behaviour" could be given, but in this context they are rather irrelevant. The "light" zone embracing the two northern provinces of Groningen and Friesland, the province of North Holland and the adjacent part of the province of South Holland is almost identical with that part of the Netherlands where modern trends are most clearly visible. It should be added that the modernization of life (technique, secularization, socio-cultural differentiation, and individuation) began very early in this section of the country, well before the beginning of the nineteenth century. The small republic which played such an important role in international politics in the sixteenth and seventeenth century was always only formally the Republic of the Seven United Netherlands. Endowed with an excellent geographical situation and a high natural soil fertility, the Groningers, Frieslands, Hollanders, and Zeelanders were those who represented the spirit and determined the policy of this remarkable republic which so successfully competed with Spaniards, Portuguese, French, and English. The population of the non-coastal provinces which did not lie along the great traffic roads and were not blessed with a fruitful soil missed that window upon the world necessary for a mobilization of its possibilities. In Drente, Overijssel, Guelderland, and the

other non-coastal parts of the country modern life hardly pene-
trated before the foundation of industry, the extension and the
improvement of the road system, and the introduction of artificial
fertilizers in the late nineteenth century.[14]

Until now nuclear family individualization in the Netherlands
has only been considered in its undeniably strong dependence on
regionally bound culture. It is time now to investigate whether
notwithstanding this strong dependence nuclear family individualization depends still more on urbanization. Table 2 contains
the answer. This table measures the degree of nuclear family
individualization (measured with the formula) in each urbanization class in each of the eleven provinces of the country as well
as in the Netherlands as a whole.

Table 2 does not leave the slightest doubt that nuclear family
individualization in the Netherlands is considerably more dependent on regional culture than on the degree of physical
urbanization. Indeed, in the country as a whole as well as in seven
of the eleven provinces, the percentage of the B category is lower
than that of the A category, while that of the C category falls
below that of the B class. For the Netherlands the difference
between the percentages of A and C is 3.9, for the seven provinces
(Overijssel, Guelderland, Utrecht, North Holland, Zeeland,
North Brabant, and Limburg) it is respectively 8.9, 8.1, 4.4, 0.9,
2.9, 3.7, and 9.3. For the rest of the provinces (Groningen,
Friesland, Drent, and South Holland) the percentage of B is
higher than that of A, that of C is higher than that of B, or that
of C is as high as that of B. Nevertheless, there the score of the
A category is also higher than that of the C category—in Groningen 1.0, in Friesland 0.4, in Drente 4.7, and in South Holland
2.1. From the foregoing it appears indeed, that urbanization
exercises an incontestable influence upon nuclear family individualization in the Netherlands. At the same time it is clear that

---

[14] As is quite understandable, a large number of historical studies on the
Netherlands exist. The foreign reader can find some indications of diverging
evolution between the diluvial and the alluvial Netherlands in Bernard Vlekke:
Evolution of the Dutch Nation (London, 1951, pp. 377).

TABLE 2. RELATED HOUSEHOLDS IN ... RELATIVES THAN NUCLEAR FAMILY MEMBERS AS PERCENTAGE OF ALL HOUSEHOLDS, 30 JUNE 1956

Urbanization class	Gr.	Fr.	Dr.	Ov.	Ge.	Ut.	NH.	SH.	Ze.	NB.	Li.	Neth.
A1	7.1	6.6	17.7	20.4	27.5	20.0	7.1	9.9	10.6	16.9	20.7	12.0
A2	7.4	7.0	12.7	20.4	19.8	13.0	7.0	10.3	10.6	13.8	21.4	12.2
A3	7.4	6.3	11.0	16.2	16.2	11.3	6.4	9.3	11.2	12.4	19.0	12.3
A1–A3	7.3	6.6	14.8	18.9	18.1	12.1	6.9	9.7	10.8	13.1	19.8	12.2
B1	6.8	7.7	—	16.3	16.0	8.7	6.6	8.3	9.5	10.7	14.9	11.7
B2	7.8	—	—	15.9	—	8.8	5.6	6.8	6.5	10.4	10.2	9.4
B3	8.4	—	—	—	10.5	8.5	6.5	6.8	—	7.9	—	7.6
B4	7.8	7.0	7.4	—	9.2	—	6.4	6.8	—	11.7	13.5	9.3
B1–B4	7.5	7.3	7.4	16.1	14.6	8.6	6.4	7.6	8.8	10.6	13.8	10.4
C1	6.0	6.3	11.8	13.4	10.2	9.7	6.5	8.9	9.9	12.8	10.2	9.3
C2	7.0	6.5	11.6	9.8	11.7	—	6.9	8.2	8.2	10.4	12.8	9.0
C3	—	—	6.8	8.4	7.8	—	5.5	6.6	6.3	8.6	10.6	7.7
C4	—	5.0	—	7.9	7.5	5.8	6.3	5.9	—	7.9	9.8	7.1
C5	4.8	—	—	9.9	7.2	5.7	5.5	6.1	—	7.6	—	6.7
C1–C5	6.3	6.2	10.1	10.0	7.7	6.0	7.6	7.9	9.4	10.5	10.5	8.3
A1–C5	7.2%	6.6%	14.0%	16.6%	16.1%	10.7%	6.6%	9.0%	10.5%	12.2%	16.3%	11.4%

Key: Gr. Groningen; Fr. Friesland; Dr. Drente; Ov. Overijssel; Ge. Guelderland; Ut. Utrecht; NH. North Holland; SH. South Holland; Ze. Zeeland; NB. North Brabant; Li. Limburg; Neth. Netherlands.

this influence is considerably less important than that of regional culture. The latter is indicated by the A percentages of Groningen, Friesland, and North Holland as against the C percentages of Drente, Overijssel, Guelderland, and Limburg. While these A percentages are respectively 7.3, 6.6, and 6.9, the C percentages compared with them are respectively 10.1, 10.0 and 10.5. There seems to be no need for a further proof of the preponderance of regional culture over urbanization, but a crucial point has not yet been explicitly noted. It is the influence of urbanization in regions with a low and with a high degree of nuclear family individualization. The conclusion appears to be justified that as a rule the influence of urbanization upon nuclear family individualization is substantially higher in regions with a low individualization degree than in those with a high degree. While in Groningen, Friesland, and North Holland with their high degree of nuclear family individualization the percentage difference between the categories A and C is 1.0, 0.4 and 0.9, in Drente, Overijssel, Gelderland, and Limburg—the least individualized provinces— it is 4.7, 8.9, 8.1, and 9.3.

SUMMARY

Urbanization is only a *secondary* factor in the process of nuclear family individualization in the Netherlands in the second half of the twentieth century. In this country its role in this process is almost negligible in those provinces where the basic trends of the present Western cultural phase are most advanced. The regions where urbanization is apparently a fairly weighty factor in the individualization process are these parts of the country which have been isolated and poor for ages and are now rapidly being taken into the modern cultural pattern of the West. This investigation shows that nuclear family individualization and urbanization are less connected than many are inclined to believe. Physical urbanization is at most a secondary factor in the process of socio-cultural change in the Netherlands of today.

INTERPRETATION OF FINDINGS: AN EPILOGUE

Why and how the city developed as a historical phenomenon is not entirely relevant. However, it is important, that as the city gained in significance it became more clearly marked in a socio-cultural sense. This development has been accompanied, of necessity, by the countryside becoming more clearly marked as well. From what was not differentiated before (at least not visibly) developed two-sided picture more or less in antithesis: city and countryside.[15] The two social categories can be described by enumerating their antithetic socio-cultural characteristics. Whereas the city in its more pronounced form had a relatively high population density and its inhabitants conducted preponderantly non-agrarian activities, the rural districts had a relatively low population density and its inhabitants found their subsistence in agriculture. It seems plausible that this explains the socio-cultural differences between city and countryside which are so striking to sociologists. The differences mentioned are in brief—internal heterogeneity and frequent but variegated contacts with the inhabitants of another territory among the city population against internal homogeneity and the infrequent and invariegated contacts with outsiders among the country population.

It should be remembered that the "world" of the country dweller was not the countryside in its totality, but the very small "world" of neighbourhood or village. It is quite understandable that the life of the city dweller in general was far less "past bound" than that of the country dweller. The city was the environment of economic and technical specialization of the social and religious "experiment", the countryside was the environment where life was mainly conducted along traditional lines.

For a long time the countryside refused to adopt new ways, or followed the urban milieu only very hesitatingly on the ways which the latter readily welcomed. However, when life in a number of Western countries is becoming dominated by modern

[15] The author dealt more extensively with this picture in his *De leefbaarheid van het platteland*, Verslag 106de Landhuishoudkundig Congres, pp. 63–74.

techniques—not least the modern technique of communication—
and by the modern ideology of democracy, the old contrast of
the standards of life within these countries fades away. Of course,
the countryside remains relatively homogeneous, but the frame
of reference of the country dweller, which was formerly his neighbourhood or village, may come to include the dynamic metro-
polis. Living and working in the countryside, and therefore
being an inhabitant of the country, means no longer that only
old local values are referred to.[16] It may now include an attitude
of adaptation-mindedness, more dynamic than that possessed by
many a large city dweller. We see, therefore, that in the countryside of Western countries, a mental differentiation is developing
within one and the same village or within one and the same
region. This creates a gap between those who are conservative
and those who desire innovation. What did not and could not
exist before is now taking place: country dwellers are becoming
estranged from one another by referring morally and affectively,
either to a local past or to a present reaching far beyond the local
boundaries. The contrast of town and country in the sense of a
progressive–dynamic versus conservative–static attitude to life
disappears and is replaced by a new contrast, viz. progressiveness
versus conservatism which cannot be explained by structural
differences between city and countryside. It is extremely difficult
to establish reasons here with accuracy. At any rate, it is far more
a question of differences in disposition than of objectified differences in overt behaviour. This difference in disposition, it should
be added here—presumably is due less to personal disposition
of character than to the mental climate of primary groups and
the degree of formal training which is stimulated by this climate.

In the foregoing it has been assumed implicitly that the urbanization hypothesis seems plausible in situations where the social
distance between city dweller and country dweller is still wide
and where, therefore, their mutual contact is slight. The hypothe-

[16] The characteristics of modern country life form the subject of the author's
attention in "The modern countryside—a sociological approach", *Notes and
Studies*, April 1962.

sis cannot be maintained, however, in situations where the social distance between city dweller and country dweller is small. Whether this revision is correct can be shown only through new and accurate inductive tests. In the meantime there is sufficient reason for sociologists to be a little more cautious with the term "urbanization". The suspicion arises that this factor, accounting for everything in the opinion of some, may actually explain little or nothing.

Old Age

The Extended Family in Transition: A Study of the Family Life of Old People in the Netherlands*

P. TAIETZ

SUMMARY—The data for this study were gathered in two Dutch townships, where a high proportion of the aged lived in extended families. Personal interviews were held with a total of 355 old persons. The attitudes and behaviour of the aged respondents toward sharing a household with children suggest that this norm does not have the salience nor is it as extensive as has been assumed. This conclusion is supported by the following pieces of evidence gleaned from the study: the deviations from the extended family norm; some indications of avoidance of joint living arrangements; an absence of common meanings and values between the aged and their children; and the high proportion of old people who express themselves negatively toward the extended family. The practice of leaving the farm to the oldest son and the limited occupational opportunities in the rural townships contribute to the decline in the prevalence of the extended family by virtue of the occupational and residential mobility of the sons. Given the above, one can predict that the emerging family structure in the eastern part of the Netherlands will be a household separate from children, a type that is characteristic of industrial society. But we can suggest on the basis of the evidence in the study that this set of events need not lead to the isolation and alienation of the aged from the adult generation.

* The data for this study were collected in The Netherlands in 1958 under a Fulbright Research Grant. Supplementary funds for the field work were provided by the United States Educational Foundation in the Netherlands and the Ministry of Social Work of the Netherlands. Funds for the analysis of the data were provided by the Faculty Research Grants Committee of Cornell University. I am most grateful to E. W. Hofstee, Head, Department of Rural Sociology, Agricultural University, Wageningen, The Netherlands, for making available to me the facilities of his department and for many other courtesies. Thanks are also due G. A. Kooy for his assistance in making arrangements with officials of the two townships and to W. J. Vriezen who most ably directed the field work operations.

THE RESEARCH PROBLEM

Interest in the present study developed from the hypothesis put forth by Hofstee (1957) concerning the attenuation of the extended family norm in the eastern part of the Netherlands. In this part of the Netherlands, the locus of the study, the extended family is still a meaningful social structure (Petersen, 1960). In its typical form it is characterized by the high value placed on maintaining the farm, undivided, in the same family. Toward this end, one of the sons, usually the oldest, is designated as the sole heir. His wife is subject to considerable supervision and guidance by the mother-in-law.

The patriarchal family is marked by strong obligations of filial responsibility based on traditional norms. The children must take care of the ageing parents and continue to obey them. When the children marry it is expected that the parents will share their household if the parents are not already part of the household of another child.

However, the social and economic modernization which this isolated part of the Netherlands is undergoing and the increasing individualism of the younger generation have brought into question the desirability of the extended family in its traditional form. There is resentment on two counts: (1) the young couples want their own home, and (2) those with children object to the excessive participation of the grandparents in the socialization of their children.

We cannot speak of a decline in the extended family in a statistical sense because we do not have comparative data from some previous points in time. Our contention is that if the norm of sharing a household with children is indeed undergoing transition then the present study should uncover the following tendencies: (1) lack of clarity in the norms of sharing a household with children and a certain amount of deviation from these norms; (2) lack of congruity between behaviour and attitudes toward living arrangements.

The data for the present study were gathered in February 1958 in the townships of Eibergen and Hedel in the province of Gelderland. These townships were selected as a sampling context because it was known that a high proportion of the aged in Eibergen and a somewhat smaller proportion of those in Hedel lived in extended families and because we were interested in investigating the differential behaviour and attitudes of the aged in these two communities toward the extended family.

THE SURVEY SAMPLE

Personal interviews were held with a total of 355 non-institutionalized old persons, 154 men and 118 women in Eibergen and 46 men and 37 women in Hedel. This represents almost a third (30 per cent) of all persons over 65 in the first and almost one-half (48 per cent) of those in the second community. A table of random numbers was used to select the samples from the municipal registers.

On most of the compositional characteristics the respondents in the two communities are quite similar. The people studied range in age from 65 to well over 90 with a median of 71.7 years. In terms of nativity and place of residence the older people constitute an extremely homogeneous and stable segment of the population. They are predominantly Protestant, few have gone beyond elementary school and none has ever attended a university. The women are more often widowed than the men. The modal income is less than 2000 guilders a year. Somewhat more of the men in Eibergen than in the other community are or have been farmers (55 per cent compared with 42 per cent). The men are typically retired, 63 per cent in Eibergen and 74 per cent in Hedel.

THE SHARING OF
A COMMON HOUSEHOLD WITH CHILDREN

However, it is in the family structure of the two communities that differences are sharpest. Considering the respondents who have living children, 84 per cent in Eibergen, compared with

64 per cent in Hedel, live in a household which includes one or
more of their children (Table 1). If we consider the proportion of
the aged who live in a three generation family as our criterion, the
difference between the two communities is even more striking:
62 per cent of the aged in Eibergen live in such families compared
with only 17 per cent in Hedel. In Eibergen living with children
is the modal pattern for both the aged farmers and non-farmers.
In Hedel whether the aged person is a farmer or not makes a
difference in his living arrangement: farmers live in a household
containing one or more of their children significantly more often
than nonfarmers (Table 2). Furthermore, aged parents in Eibergen typically share a household with their son and his family

TABLE 2. PERCENTAGE DISTRIBUTION OF LIVING ARRANGEMENTS
ACCORDING TO OCCUPATION AND COMMUNITY

	Eibergen		Hedel		Total	
	Farmer	Non-farmer	Farmer	Non-farmer	Farmer	Non-farmer
Children in household	80	70	70	38	78	60
No children in household	20	30	30	62	22	40
Total	100	100	100	100	100	100
Number of cases	83	61	20	29	103	90
	$\chi^2 = 1.5570$		$\chi^2 = 4.8713$		$\chi^2 = 7.0656$	
	D.F. = 1		D.F. = 1		D.F. = 1	
	$P = > 0.05$		$P = < 0.05$		$P = < 0.01$	

whereas aged parents in Hedel live more often with an unmarried
daughter (Table 3). It should be noted that sharing a household
with children does not mean bei ng dependent on the children.
In fact, in both communities adult children more often live in
the household of their elderly parents than the other way around
(Table 4).

TABLE 3. PER CENT OF OLD PEOPLE WHO SHARE HOUSEHOLD WITH
CHILDREN ACCORDING TO SEX OF CHILDREN AND COMMUNITY

	Eibergen	Hedel	Total
Has sons and daughters. Shares a household with:			
Son(s) only	61	32	56
Daughter(s) only	16	50	21
Daughter(s) and son(s)	23	18	23
Total	100	100	100
Number of cases	159	28	187

TABLE 4. PERCENTAGE DISTRIBUTION OF FAMILY STATUS OF AGED
ACCORDING TO COMMUNITY

	Eibergen	Hedel	Total
Head of household; children in household	52	35	48
Head of household; no children in household	22	47	28
Not head of household; children in household	22	14	20
Not head of household; no children in household	4	4	4
Total	100	100	100
Number of cases	272	83	355

The consequences of being without children are clearly shown in
Table 1. Only 3 per cent of the total sample who have children
live alone or in a household with unrelated persons compared
with 19 per cent in Eibergen and 47 per cent in Hedel who
have no children.

DEVIATIONS FROM
THE NORM OF THE EXTENDED FAMILY

Having children in the community and not sharing a household with them would seem to be an obvious instance of deviation from the norm of the extended family. In Eibergen, 13 per cent of those who have children in the community do not live with any of them. The proportion of deviant families is 44 per cent in Hedel. Furthermore, in both communities there are modifications of the extended family structure such as the old people having their own living room and eating alone, or living in the same dwelling but not the same household as the children, separate entrances, and other mechanisms of separation.

GEOGRAPHIC MOBILITY AND VISITING

Only 33 of the respondents have all of their children living at home. The remaining 273 have contacts of varying frequency with their children who live away from home. Table 5 shows that the frequency varies between communities and according to the residence of the children. The impact of geographic mobility in separating parents from children is rather vividly shown. Three out of four who have children in the community see one of them at least weekly. In contrast, only 10 per cent of the old

TABLE 5. PER CENT OF OLD PEOPLE WHO SEE A CHILD ONCE A WEEK OR MORE OFTEN, BY RESIDENCE OF CHILDREN AND COMMUNITY

	Eibergen	Hedel	Total
Children live within 10 km of parents	69 (187)	91 (55)	74 (242)
Children live elsewhere in Holland, Europe, or overseas	10 (144)	8 (36)	10 (180)
Total—children live away from home	64 (213)	86 (59)	69 (272)
All children, living at home or away from home	92 (240)	97 (66)	93 (306)

people who have children living outside of the community see one of them at least weekly. A significantly higher proportion of the old people in Hedel than in Eibergen have at least a weekly contact with one of their children who are away from home (86 per cent compared with 64 per cent, $\chi^2 = 48.029$, $P = 0.01$).

FAMILY STRUCTURE AND VISITING PATTERN

The finding that the old people visit with their children more often in Hedel than in Eibergen is rather surprising. We expected that the greater conformity to the extended family in Eibergen would result in a higher incidence of visiting in that community than in Hedel. This expectation is based on the implicit assumption of a positive relationship between visiting and sharing a household with children. However, an assumption of a negative association between visiting and extended family living is equally valid. Such a relationship can be interpreted by supposing that children will more likely make visits to aged parents who live alone than to those who already have one or more children living in the household. A third possibility is that visiting and sharing a household are independent of each other. And this indeed is the case as Table 6 shows. The old people who share a household with children do not have more frequent visits from other children than those who live without children. This suggests that the visiting pattern may not be a criterion of the extended family structure as we have supposed.

PREFERRED AND ACTUAL LIVING ARRANGEMENTS

If as the Dutch sociologists contend, the younger generation is dissatisfied with the extended family system, then it can be expected that many aged parents who shared a residence with their children will be in a situation of cross-pressure between the traditional norms which they hold and the transitional norms of the children. One of the findings of this study suggests that there is

TABLE 6. FREQUENCY OF VISITING ACCORDING TO FAMILY STRUCTURE AND COMMUNITY

Frequency of visiting	Eibergen		Hedel		Total	
	Children in household (per cent)	No children in household (per cent)	Children in household (per cent)	No children in household (per cent)	Children in household (per cent)	No children in household (per cent)
Low	38	49	30	4	37	33
Medium	38	36	35	67	37	47
High	24	15	35	29	26	20
Total	100	100	100	100	100	100
Number of cases	175	39	34	24	209	63

an absence of common meanings and values between the aged respondents and their children. Four out of five of the respondents agree that "So far as ideas are concerned, parents and children live in different worlds."

To measure the attitudes of the aged toward the extended family we asked them to react to the following: "If you had your choice which of the following living arrangements would you choose for yourself—to live in your own house; to live in your own house, but near children; to live in an old age centre; to live in a home for the aged; or to live with your children?" In Eibergen 56 per cent express a preference for living in a household with one of their children while only 24 per cent in Hedel state such a preference.

The preferred living arrangement is of greater significance when it is related to the actual living arrangements of the old people. For here we can uncover the presence of any disparity

TABLE 7. PREFERRED AND ACTUAL LIVING ARRANGEMENTS OF
RESPONDENTS WITH LIVING CHILDREN ACCORDING TO COMMUNITY

	Eibergen (per cent)	Hedel (per cent)	Total (per cent)
1. Prefers to live with children; does live with children	55	22	48
2. Prefers to live with children; does not live with children	a	2	a
3. Prefers not to live with children; does live with children	28	40	31
4. Prefers not to live with children; does not live with children	17	36	21
Total	100	100	100
Number of cases	234	64	298

ᵃ Less than 1 per cent.

between aspiration and achievement and it is this disparity which can lead to dissatisfaction. When the distributions of the variables measuring preference and actual living arrangements are dichotomized and cross-tabulated, four types of preference and achieved combinations result (Table 7). Types 2 and 3 show disparity and types 1 and 4 show congruity between preference and achievement. In Eibergen, 28 per cent are frustrated in their living arrangement aspirations compared with 42 per cent in Hedel.

Thus the two communities differ in the proportion of aged who are dissatisfied with their living arrangements. Another way of showing this difference is to note the modal type in the two communities. We observe that type 1 is modal in Eibergen. Here the aged prefer to live with children and actually do so. In Hedel, however, type 3 is modal; the old persons typically live with children but prefer another arrangement.

OCCUPATIONAL STRUCTURE AND FAMILY STRUCTURE

The relationship of the family system to the occupational system is most easily discernible in the extended farm family. Here, in sharp contrast to the situation in the nuclear family, occupational and familial roles are played within the same social system and the distinction between what is occupational and what is familial becomes blurred. Interpersonal relations are significant not only because of their impact on the kinship structure but also on the occupational structure. Success in the kinship and occupational structures is interdependent.

Two elements of the social structure contribute to an explanation of occupational mobility in the two communities: the farm succession pattern and the opportunity structure. In 59 per cent of the cases the oldest son only works on the farm with the father and is presumably the heir. This practice of primogeniture encourages some of the more ambitious sons to leave the family farm and even the community to seek better opportunities elsewhere. To remain on the farm where there is already an heir means being relegated to the permanent position of a farm labourer. Non-farm job opportunities are also relatively few in these townships and migration to Canada or the United States or moving to a larger city in the Netherlands is the answer for many of the sons. Our data bear out these contentions. Table 8

TABLE 8. PERCENTAGE DISTRIBUTION OF OCCUPATION OF SONS BY RESIDENCE AND COMMUNITY

Residence of sons	Eibergen				
	Farmer	Non-manual	Manual	Total	Number of cases
Same household with parents	53	11	36	100	180
In the community but not with parents	18	22	60	100	225
10–40 km away	9	37	54	100	67
Elsewhere in Europe and overseas	13	56	31	100	70
	Hedel				
Same household with parents	50	14	36	100	22
In the community but not with parents	11	33	56	100	80
10–40 km away	0	45	55	100	11
Elsewhere in Europe and overseas	6	72	22	100	18
	Total				
Same household with parents	54	10	36	100	202
In the community but not with parents	16	25	59	100	305
10–40 km away	8	38	54	100	78
Elsewhere in Europe and overseas	11	59	30	100	88

shows that half of the sons in both communities who live at home are engaged in farming with their parents and only 11 per cent in one community and 14 per cent in the other are engaged in non-manual occupations. As we move away from the household of the parents into the larger world, the proportion of sons engaged in professional and other white collar occupations increases to 56 per cent of those who originated in Eibergen and 72 per cent of those who had their origins in Hedel.

Education is a recognized channel for social mobility and is associated with geographic mobility. Of the 16 sons who have some university education 56 per cent migrated to other parts of Holland or other European countries, 19 per cent migrated to Canada, the United States or Australia, and 25 per cent live within 50 kilometers of their home. None of the sons who live at home or in the home community have been to college. (It is interesting to note parenthetically that none of the daughters have any college education.)

What of the sons who have been able to break away from the extended family and have moved up or down the social ladder? Do they maintain as frequent contacts with their parents as do those who have experienced no mobility? In short, we are interested in the relationship between social mobility and extended family relations, a topic which has received both theoretical and research interest in recent years.[1]

Before presenting our findings a few words about the measurement of occupational mobility are in order. We combined the

[1] Talcott Parsons (1949) has suggested that occupational mobility is antithetical to extended family relations. Gordon F. Streib (1958) suggests that social mobility of children may not have an adverse effect on family cohesiveness. E. E. LeMasters (1954) in an early study of the subject concludes that families which have not experienced social class mobility are those families "in which the aged parents live with their grown children with considerable consensus and mutual enjoyment". Recent research by Eugene Litwak (1960) posits an ideal type of family which he calls "modified extended" which differs from the classical extended family in that while it supports extended family values it is characterized by a high degree of structural differentiation in the familial and occupational systems. Litwak presents evidence to support his hypothesis that a modified extended family is consonant with occupational mobility.

occupations into three broad categories of *manual, non-manual,* and *farm* occupations. Two assumptions underlie the direction of movement: (1) a move from manual to non-manual employment constitutes upward mobility. This assumption is based on the generally accepted grounds that most male non-manual occupations receive higher prestige than most manual occupations; (2) a move from manual to farm constitutes upward mobility and a move from non-manual to farm constitutes downward mobility. This assumption can be defended by the evidence in this study that farmers are in an intermediate position between manual and non-manual respondents on education and income (Tables 9 and 10). For our measurement of family contacts we used weekly visits from sons to their parents.

TABLE 9. INCOME ACCORDING TO OCCUPATIONAL STATUS

Income	Non-manual (per cent)	Farmer (per cent)	Manual (per cent)
Low	24	41	67
High	76	59	33
Total	100	100	100
Number of cases	46	93	49

$\chi^2 = 18.3444.$
D.F. $= 2.$
$P = < 0.01.$

Table 11 shows that when geographic mobility is taken into account there is a relationship between occupational mobility and frequency of visits in both communities. Of the sons who live in the parents' community, those who are mobile with respect to their parents tend to visit less often than sons who are in the same stratum as their parents. This finding supports Parsons' hypothesis that occupational mobility is antithetical to family relations (Litwak, 1960).

TABLE 10. EDUCATION ACCORDING TO OCCUPATIONAL STATUS

Education	Non-manual (per cent)	Farmer (per cent)	Manual (per cent)
Low	50	60	84
High	50	40	16
Total	100	100	100
Number of cases	50	101	49

$\chi^2 = 13.383$
D.F. $= 2$.
$P = < 0.01$.

TABLE 11. PER CENT OF PARENTS WHO RECEIVE AT LEAST WEEKLY VISITS FROM SONS WHO LIVE IN THE COMMUNITY, ACCORDING TO OCCUPATIONAL MOBILITY OF SONS AND COMMUNITY

	Eibergen		Hedel		Total	
	Occupational mobility of sons					
Frequency of visits	Not mobile	Mobile	Not mobile	Mobile	Not mobile	Mobile
At least weekly	61	46	100	75	73	51
Less frequently	39	54	0	25	27	49
Total	100	100	100	100	100	100
Number of cases	130	93	58	20	188	113
	$\chi^2 = 4.621$ D.F. $= 1$ $P = < 0.05$		$\chi^2 = 11.606$ D.F. $= 1$ $P = 0.01$		$\chi^2 = 14.260$ D.F. $= 1$ $P = < 0.01$	

REFERENCES

HOFSTEE, E. W. (1957) *Rural Life and Rural Welfare in the Netherlands* (The Hague, Government Printing and Publishing Office), 12.
LEMASTERS, E. E. (1954) Social class mobility and family integration, *Marriage and Family Living* 16 (August), 226–32.

LITWAK, E. (1960) Occupational mobility and family cohesiveness, *Amer. Sociol. Rev.* **25** (Febr.), 9–21.

PARSONS, T. (1949) The Social Structure of the Family. In R. N. Anshen (Ed.) *The Family: Its Function and Destiny*, New York, Harper, pp. 191–2.

PETERSEN, W. (1960) The demographic transition, *Amer. Sociol. Rev.* **25** (June), 334–47.

STREIB, G. F. (1958) Family Patterns in Retirement, *The Journal of Social Issues* **14**, 46–60.

Relations between Generations and the Three-generation Household in Denmark*

J. STEHOUWER†

UNTIL about the beginning of this century it was still common and sometimes even preferred that one of the adult children remain with his parents, even after marriage. This has changed. Urban growth, industrialization, and mechanization of agriculture have contributed to the individualization of the nuclear family and have made generations less dependent on each other in both urban and rural areas. There is considerable evidence that elderly people now want to live near their adult children, but not with them.[1]

Considering this development, one is inclined to wonder what has happened to the household of three generations as well as to relations between generations not living under the same roof. This paper deals with these questions in relation to the situation in Denmark. The paper is divided into three parts.

In the first part, the living arrangements of elderly people in Denmark, their proximity to children, and their contact with children are described briefly. It has often been assumed that the aged in modern industrial societies are isolated from their children, especially in urban areas. The first part of this paper will deal with this question. Further, the situation of the aged in

* This research has been financed by a grant from the United States National Institutes of Health, MH 05509 and the Public Health Service, Chronic Disease Division, CH 0052-03.
[1] Gordon F. Streib, "Family Patterns in Retirement," *Journal of Social Issues* **14** (2) (1958), 46–60, Leopold Rosenmayr and Eva Köckeis, "Propositions for a Sociological Theory of Ageing and the Family," *International Social Science Journal* **15** (3) (1963), 410–26.

Denmark will be compared with equivalent data from sample surveys in Great Britain and the United States.

The second part of this paper will deal with factors which contribute to the establishment and maintenance of three-generation households and to the occurrence of such households in Denmark. Compared with non-Scandinavian European countries, Denmark has remarkably few people who live in three-generation households.

This observation leads to the third part of this paper, which deals with the relations between generations in Denmark. The fact that Denmark has a long-established tradition of social pension systems, health insurance, and housing policy for the aged makes the study of relations between generations an attractive object for cross-national comparisons.

The data of this paper derive from two sources. The first source is the study of the social well-being of the aged in Denmark, which is a part of a cross-national study in social gerontology, carried out in Britain, the United States, and Denmark.[2] The second source is the screening interview on household composition and health conditions, carried out by the Danish National Institute for Social Research in 1961, which was used as the sampling basis for three national sample surveys in Denmark. The data about the number and the composition of three-generation households in Denmark are a by-product of this sample survey.[3]

---

[2] This study is financed by grants from the United States National Institute of Mental Health and the United States Public Health Service, Community Health Services, Bureau of State Services, in all three countries. The general aim of this study is to secure comparable data about health, physical capacity, the employment status, the family relations, and the economic status of elderly people in these countries. In each country roughly 2500 persons aged 65 and over were interviewed during April–July, 1962. The national teams used the same sampling methods, questionnaires which included mainly comparable cross-national questions, similar definitions of variables, and similar interviewer instructions. The results of this study are published in: E. Shanas, P. Townsend, D. Wedderburn, H. Friis, P. Milhøj and Jan Stehouwer, "Old People in Three Industrial Societies", The Atherton Press, New York 1968, Routledge & Kegan Paul, London 1968.

[3] A 0.7 per cent stratified area probability sample of about 10,000 households.

THE LIVING ARRANGEMENTS OF ELDERLY PEOPLE:
THE PROXIMITY OF CHILDREN AND THE
FREQUENCY OF CONTACT

Urbanization and industrialization in Denmark started relatively late compared with other Western European countries. Denmark has a population of about 4.5 million people, one-third of whom live in the metropolitan area of Copenhagen. Another third live in the provincial towns, which range from less than 2000 to almost 180,000 inhabitants. Approximately half of those in provincial towns live in communities with less than 30,000 inhabitants. The rest of the population live in the rural areas of the country.

Approximately 6 per cent of the people aged 65 and over live in institutions.[4] Among older people who live in private households it is more common to live apart from children than together with them. Those elderly who live with children live with unmarried children. Very few elderly people in Denmark live with married children.

Differences within Denmark

As one might expect, we find the largest proportion of married elderly people living with children in the rural parts of the country. Our results show that in Denmark in rural areas nearly one-fifth of the elderly people live together with children. This, however, does not mean that these households function as traditional farm families of more than two generations living and working together. This type of household has nearly disappeared in Denmark.

The elderly living in the provincial towns differ from the elderly in Copenhagen as well as from those in the extreme rural areas in living arrangements as well as in relations to their children.[5]

[4] There are only estimates about the number of elderly people in nonprivate households. Census data are not yet available.

[5] Extreme rural areas are areas with less than 10 per cent of the population living in the built-up area of the community.

TABLE 1. THE LIVING ARRANGEMENTS OF PEOPLE AGED 62 AND OVER,
THEIR PROXIMITY TO NEAREST CHILD, AND CONTACT WITH CHILDREN
IN AREAS OF DENMARK[a]

Marital status and living arrangements	Copen-hagen (per cent)	Provincial towns (per cent)	Rural areas (per cent)	Extreme rural (per cent)	Whole country (per cent)
Married					
Total	100.0	100.0	100.0	100.0	100.0
Living with:					
Spouse only	77.9	84.0	75.3	60.8	77.8
Unmarried children	17.3	12.3	17.6	19.6	16.5
Married children	0.3	0.4	2.8	8.4	1.4
Others	4.5	3.3	4.3	11.2	4.3
$N =$	353	559	324	396	1632
Unmarried					
Total	100.0	100.0	100.0	100.0	100.0
Living alone	61.8	73.7	43.9	47.0	60.8
Living with:					
Unmarried children	19.2	14.5	30.3	22.6	19.6
Married children	5.5	3.9	12.1	19.5	8.4
Others	13.5	7.9	13.7	10.9	11.2
$N =$	297	330	132	164	923
Married (not living with children)					
Nearest child, more than hour away	6.4	25.0	17.4	19.0	18.1
Child not seen in last month	4.0	8.3	8.5	4.3	6.5
$N =$	296	492	260	300	1348
Unmarried (not living with children)					
Nearest child more than hour away	8.6	17.9	16.7	12.0	14.5
Child not seen in last month	10.3	8.4	12.8	10.1	9.8
$N =$	233	274	78	99	648

[a] Includes only persons with living children.

SOURCE: Jan Stehouwer, "Urban–Rural Differences in Contact between the Aged and their Children in Denmark," paper prepared for the International Social Science Research Seminar in Gerontology, Markaryd, Sweden, 1963.

In the provincial towns we find the largest proportion of elderly married people who live only with their spouse and the largest proportion who have their nearest child at a distance of more than 60 transport minutes, and the number of those who have not seen a child within the last month is about twice as high as that reported for Copenhagen or the extreme rural areas.

Among the unmarried aged we find almost the same pattern. Again the proportion of those who live alone is highest in the provincial towns. About twice as many in the provincial towns as in the Copenhagen area have their nearest child at a transport distance of more than 60 minutes. Contrary to the situation of married people, we find no significant differences in the frequency of contact with children for those who are single whether they live in Copenhagen, the provincial towns, or the rural areas.

Table 1 indicates that the probability that all children move away from the areas where their parents live is highest in the provincial towns, somewhat lower in the rural areas, and lowest in Copenhagen.

Our data reveal that one has to be careful with the hypothesis that urbanization leads to spatial separation between generations and towards isolation of the aged. The inclination for parents and children to see one another may still be greatest in the rural areas, but the possibilities of contact are greatest in Copenhagen —because the parents will more frequently find a child within the limited and densely populated area of Copenhagen than within any other area of the same size.

The Living Arrangements of People with Living Children, in Denmark, Great Britain, and the United States

Nearly three out of four elderly persons aged 65 or over in Denmark, Britain, and the United States have at least one living child. The proportions without children are: Great Britain 23.6 per cent, United States 24.4 per cent, and Denmark 24.5 per cent. Compared with Britain and the United States, however, we

TABLE 2. THE LIVING ARRANGEMENTS OF PEOPLE AGED 65 AND OVER
WHO HAVE LIVING CHILDREN

Marital status and living arrangements	Britain (per cent)	United States (per cent)	Denmark (per cent)
Married			
Total	100.0	100.0	100.0
Living with:[a]			
Spouse only	63.8	77.9	79.8
Married daughter	4.7	1.0	0.4
Married son	0.8	1.1	1.2
Unmarried child	25.9	14.6	14.9
Sibling	1.5	1.3	0.3
Grandchild	1.5	2.3	0.7
Other relative	0.6	0.8	0.3
Nonrelative only	1.2	1.0	2.4
$N =$	1022	1169	1183
Divorced, widowed, or single			
Total	100.0	100.0[b]	100.0
Living alone	38.7	46.5	61.1
Living with:[a]			
Married daughter	19.7	14.5	4.5
Married son	7.4	4.1	4.1
Unmarried child	26.8	24.1	18.4
Sibling	2.6	2.5	1.0
Grandchild	0.7	2.2	1.4
Other relative	0.9	1.4	0.8
Nonrelative only	3.2	4.6	8.7
$N =$	889	843	828

[a] Listing in priority order.
[b] Per cents do not add to total because of rounding.

find that Denmark has the lowest proportion of elderly people—
single or married—who live together with their children. As
Table 2 shows, we find in Denmark only 8.7 per cent of the aged
who are unmarried living together with married children compared to 18.6 per cent in the United States and 24.2 per cent in
Britain. In Denmark we find no difference in the proportion of
elderly people living together with the family of the married
daughter or married son. In Britain, the majority of the elderly,

single as well as married, who live with married children live together with the family of a married daughter.[6] In the United States typically single persons living with married children, live together with a daughter's family.

The Proximity of Children and the Frequency of Contact between Aged Parents and their Children

Although relatively few people in Denmark live together with their children, most old people live within a short distance from at least one child. Table 3 shows that about one out of eight elderly people in Denmark and Britain have their nearest child at a distance of more than 60 transport minutes. In the United

TABLE 3. THE PROXIMITY OF THE NEAREST CHILD TO PEOPLE AGED 65 AND OVER IN GREAT BRITAIN, THE UNITED STATES, AND DENMARK[a]

Proximity of the nearest child	People with living children		
	Britain (per cent)	United States (per cent)	Denmark (per cent)
Total	100.0[b]	100.0	100.0
Same household	41.9	27.6	20.1
10 minutes' journey or less	23.5	33.1	32.0
11–30 minutes' journey	15.9	15.7	23.0
31 minutes—1 hour	7.6	7.2	12.4
Over 1 hour but less than one day	9.1	11.2	11.2
1-day journey or more	1.9	5.2	1.3
$N =$	1911	2012	2009

[a] Unclassifiable 0, 0, and 4 respectively.
[b] Per cents do not add to total because of rounding.
SOURCE: Adapted from Peter Townsend, "Family of Three Generations", paper prepared for the International Social Science Research Seminar in Gerontology, Markaryd, Sweden, August 1963.

---

[6] Peter Townsend, "The Family of Three Generations," paper presented at the International Social Science Research Seminar in Gerontology, Markaryd, Sweden, August, 1963.

States the proportion is one to six. Our data support results from other surveys, which show that parents and children generally settle in the vicinity of each other.[7] In this respect, we find striking similarities among the three countries. Looking at the proportion of children living at a long distance from their parents, we must remember that the three countries vary greatly in size, which makes the relatively small number of elderly people with their nearest child within more than 60 transport minutes in the United States even more surprising compared with the corresponding proportions found in Denmark and Great Britain.

The majority of elderly people with living children are in daily or weekly contact with at least one of them. The proportion of people who have not seen a child within the last week is one in six in the United States and even smaller in Denmark and Britain. In Denmark this means that although very few elderly people live together with their children, the majority of them have daily or weekly contact with at least one child. Table 4 shows that

TABLE 4. WHEN PEOPLE AGED 65 AND OVER LAST SAW ONE OF THEIR CHILDREN[a]

Last time child seen	People with living children		
	Britain (per cent)	United States (per cent)	Denmark (per cent)
Total	100.0	100.0	100.0
Today or yesterday	69.3	65.0	62.3
Within previous seven days	17.3	18.7	21.8
Within previous month	7.4	6.8	9.8
Within previous year	4.2	7.0	4.8
More than a year ago	1.8	2.5	1.3
$N =$	1906	1996	2001

[a] Unclassifiable: 6, 16, and 12 for Britain, the United States, and Denmark respectively.

[7] Leopold Rosenmayr and Eva Köckeis, "A Method to Assess Living Arrangements and Housing Problems of the Aged," paper presented at the International Social Science Research Seminar in Gerontology, Markaryd, Sweden, August, 1963.

about two-thirds of the elderly in each country have seen at least one of their children today or yesterday. Among the British about 40 per cent of those with children live with a child, in Denmark only about 20 per cent. The data in Table 4 indicate that "not living together in Denmark" is highly compensated for by daily contact.

Summarizing our major results as to the living arrangements of the aged in Denmark, the proximity of children, and the frequency of contact with children, and the comparison with Great Britan and the United States, we can conclude that in spite of the fact that Denmark has a very high proportion of aged who live apart from their children, we find no differences in the proximity of the nearest child and the frequencies of contact with children between Denmark and the two other countries involved in this cross-national survey.

These results raise two questions: first, what has happened to the household of three generations in Denmark and, secondly, what are the relations between generations when elderly people do not live together with their children. In the next two sections we will try to throw some light on these problems.

THE THREE-GENERATION HOUSEHOLD

Why do so few elderly people in Denmark live in households consisting of three successive generations? Why in general do we find so few elderly people in Denmark who live with their children? The higher degree of institutionalization of elderly people in Denmark, compared for example with the United States, 6 per cent compared to 4 per cent, may have caused some of the difference—but evidently not the whole. The next pages first deal with factors which contribute to the establishment of three-generational living, secondly we summarize some recent evidence about the occurrence of three-generation households in Western European countries, and finally we describe the structure of the three-generation households which are still found in Denmark.

The Establishment of Three-Generation Households

Various reasons exist for the establishment of temporary or permanent three-generation households. In general, two main causes for such households can be distinguished: (1) dependence originating because the family functions as a joint enterprise involving two or more generations working together, and (2) need for help and care, offered either by first or second generation.

Economic dependence has traditionally been considered as one of the main reasons which have led to the establishment of three-generation households. Le Play's "La Famille Souche" in which one of the sons inherits the farm or business owned by his father, and continues to keep it for the family, is a good example of this kind of economic and functional dependence which leads to three-generational living, especially among farmers and small entrepreneurs.[8] In rural areas of Western Europe this type of farm family has been rather common and mainly patrilocal in structure.[9]

The need for help and care can be the reason for three-generational living in various circumstances. In some instances, the first or older generation offers help. Some such households are established, more or less on a temporary basis, for example, when an adult child marries, and the young couple must wait to get a dwelling for themselves. In these cases, a housing shortage may be a factor which contributes to the establishment of temporary three-generation households. A recent study of the housing conditions of newly married couples in Copenhagen, for example, has shown that 23 per cent of all couples start married life living with either his or her parents, and in a great number of cases the first child is born in this household.[10] Young and Willmot

[8] Frédéric Le Play, *L'Organisation de la famille*, 3rd edn. Tours: A. Mame et fils, 1884.

[9] J. P. Kruijt. Het gezin sedert de middeleeuwen, *Sociologisch Bulletin*, 4ᵉ Jaargang, No. 3 (1950) p. 81.

[10] K. Auken, *Familien lever*, Copenhagen, Gad, 1962, pp. 59 ff.

reported the same sort of households in East London.[11]

Another typical example of help offered by the first generation is seen when an unmarried daughter (or married, but temporarily separated from her husband) continues or returns to live with her own family. This has been a common pattern especially in times of war.[12]

Evacuation and acute shortage of houses caused by the destruction of war have also been common reasons for temporary and even permanent establishment of three-generation households, either in the family of the first or second generation.[13]

Finally, declining health among elderly people and the reduction of their capacity to take care of themselves are common reasons for the establishment of three-generation households in many countries. Instead of moving into an institution, the aged parents move to live with their children.

Discussing the structure of the three-generation household in Germany, Baumert makes the distinction between the new and the old type of three-generational living.[14] In the old traditional type of three-generation household, at least one of the children remains with the parents and in many cases continues to work on the farm or in the business which has been owned by the family for generations. In this type of household economic and

[11] Michael Young and Peter Willmott, *Family and Kinship in East London*, Pelican, A 595, Harmondsworth, Middlesex: Penguin Book Company, 1962, p. 31.

[12] William M. Smith, Jr., Joseph H. Britton, and Jean O. Britton, *Relationships Within Three-Generation Households*, College of Home Economics Research Publication No. 155, University Park: The Pennsylvania State University, 1958, p. 16. See also K. Ishwaran, *Family Life in the Netherlands*, The Hague, Van Keulen, 1959, chapter on: The Impact of the War on the Family, pp. 92 ff.

[13] Enrico Quarantelli, A note on the protective function of the family in Disasters, *Marriage and Family Living*, **22** (August 1960), 263–4. See also Marvin B. Sussman's review of the literature on this topic in his contribution in chapter IV of this volume.

[14] Gerhard Baumert, Changes in the family and the position of older persons in Germany, *Social and Psychological Aspects of Aging*, Clark Tibbitts and Wilma Donahue (Eds.), New York, Columbia University Press, 1962, pp. 416 ff.

occupational dependence together with family traditions is the main reason for three-generational living. In the new type, according to Baumert, the members of the second generation move away from the parental home, establish their own families, and later invite the parent(s) to live with them in cases of the former's widowhood, declining health, or physical incapacity.

Having no data for retrospective comparisons, it is doubtful whether we are able to speak about old and new types of three-generation households. It is indisputable that the number of three-generation households was larger about a century ago than it is now. It is also correct that the so-called "old type" or Le Play's "La Famille Souche" has been a frequent household type in the rural areas of Western Europe. This does not allow us to assume, however, that the other type of household, in which the first generation moves into the household of the second, is particularly new. Perhaps, this latter type is more urban than rural in origin. The lack of public care for the aged, the absence of medical care, and the very unattractive institutions for the aged 100 or even only 50 years ago must have been conditions which frequently contributed to the establishment of the three-generation household in urban areas. The three-generation household in which the children take care of their parent(s) who have moved into their household is not a new one. It may well be the remainder of an old, and perhaps traditionally urban type.

The Three-generation Household in Western Europe

Does the three-generation household still exist in Western Europe, and where do we find it? This is the next question which should be answered before we turn to a more detailed analysis of three-generational living in Denmark. There is evidence that the three-generation household is still a common arrangement among the population of poor agricultural and economically backward regions within a number of Western European countries, such as Italy,[15] the Netherlands,[16] and even Germany.[17]

The number of three-generation households in Europe is smallest in urban areas. In rural areas their frequency seems to vary with the regional traditions and the prosperity of agriculture. Rural sociologists in the Netherlands have ascertained that relatively many three-generation households still exist along the German frontier. The extended family system in Holland is confined to the sandy areas in the east and the middle of the country—which, up to the beginning of this century, as a result of geographical as well as social factors, have been extremely isolated. The farm family in these areas until recently has been a production as well as a consumption unit. Being small, the

TABLE 5. NUMBER OF GENERATIONS LIVING TOGETHER IN URBAN AND RURAL FAMILIES IN A WEST GERMAN CITY AND ITS HINTERLAND, PERCENTAGE DISTRIBUTION

Number of generations	Urban families ($N = 387$)	Total ($N = 434$)	Rural families		
			Nonfarm	Part-time farm	Full-time farm
One	36	25	27	35	7
Two	59	62	64	49	51
Three	5	12	9	15	37
Four		1		1	5

SOURCE: Gerhard Baumert, Changes in the Family and the Position of Older Persons in Germany, *Social and Psychological Aspects of Aging*, Clark Tibbitts and Wilma Donahue (Eds.), New York: Columbia University Press, 1962, p. 420.

[15] Aurelia Florea, *L'Anziano in Famiglia* (Roma: Comitato Italiano Per Gli Anziani, 1962) and some unpublished tabulations from a sample survey in rural parts of North and South Italy.

[16] E. W. Hofstee and G. A. Kooy, Traditional households and neighborhood groups, survivals of the genealogical-territorial societal pattern in Eastern parts of the Netherlands, 1954 (Reprinted above, p 263).

[17] Baumert, Changes in the family and the position of older persons in Germany, *op. cit.*

farms need no hired labor. Each member of the family and even sometimes members of the extended kin group are to some degree engaged in the farm work.[18]

In Baumert's study of Darmstadt in 1950 (see Table 5) 42 per cent of the full-time farm families had an extended family system of three or more generations living together. In contrast, only 5 per cent of the families in the city he studied lived in a three-generation household.

In Vienna, Rosenmayr and Köckeis found that almost 4 per cent of all households consist of three generations living together.[19] In one of six of these households the members of both adult generations were still married. In all other cases, either the grandparent or the parent (or even both) were widowed. From this, Rosenmayr and Köckeis conclude that "joint households thus seem hardly even to be maintained throughout adult life in urban industrial society but rather re-established when other relationships break off".[20]

The Three-generation Household in Denmark

Two of every hundred households in Denmark include three or more generations. Although the majority of the three-generation households in Denmark include aged persons, in a substantial proportion the first or grandparent generation is still at the stage where the youngest children are about to get married and leave the household. Both in absolute and relative terms we find

[18] Hofstee and Kooy, Traditional households and neighborhood group, *op. cit.* See also: K. Ishwaran, *Family Life in the Netherlands, op. cit.*, p. 40: "The extended family is confined to those areas which the Netherlanders themselves describe as 'old', 'primitive', 'outdated', and 'undeveloped'."

[19] Rosenmayr and Köckeis, A method to assess living arrangements and housing problems of the aged,. *op. cit.*, p. 5.

[20] *Ibid.* A similar conclusion is reported by Robins in an American study. Robins found that in Columbia, Missouri, the combined household was formed on an average of ten years after the children's marriage. Arthur J. Robins, Family relations in three-generation households, *Social and Psychological Aspects of Aging*, Clark Tibbitts, and Wilma Donahue (Eds.), New York, Columbia University Press, 1962, p. 470.

most of these in the country and only a few in the Copenhagen metropolitan area and in the provincial towns.

When we look at the population aged 65 and over who have children, we find that 5.1 per cent live in three-generation households. In the United States the proportion is 8.1 per cent and in Great Britain 13.4 per cent.

Why is the number of three-generation households so limited in Denmark? There are two main conditions in Denmark which may have prevented three-generational living and diminished the number of households of this kind. First, for the country as a whole, the long tradition of care and the housing policy for the aged have diminished dependency among generations. This tradition may have contributed to the fact that there has been far less pressure in Denmark, than, for example, in the Netherlands and the United States to make adult children take care of their aged parents.[21] Recent trends in the housing policy for the aged show that everything possible is done to keep old people independent in their own dwellings. Institutionalization is a final solution only in cases where the elderly person is not able to take care of himself. Second, the housing conditions of Denmark serve to prevent three generations from living together. Three-generational living is dependent on large housing units, and this condition exists in Denmark only to a very limited extent, especially in urban areas. In Denmark, as well as in the other Scandinavian countries, the average dwelling has only two or three rooms.

Furthermore, in rural areas, the structure of agriculture and the high degree of mechanization of farm work have limited the need of unpaid family workers (except for the wife of the smallholder). Rural areas with a long tradition of three-generation households, such as can be found in the Netherlands, do not exist in Denmark. Finally, we must take into account that Den-

[21] See, for example, Ethel Shanas, *The Health of Older People: A Social Survey*, Cambridge, Mass., Harvard University Press, 1962, chapter VI, "Older People and Their Families," pp. 107–41; and J. Diederich, *Levensomstandigheden van bejaarden in kleinere en middelgrote gemeenten van Nederland*, Amsterdam, Nationale Raad voor Maatschappelijk Werk 'sGravenhage, Netherlands, 1958.

mark has had no major part in either the First World War or the Second. The country has not had the problem of war-widows, nor the acute housing shortage caused by war destruction which is still apparent in much of Western Europe.

The Composition of Three-generation Households in Denmark

The most common arrangement in three-generation households in Denmark is that of widowed parents living with their married children and grandchildren (Table 6).

In only one of the six cases do three-generation households consist of two married couples of successive generations. Households

TABLE 6. THE COMPOSITION OF THREE-GENERATION HOUSEHOLDS
IN DENMARK

Head of household	Per cent
Total	100.0
1st generation	
Married couple, married child(ren), possibly other child(ren), grandchild(ren) and possibly others	10.5
Married couple, unmarried child(ren), and grandchild(ren) and possibly others	14.8
Unmarried head, married child(ren), and grandchild(ren) and possibly others	8.6
Unmarried head, unmarried child(ren), and grandchild(ren) and possibly others	11.7
2nd generation	
Married parents, married child(ren), and grandchild(ren) and possibly others	6.2
Married parents, unmarried child(ren), and grandchild(ren) and possibly others	1.9
Unmarried parent, married child(ren), and grandchild(ren) and possibly others	44.4
Unmarried parent, unmarried child(ren), and grandchild(ren) and possibly others	1.9
$N =$	162
Total number of households in sample	8634

consisting of a married couple and single children and grand-children also occur in the same proportion.

Nearly 70 per cent of the households in which the parent(s) live in the household of one of their children are found in rural areas of the country. About 50 per cent of the households with a member of the first generation as head are also found in the rural areas of the country. Neither these households, nor the ones where the parents have moved into the household of one of the children, however, represent a typical rural tradition in three-generational living. The very small numbers of different types of three-generation households indicate in themselves that we are unable to speak of tradition in this respect.

The observation that there are households in urban areas in which two younger generations stay in the household of the first generation (Table 7) can be explained by current housing conditions. The proportion of elderly people who occupy large dwellings is larger than the proportion of young families with space for three-generational living.

There is considerable evidence that the three-generation household, as it has survived in Denmark, is a subsidiary system rather than a system kept together by occupational and economic

TABLE 7. DISTRIBUTION OF THREE-GENERATION HOUSEHOLDS, URBAN
AND RURAL DENMARK

Area	All three-generation households (per cent)	Generation of head		Frequency in total sample (per cent)	Distribution of total sample (per cent)
		First (per cent)	Second (per cent)		
Total	100.0	100.0	100.0	1.9	100.0
Copenhagen area	19.1	20.3	18.2	1.2	29.9
Provincial towns and suburbs	21.6	32.4	12.5	1.2	35.1
Rural districts	59.3	47.3	69.3	3.1	35.0
$N =$	162	74	88		8636

dependence. Very few households consist of two married couples. The majority consists of a single parent, usually widowed, living with children. Of these parents, the majority are women. Data about health and physical capacity of all family members of the household (Table 8) show that 55.4 per cent of all three-generation households in Denmark, compared to 15.4 per cent of all households, have at least one member with health troubles or physical handicaps.

Our results correspond very closely to observations made by Rosenmayr and Köckeis. They summarize their findings from a micro-census in Vienna and two federal states in Austria by saying "that intergenerational households are nearly always retained or re-established only if and when one of their members (either of the older or of the younger generation) would otherwise have to live quite alone, or at least not in a family household".[22]

TABLE 8. ILLNESS, HEALTH TROUBLES, AND PHYSICAL HANDICAPS AMONG MEMBERS OF THREE-GENERATION HOUSEHOLDS IN DENMARK[a]

Members with complaints	Number of house-holds (per cent)
Total	100.0
None	44.6
Head of household only	13.6
Spouse of head only	11.7
Both head and spouse	5.6
Other member, related to head	12.3
Head and other related member	6.8
Spouse of head and other related member	1.8
Head and spouse of head and other member	1.8
No information	1.8
$N =$	162

[a] Households with member(s) who are ill, have complaints about health, or have a physical handicap. Refers to long-term, not temporary illness.

[22] Rosenmayr and Köckeis, A method to assess living arrangements and housing problems of the aged, op. cit.

RELATIONS BETWEEN GENERATIONS IN SEPARATE
HOUSEHOLDS

Since we find that Denmark has very few three-generation households, one is inclined to ask: How about relations between generations in Denmark in general? Is the vanishing three-generation household a sign of a weakening of relations between the elderly and their children?

In the beginning of this paper, we have shown that, in spite of certain marked differences in the living arrangements of the elderly in Denmark, compared with Great Britain and the United States, we find remarkable similarities between the elderly population of the three countries as far as the frequency of contact with their children and the proximity of their children is concerned.

Living together in a common household imposes a functional as well as an emotional dependence on all household members apart from the dependence which exists because of family and kinship ties. To what extent is the fact that generations live apart from each other in Denmark a symbol of functional independence between generations, although a pattern of regular contact is maintained? In the last part of this paper we will deal with some aspects of relations between generations which may give some answers to this question.

Patterns of Mutual Help and Assistance in Denmark

Help given to children is one of the indicators of the extent to which the aged parent is involved in the daily life of the adult children. In Denmark as a whole, 27.7 per cent of the people aged 65 and over reported that they are able to help their children with various things, such as repairs, housekeeping, and taking care of the grandchildren. The proportion of elderly people who say that they help their children is largest in the rural areas, nearly as large in Copenhagen, and lowest in the provincial towns (Table 9).

TABLE 9. ARE YOU ABLE TO DO ANYTHING FOR YOUR CHILDREN?

Answers of persons aged 65 and over with living children	Copenhagen area (per cent)	Provincial towns (per cent)	Rural areas (per cent)	Whole country (per cent)
Total	100.0	100.0	100.0	100.0
Yes	28.1	22.6	31.9	27.7
No	70.7	76.7	67.3	71.5
No information	1.2	0.7	0.8	0.8
	$N = 516$	707	789	2012

When people become ill, they become dependent on help. All elderly people in the national sample survey were asked whether they had been in bed because of illness during the last 12 months. Those who had been ill were asked some further questions about who helped them with various things, such as preparing meals, housekeeping, shopping, and care. Those who had not been ill were asked questions about who would help them in case of illness. The answers given by those persons with living children tell us something about the extent to which children in fact do help the elderly and to what extent the elderly expect help from them (Table 10).

About four out of five elderly married people expect their spouses to prepare their meals during illness, and about the same proportion in fact receive help from their spouses in this situation. Less than one of ten married elderly people expect their children to help them with meals, but the proportion of those who actually get help from their children with the preparing of meals is slightly larger.

Three out of five single people who live with a child expect one of their children to take care of meals, and something less than this proportion get this help. Among those who are single and live alone, only two of five expect and get help from children with meals. Unmarried elderly people who live alone are in the worst situation when ill. About 10 per cent of those who had not been ill during the last 12 months answered that there would be

TABLE 10. EXPECTATIONS OF HELP WITH MEAL PREPARATION DURING ILLNESS COMPARED WITH THE HELP GIVEN[a]

Persons aged 65 and over with living children	Ill during last 12 months: who helped with your meals?				Not ill during last 12 months: who would help with your meals, if you became ill?			
	Unmarried		Married		Unmarried		Married	
Priority code	Alone (per cent)	With others (per cent)	Spouse only (per cent)	Spouse and others (per cent)	Alone (per cent)	With others (per cent)	Spouse only (per cent)	Spouse and others (per cent)
Total	100.0	100.0	100.0	100.0	100.0	100.0	100.0	100.0
No one	20.6	3.6	2.5	1.5	9.3	2.0	0.6	1.2
Spouse only	—	—	65.0	61.7	—	—	71.6	63.2
Spouse and others	—	—	12.8	10.3	—	—	9.6	18.7
Child in household	4.8	58.9	0.6	16.2	3.0	51.2	0.6	7.6
Child outside household	35.8	7.1	7.2	—	36.8	9.2	5.3	1.7
Relative in household	—	11.6	—	—	0.9	16.6	—	0.6
Relative ouside household	13.3	5.4	0.9	4.5	15.6	3.4	1.3	0.6
Social services	15.2	4.5	3.8	—	29.0	14.6	8.7	5.8
Others	10.3	8.9	6.9	5.8	3.6	3.0	1.3	0.6
No information	—	—	0.3	—	1.8	—	1.0	—
N =	165	112	320	68	334	205	619	171

[a] Total sample interviewed except 17 persons who are bedfast and 5 who did not respond to the question whether they had been ill during the last 12 months.

no one to help them with meals during illness. Among those who had been ill, we found about 20 per cent who had no help with meal preparation during their illness.

Finally, it is interesting to see that relatively more elderly people expect to receive help from local social agencies, such as community home helpers, than people who actually get help from these authorities. For the elderly population as a whole, we find that about one of eight expect that they will receive help during illness from local social agencies, but about one out of eighteen gets this kind of service. Table 10 shows the difference between the number of people who expect help and those who get help from social services for all categories.

Relations between Generations in Denmark, compared with Great Britain and the United States

As already mentioned, we find that in Denmark about one of four elderly people report that they were able to help their children. In Great Britain as well as the United States we find that the proportion of elderly people who help their children, and thus take an active part in the life of their children and grandchildren, is much higher. In Great Britain nearly half, and in the United States more than half of the elderly population aged 65 or over, reported that they helped their children (Table 11).

The same pattern is observed concerning help to grandchildren. Only 13.3 per cent of the Danish respondents reported that they helped their grandchildren, while the percentages in Britain and the United States are 46.9 per cent and 52.5 per cent respectively.

To stay overnight with children or to have the children staying during holidays and other occasions is relatively uncommon in Denmark, where about one out of five parents has stayed with his child(ren) or has had a child(ren) staying with him in the previous year. In the United States little less than half of all older people with children have stayed with children or have had children

TABLE 11. THE LIVING ARRANGEMENTS, THE PROXIMITY OF THE
NEAREST CHILD, THE CONTACT WITH CHILDREN, AND PATTERNS OF
MUTUAL HELP OF PEOPLE AGED 65 AND OVER WITH LIVING CHILDREN,
IN DENMARK, GREAT BRITAIN, AND THE UNITED STATES

Living arrangements and relationships with children	Denmark (per cent)	Britain (per cent)	United States (per cent)
Proximity of children:			
Children in the same household	20.1	41.9	27.6
Nearest child at more than one hour's transport distance	12.5	11.0	16.4
Contact with children:			
Have seen at least one child today or yesterday	62.3	69.3	65.0
Have stayed overnight with child within last 12 months	20.0	29.5	42.9
Have had children staying overnight within last 12 months	20.1	26.2	46.0
Help to children:			
Those able to do anything for children	27.7	46.9	52.5
Those able to do anything for grandchildren*	13.3	32.8	49.6
Help from children:			
Received a regular money allowance within last 12 months	2.5	4.1	4.2
Received occasional money gifts within last 12 months	6.2	20.3	34.9
N =	2012	1911	2012

* Percentage computed only for those who have grandchildren. Denmark
N = 1845, Britain N = 1719, and United States N = 1873.

staying overnight with them. These differences are even more
striking when we take into account that there are relatively fewer
elderly people in Denmark who live with their children than in the
United States.

We must, however, take into consideration, that there may be several conditions which may make staying overnight more common in the United States than in Denmark. First of all, housing conditions in the United States permit overnight visitors to a larger extent than is true in Denmark. Secondly, we must remember that Denmark is a small country, whereas the geographical conditions in the United States make it probable that at least one of the children lives at a long distance from the parents, which makes overnight stays desirable during visits.

A regular money allowance from children is rather uncommon in all three countries. The proportion of elderly people who have received a regular allowance during the past 12 months is smallest in Denmark and highest in the United States. Receiving occasional money gifts from children is a regular phenomenon in Britain and the United States, but rare in Denmark. In Denmark, one of every seventeen old people reported that they had received money gifts from their children during the last 12 months. In Britain, one of five, and in the United States, one of three had received occasional money gifts.

In comparing economic support given by children to their elderly parents in Denmark, Britain, and the United States we have to take into account that the Danish taxation system, in contrast to that of the other two countries, does not permit the deduction of economic support to relatives in the annual income declaration. We should also mention that as far back as to the first codified rules on help to the poor, the sick, and the aged (1799), the Danish Social Security Acts never have had a rule that public relief of the aged (and other groups) is given on the condition that the children are unable to support their parents.

Summarizing the few comparable observations about relations between generations in the three countries, which are available at this stage of our cross-national research, it seems that elderly people in Denmark are in regular contact with their children and live close to them. Unlike Great Britain and the United States, however, contact seems to be limited to visiting and is not the result of functional dependence. Compared with Britain and the United States, the elderly in Denmark seem to take a less active part in the lives of their children. Neither do they seem to be as dependent on help from their children as are the aged in England and the United States.

In evaluating these preliminary results from our cross-national survey one has to make certain reservations. First of all, we must be aware of the fact that some of the differences in the help patterns among generations in the three countries can be explained by structural differences in the populations concerned. The fact that we find a very large number of people in Britain saying that they are able to help their children can be a function of the extremely large proportion of elderly people in Britain living with their children. In this respect the Danish and American populations are more alike—which makes the differences in help patterns between these two countries more striking. Other structural differences between the three national samples will also have to be taken into account, such as proportions of married and unmarried elderly people, and the average number of children.[23]

We have already mentioned that Denmark has a long tradition of care for the aged—and especially a long-established pension system. Health insurance societies were formed in the middle of the nineteenth century and furnished the basis upon which the present nationwide system in Denmark is established.

The movement towards keeping the aged out of institutions— and if possible, in their own homes or in special apartment houses with a low rent—has been supported by a system of municipal home care. In this respect, the aged in Denmark are able to be more independent of their children, as far as housekeeping, nursing, and other sorts of help are concerned.

Apart from these factors, however, there are other circumstances which should prevent a complete detachment of genera-

[23] We have to take into account that the observations in intergenerational relations in the three countries are based on sample surveys with the aged in private households only. Differences in the degree of institutionalization of the aged in the three countries, however, is not great enough to be the cause of the observed difference.

tions. More than 30 per cent of the married women in Denmark are in the labor force, and in the large towns the proportion is even higher. Nevertheless, it seems that the grandmother in Denmark has taken the place of the mother only to a very limited extent in regard to taking care of children. The environment of the small town and the rural areas which is typical of the country ought to be ideal for the development of intensive relations between generations. This does not seem to be the case in Denmark where we find nearly equal and low proportions of elderly people in Copenhagen and rural areas who say that they help their children. Denmark seems to be an example of a country in which generations live in close contact with each other but with a relatively low degree of functional dependence.

Obviously the differences in mutual help patterns reported here only tell us something about the degree of functional interdependence of aged parents and their children and nothing about the emotional quality of intergenerational relations in these three countries.

But, in spite of these reservations, one cannot help but ask about the causes of such pronounced differences in patterns of mutual help between Denmark on one side, and Britain and the United States on the other.

SUMMARY AND CONCLUSIONS

The lengthening of the average lifetime of man in modern Western societies has increased the possibility of having family members or relatives in two or three generations apart from one's own. In spite of this development the household consisting of members from three successive generations seems to be a disappearing structure in most parts of Western Europe as well as in the United States. The increasing proportion of elderly people in the populations of almost every country with a high degree of industrialization and urbanization makes the study of intergenerational relationships a topic of general interest for theorists as well as social practitioners.

In this paper we have dealt with three aspects of intergenerational relations in Denmark. In the first part we have described living arrangements of elderly people in Denmark, their contact with children, and the proximity of children.

Observations within the country show that:

1. Urbanization has not led to spatial separation of elderly parents and their children. As expected, we find the largest proportion of elderly people who live together with adult children in the rural areas of the country. Nevertheless, relatively more elderly people in the small provincial towns than in the metropolitan area of Copenhagen live apart from their children.

2. Urbanization has not contributed to a reduction of regular visiting between the aged and their children. The largest proportion of elderly people who have not had contact with at least one child within the last month is found in the provincial towns. The lowest proportion is found in the Copenhagen area and not in rural areas as one might expect.

Cross-national observations in this research area reveal that:

3. The proportion of people aged 65 and over with living children who share a household with their children is largest in Britain and lowest in Denmark.

4. Elderly people in all three countries tend to live in the vicinity of their children.

5. Most elderly people in all three countries are in regular contact with at least one of their children.

The second part of this paper has dealt with the household of three generations in Denmark.

In Western Europe as well as the United States the three-generation household still exists, but it is a disappearing structure especially in highly industrialized regions, where we find only very small proportions of the population living together in households of three or more generations. Denmark, in particular, is an example of a country with a very small proportion of three-generation households, in spite of the fact that about 25 per cent of the population lives in rural areas. This situation, which may seem to contradict some beliefs about the association between rural life and three-generation households, has to be evaluated against the background of a long tradition of social policy for the aged and a typical Scandinavian tradition of small housing, factors which limit the need and the possibilities of three-generational living.

Observations based on a national household sample show that:

6. The majority of three-generation households in Denmark are found in the rural areas of the country, whereas the remainder are equally divided between Copenhagen and the provincial towns.

7. There are nearly equal proportions of households in which the first and second generations are reported to be the head of the household.

8. One-third of all three-generation households consist of a married couple in the first generation. Only one of six households consists of two married couples of successive generations. In two out of three households we find a single member, either among the first or the second generation.

9. In more than half of all three-generation households, at least one member has health complaints or a physical incapacity.

10. Married elderly people who share a household more often live with the family of their married son than with the family of a married daughter. These households are found only in rural areas.

11. Widows more often live with married daughters than with married sons.

The traditional extended family system, consisting of three or more generations closely related to each other in an occupational and economic interdependent unit, is a type which is nearly nonexistent in Denmark. Among the disappearing three-generation households in Denmark, that which remains functions as a subsidiary system in which either first- or second-generation members are dependent on care and help from other family members. This is a type of household which has a less traditional reputation but which nevertheless must have existed for centuries, perhaps especially in urban areas.

In the last part of this paper we deal with relations between generations not living together in Denmark, Great Britain, and the United States.

Our main observation is that, in spite of similarities in regard to the proximity of the children and contact with children, there are striking differences between Denmark and the other two countries. In regard to an older parent's staying overnight with children, children's staying overnight with parents, and patterns of mutual help and assistance, we find that:

12. More than twice as great a proportion of elderly people in the United States as in Denmark stay with children overnight or have children staying with them.

13. In Denmark about one of four elderly people reports that he is able to help his children. In Britain and the United States, about one of two was able to help his children.

14. Correspondingly, we find that relatively few Danish grandparents were able to help their grandchildren with various things.

15. Regular financial support from children is a rare phenomenon in all three countries. Occasional money gifts from children occur more frequently than regular financial support. The proportion of elderly people who receive occasional financial support from their children is lowest in Denmark and highest in the United States.

Our cross-national observations show that Denmark is an example of a country in which the generations live in close contact with each other but with a very low degree of mutual functional dependence. In spite of the fact that the same proportion of elderly people in Denmark, Britain, and the United States are in regular contact with their children and live near them, we find in Denmark very low proportions of elderly people who are able to help their children or who are supported by their children.

These observations have to be evaluated against the background of two conditions. First, we must remember that Denmark, being a country with a relatively moderate degree of urbanization, many small towns, and large rural areas, must be in many respects the ideal environment for the development and maintenance of strong intergenerational relations. This is confirmed by the large proportions of elderly people who are in nearly daily contact with children, and who live in the neighbourhood of their children. Second, we must take into account that Denmark has a long tradition for social security and care for the aged. This tradition may have reduced functional dependence among generations, but it does not seem to have influenced the frequency of contact between generations. Compared with the United States and Britain, Denmark seems to be a country where expectations about help between generations are reduced to a minimum, without influencing the degree of voluntary contact.

Family Relations of the Elderly*

L. ROSENMAYR†

SUMMARY—The paper reviews research findings from various European countries (including the author's own studies in Vienna) on
intergenerational relations between parents and their grown-up
children. Numerous data disprove certain important features of the
classical theory of the isolated nuclear family in industrialized and
urbanized society. Although, according to newer data, joint living is
a minority pattern, effective interaction (economic support, help in
both ways and mutual visiting) is frequent and emotionally important
particularly to the elderly. "Intimacy—but at a distance—corresponds to wishes of both generations." A special section of the paper is
dedicated to propositions for theoretical innovation in the problem
area studied including, e.g., a criticism of role theory, a criticism of
statements on family cohesion based on findings of help patterns only.
The paper postulates an amalgamation of major aspects of social
gerontology with a sociology of the family cycle.

THE sociological study of family relations of the elderly has
many practical implications for social work, social and economic
policy, housing and regional planning, and, last but not least,
medicine. Studies have shown that the life expectancy of older
persons diminishes when they are removed to an institution.
This change of environment may sometimes be due to the fact
that adult children were unable or unwilling to provide a sufficient amount of care for their parents at home.[1] Public and private

* Revised version of a paper given at the 7th International Congress of
Gerontology, Vienna, Austria, 26 June–2 July 1966.

† *Leopold Rosenmayr, Dr. Phil., is Director of the Social Science Research Center
and Chairman of the Department of Sociology at the University of Vienna.*

[1] Margaret Blenkner, Social work and family relationships in later life, in
Social Structure and the Family: Generational Relations, edited by Ethel Shanas and
Gordon F. Streib, Englewood Cliffs, New Jersey, Prentice-Hall, Inc., 1965,
p. 53.

agencies are interested in optimizing the supportive capacity of the family vis-à-vis its aged members.

Knowledge of family processes and development furnished the basis for adult and self-education, and such education may have preventive functions. It may help welfare organizations to save effort and money by redirecting their activities. Individual and organized medical treatment (including psychosomatic and sociopsychiatric cases) may, on the basis of a specific knowledge of family ties and interactions, become more effective. Therapeutic measures and organizations require information about the ways in which they may or may not count on family support.

Last but not least, sociological studies may, if they are critical and precise, prevent stereotypes and popular misconceptions of the aged from becoming too influential. Catch phrases like the one about the role-uncertainty of the aged tend to become self-fulfilling prophecies. Misconceived and undue generalizations from the notion of disengagement may develop in the same direction. Sociological research and its theoretical formulation are a means to prevent such effects.

It is the purpose of this paper to review new scientific findings on one special but central problem of the elderly: their relations to their grown-up children. Here, too, it will be necessary to deal with stereotypes, and even such ones which are due to over-simplified generalizations from observations and findings.

Historically, the study of family relations of the elderly had two main roots. One was the prevailing sociological theory of the so-called nuclear or conjugal family. This theory stated that the processes of industrialization and urbanization lead to the dissolution of the extended or multigenerational family. The family as a system, according to this view, contracts itself to the conjugal couple and their young children.[2] The elderly are excluded; this

[2] See, for instance, the papers on "Age and Society" in *Old Age in the Modern World*, Report of the Third Congress of the International Association of Gerontology in London, 1954, Edinburgh and London: E. & S. Livingstone, 1955. For a prominent theoretical statement of this position of the "nuclear" family, see Talcott Parsons and Robert F. Bales, *Family, Socialization and Interaction Process*, Glencoe, Illinois, The Free Press, 1955; and Talcott Parsons, "The

is—according to these earlier theories—one of the main reasons for their alleged role-uncertainty in modern society.

Intergenerational relations within the family were therefore studied by sociologists in connection with this earlier theory of double isolation, leading to the definitions of the self-sufficiency of the nuclear family and the disjointed life of the elderly. This theory originally was developed in the United States in a period in which immigration and horizontal and vertical mobility were extensive. European sociologists were impressed with the theory of the disintegration of the extended family; authors like Helmut Schelsky emphasized nuclearization and the postwar significance of this type of family in defeated countries.[3]

The second root of sociological research on family relations of persons of higher age lay in the perspective of professional social workers. As an eminent theorist of social work, M. Blenkner, put it: they "seem mainly the aged who are without families or who have been alienated from their families".[4]

The theory of the isolated nuclear family and the isolated aged, however, did not hold as a general sociological frame. There was too much even prescientific evidence from Europe suggesting traditional bonds in the extended family and underlining the importance of the grandmother as a pillar of the family system whenever the mother went out to work and the grandmother was fit enough to take over segments of the mother's role.

As immigration and rural-to-urban migration became less important in the United States, there too sociologists started to question the thesis of the all-importance of the nuclear family, and their work during the last decade has lead to what Marvin B. Sussman rightly calls a "plethora of studies".[5]

Aging in American Society," *Law and Contemporary Problems* **27** (1), (1962), 22–35. This position is characterized and criticized by Marvin B. Sussman, Relationships of adult children with their parents, in Shanas and Streib, (Eds.), *op. cit.*, particularly on pp. 63–68.

[3] Helmut Schelsky, *Wandlungen der deutschen Familie in der Gegenwart*, 5. Aufl., Stuttgart: Enke, 1967.

[4] Blenkner, *op. cit.*, p. 49.

[5] Sussman, *op. cit.*, p. 68

Recent research literally overthrew the theory of the nuclear family by furnishing ample empirical evidence for the existence and powerful consequences of intergenerational exchanges within the family. Also, the fact that social scientists have reached a certain new agreement upon the subject does not constitute an end but a beginning for a more detailed analysis of the various types of the patterns of interaction and relations between the elderly and their families. Propositions will be made as to how this analysis should proceed.

In the following paragraphs documentation for this thesis will be given, including data and theoretical explanation from the author's previous work. In many ways such a compilation of more or less rigidly comparable data from various countries characterizes an interim phase of social research. Cross-nationally or cross-culturally designed studies allow, at least in principle, methodologically more satisfactory and thus theoretically more stringent results. Only one study with important data on family relations of the elderly up to now fulfills certain more rigid criteria;[6] as for the rest of this presentation, the author can only furnish "ex post facto" comparisons and deductions from them.

A few introductory remarks are necessary, however, to clarify the general problem of isolation of the aged before discussing the family's role in integrating them. Basic agreement has been reached by recent research that isolation in old age is a serious and complex problem, but only for a minority group.[7] Extreme isolation afflicts about 5 per cent.[8] Although having children is one of the most important general factors in avoiding isolation

[6] Ethel Shanas, Peter Townsend, Dorothy Wedderburn, Henning Friis, Paul Milhoj, and Jan Stehouwer, *Old People in Three Industrial Societies*, New York and London, Routledge (1968). For a first report see Ethel Shanas, Family help patterns and social class in three countries, *Journal of Marriage and the Family* **29** (2), (May 1967), 257–66.

[7] Jeremy Tunstall, *Old and Alone, A sociological study of old people*, London, Routledge & Paul, 1966, p. 3.

[8] Peter Townsend, The changing role of the older person in our society, *Proceedings of the First Canadian Conference on Aging*, Toronto, Canada, The Canadian Welfare Council, 1966, p. 11; Majorie Fiske Lowenthal, Social isolation and mental illness in old age, *Amer. Sociol. Rev.* **29** (1), (February 1964).

TABLE 1. PERCENTAGE OF AGED PERSONS LIVING
IN A JOINT HOUSEHOLD WITH AT LEAST ONE OF
THEIR CHILDREN[a]

	Percent of all aged persons	Percent of aged persons who have living children
Denmark	—	21
Vienna	23	—
Bâle (Switzerland)	24	—
United States	—	28
Budapest	31	54
Western Germany	32	—
Great Britain	—	42
Düsseldorf–Mettmann (a rural region of Western Germany)	40	55

[a] Results taken from the studies cited above.

of the widowed elderly, recent studies have shown that about
one-fifth of the elderly (age 65 and over) in Denmark and in the
United States and nearly a quarter in Britain are single or otherwise childless.[9] This increases their chances of being less integrated
The primary importance of marriage partners in preventing
isolation in old age however is well illustrated by research; the
functions of brothers and sisters (and to a lesser extent longstanding friendships) become important particularly if the elderly
person has not married or lost the marriage partner and if children are not alive or on hand.

JOINT LIVING—
AN IMPORTANT MINORITY PATTERN

Physical and ecological closeness is an important criterion to
measure at least opportunities for interactional frequencies,
patterns of exchange, and mutual help between the aged and

[9] Shanas, Townsend, et al., op. cit.

their grown-up children. In this sense it is important to review research results on the frequencies of the generations living together in one household.

According to the recent cross-cultural study[10] of the aged who have children, a not-unimportant minority live with at least one of them. Approximately one-fifth in Denmark, one-fourth in the United States, and 40 per cent in Britain share households; yet more than half the children who form household units with parents are unmarried, and among the parents who live with the children the proportion of widowed persons is much higher than with the parents who live separately.

In the city of Vienna, one finds that less than one-fourth of the aged parents live in one household with grown-up children.[11] This result falls in line with a stream of data from the United States, Britain, Denmark,[12] Switzerland,[13] Germany,[14] and recently from Hungary.[15]

As to the factors which make joint living more common or add to the desire for it, there are already some results available. According to German data joint living increases[16] and the preference for it rises[17] the smaller the community and the less

[10] Shanas, Townsend *et al.*, *op. cit.*

[11] Leopold Rosenmayr and Eva Köckeis, Propositions for a sociological theory of ageing and the family, *International Social Science Journal* 15 (3), (1963), 413.

[12] Jan Stehouwer, Relations between generations and the three-generation-household in Denmark, in Shanas and Streib (Eds.), *op. cit.*, pp. 142–62.

[13] Hans Guth and A. L. Vischer, *Die alten Leute in Basel-Stadt*, Ergebnisse einer stichprobenweisen Befragung der Betagten, Basel, Schwabe, 1963.

[14] K. Lange, *Forschung und Planung in der Altenhilfe; dargestellt an einer Unterschung im Landkreis Düsseldorf-Mettmann*, Köln and Berlin, 1964.

[15] Laszlo Cseh-Szombathy and Rudolf Andorka, *A Budapesti Nyugdijasok Helyzete és Problémái (Situation and Problems of the Pensioners in Budapest)*, Publication No. 6 of the Research Group for Population Studies of the Central Statistical Office and of the Committee for Demography of the Hungarian Academy of Sciences, Budapest, 1965 (with an English summary).

[16] Rudolf Tartler, *Das Alter in der modernen Gesellschaft*, Stuttgart: Enke, 1961, p. 42.

[17] Ludwig von Friedeburg und Friedrich Weltz, *Altersbild und Altersvorsorge der Arbeiter und Angestellten*, Frankfurt am Main, Europäische Verlagsanstalt, 1958, pp. 36 ff.

industrialized the region. Data from Austria[18] show that common living primarily depends on occupational and economic factors. Twenty-six per cent of the agricultural households in the federal state of Lower Austria are still three-generational. This percentage

TABLE 2. FREQUENCY OF THREE-GENERATION HOUSEHOLDS (THREE-GENERATION HOUSEHOLDS AS A PERCENTAGE OF ALL HOUSEHOLDS)

Denmark	%	Austria	%
Copenhagen area	1.2	Vienna	3.6
Provincial towns and suburbs	1.2	Non-farmers' households of Lower Austria	6.2
Rural districts	3.1	Farmers' households of Lower Austria	25.9

drops to 6 per cent for the non-agricultural population of this federal state and amounts to only 4 per cent for Vienna.

There are also some interesting structural differences within this type of joint living. In Vienna, one sixth of the three-generation households include complete couples in both generations—presently married grandparents and parents—whereas both generations are complete in one-third of the farmers' three-generation households. This supports the assumption that the extended family maintains the three-generation household throughout the family life-cycle for economic reasons and for the sake of a rational division of labor.[19] If such conditions are absent, a joint household usually arises when one family member loses his (or her) spouse.

[18] These findings are based on an analysis of a one per cent sample of the 1961 population census questionnaires carried out by Albert Kaufmann, *Demographische Struktur und Haushalts—und Familien—formen der Wiener Bevöl-kerung,* unpublished Ph.D. dissertation, Vienna University, 1966.

[19] See also Gerhard Baumert, Changes in the family and in the position of older persons in Germany, *International Journal of Comparative Sociology* 1 (1960), 207.

Furthermore, the agricultural households tended to be patri-locally structured (of those consisting of two married generations, 59 per cent contained the husband's parents) while the non-agricultural households struck a balance in favor of matrilo-cality (only 39 per cent patrilocal). As Nimkoff[20] observed, living with the daughter is the more freely chosen pattern for emotional reasons, and, one might add, living with the son is the pattern outlined by juridical norms of heritage and by the traditional division of labor. From the intercultural study one knows that widowed persons with sons are more likely to live alone than widowed persons with daughters.[21]

Additional light is shed on these data if one studies the propor-tion of women aged 65 and over who live quite on their own. In Vienna the rate is 42 per cent, i.e., approximately 77,000 aged women according to the 1961 census; whereas only 7 per cent of the elderly females of the agricultural population of Lower Austria live alone. The peasant family—at least in this area—does provide a home for nearly all its aged members.

In the urban family, old people are far more anxious to live with their children after they have lost their spouses.[22] It would be wrong, however, to conceive of these re-establishments of joint living as replacements of the losses suffered. What the re-estab-lishments show is that household separation does not entail a breach between the generations leading to their mutual isolation. On the contrary, one should speak of a revocable detachment. Thus the theory of disengagement as formulated by E. Cumming and W. E. Henry[23] does not have general application to family relations.

These findings also demonstrate the limitations of a role theory

[20] Meyer F. Nimkoff, Changing family relationships of older people in the United States during the last fifty years, in *Social and Psychological Aspects of Aging*, ed. by Clark Tibbitts and Wilma Donahue, New York and London: Columbia University Press, 1962, p. 405.

[21] Shanas, Townsend, *et al.*, *op. cit.*

[22] Rosenmayr and Köckeis, *op. cit.*, p. 417.

[23] Elaine Cumming and William E. Henry, *Growing Old*, New York, Basic Books, 1961.

TABLE 3. THE STRUCTURE OF THREE-GENERATION HOUSEHOLDS BY
MARITAL STATUS OF ADULT MEMBERS

| Marital status | Vienna (per cent) | Lower Austria | |
		Non-farmers (per cent)	Farmers (per cent)
First and second generation married	16	23	34
First generation widowed or divorced, second generation married	47	52	58
First generation married, second generation widowed or divorced	14	11	5
First and second generation widowed or divorced	23	14	3
	100 (250)	100 (209)	100 (248)

of society. Wherever high interaction frequencies between identical persons reappear after long periods of low frequencies, certain mutual identifications and emotional ties between the personalities have to be presumed and considered as important factors for the renewed role enactments.

Interestingly—but not in contradiction to the data just mentioned—a positive correlation between common living and a mutual positive evaluation of existing intergenerational relationships do not exist. Certain studies show that there are fewer tensions in families with separated households. It is quite plausible that psychological independence of the younger generation can be more easily reached outside the physical omnipresence of parents and parents-in-law. Conflict is likely to be greatest when economic reasons force the old and the young together and when traditions of subordination of the young are loosened.

FAMILY RELATIONS
DESPITE HOUSEHOLD SEPARATION

Logically, it has to be the author's next task to define the frequency, intensity, and, as far as possible, the quality of interaction between the majority of the elderly and their children who do not live in identical households. The author shall have to answer the question how the two findings can be explained simultaneously: that only a minority follows the pattern of joint living, yet the existence of effective family relations between the elderly and their grown-up children is a major social fact for the theoretical and practical consequences of social gerontology. How do the findings of household separation match with the new theoretical emphasis on the extended, the three-generational family?

Part of the explanation lies in the fact that there is a marked tendency for children to settle in the vicinity of their parents' home. The studies further reveal that old people's most frequent visitors are members of the family. The aged are seen much more

TABLE 4. THE BASIS FOR THE FAMILY RELATIONS OF THE AGED: ECOLOGICAL PROPINQUITY AND FREQUENT VISITING[a]

	Percentage of aged parents	
	Living at less than one hour's distance from the nearest child	Seeing one of their children at least every other day
Denmark	88	62
Great Britain	89	69
United States	84	65
Düsseldorf–Mettmann (rural region of Western Germany)	82	67
Budapest	74[b]	75

[a] Results taken from the studies cited in the footnotes 12, 14 and 15.
[b] Percentage living within the same city-district.

often by children and grandchildren (except when they live too far away)[24] than by neighbors and friends.[25] In the case of childless old persons, there are often more frequent contacts with other relatives.

Ample proof of mutual help between adult children and parents provides further evidence of cohesion within the multigenerational family, even when the household has split up. Under normal housing conditions in Vienna, such assistance from children or other relatives was expected by 62 per cent of the cases examined, and assistance from friends and acquaintances by only 9 per cent. A gerontological survey in Cologne revealed that 84 per cent of the old people believed that their children would gladly help them, if asked to do so.[26]

Langford and Shanas also found that old people in distress turned first to their children and relatives for help.[27] There was less question of financial support in the author's Austrian studies than in some other countries, since this was expected rather from government and welfare agencies.

There is some evidence that parent–child relations are not fully reciprocal, inasmuch as aged parents seem more attached to their children than vice versa. Old people, far more frequently than younger ones, consider that they see too little of their families.[28] Yet the children's feeling of moral obligation seems in general sufficiently strong to offset this emotional disparity.

[24] Leopold Rosenmayr and Eva Köckeis, *Umwelt und Familie alter Menschen*, Neuwied & Berlin, Luchterhand, 1965 (with an English summary), pp. 104–7.

[25] Marilyn Langford, *Community Aspects of Housing the Aged*, Ithaca, New York, Cornell University Press, 1962, p. 14; Elisabeth Pfeil, *Die Berufstätigkeit von Müttern*, Tübingen: Mohr (Siebeck), 1961, pp. 328 and 330; and also numerous American investigations, e.g., Marvin B. Sussman and Lee Burchinal, Parental aid to married children: implications for family functioning, *Marriage and Family Living*, **24** 4, (1962), 320 ff.; Marvin B. Sussman, The help pattern in the middle-class family, *Amer. Sociol. Rev.* **18** (1953), 22–28.

[26] Otto Blume, *Alte Menschen in einer Großstadt*, Göttingen: Schwarz, 1962, p. 40.

[27] Langford, *op. cit.*, p. 16; Ethel Shanas, *The Health of Older People*, Cambridge, Massachusetts, Harvard University Press, 1962, pp. 111 ff.

[28] Paul J. Reiss, The extended kinship system: correlations of and attitudes on frequency of interaction, *Marriage and Family Living* **24** (4), (1962), 337

All data which have so far come to light prove beyond any doubt that the family relations of older people can continue to exist and be operative even when they are not living with their kinsfolk. Many surveys, including the author's own in Vienna, also reveal that joint living is only readily accepted in cases where circumstances necessitate it and that, in general, it is by no means regarded as desirable. Before the results of empirical research became available, it was often believed that old people lived separately from their children only when they were obliged to do so, owing either to unwillingness on the part of the younger generation or to the fact that homes were too small. Yet whenever such a question was asked, in the most widely differing countries, only a small proportion of the aged preferred intergenerational joint living.[29]

The great practical and emotional significance of close family relations—but at the same time older people's desire to keep at some distance—came to the fore through research in the mid-fifties in Vienna.[30] This, at first, appeared paradoxical, but it soon became clear that precisely this wish to maintain some distance but not to be isolated was to be regarded as a typical attitude among the aged. The preference for a certain amount of segregation as valid in the area of family relations may also be observed in the attitudes of old people towards their local social environment. Aged persons appreciate arrangements, e.g., of gardens and green spaces, by which they are somewhat protected and withdrawn from their surroundings, but at the same time are able to take part in, or at least watch, what is going on.[31] This

[29] "Our findings reinforce the well-known view that the majority of older people with married children prefer to live independently." I. M. Richardson, *Age and Need, A Study of Older People in North East Scotland*, Edinburgh and London, 1964, p. 60.

[30] *Alte Menschen in der Großstadt*, Social Science Research Center, University of Vienna, 1958, pp. 58 ff. (mimeographed).

[31] Cf., for example, Leopold Rosenmayr and Eva Köckeis, Family relations and social contacts of the aged in Vienna, in *Aging Around the World*, edited by Clarc Tibbitts *et al.*, vol. I, New York, 1962. Similarly: *Housing Requirements of the Aged, A Study of Design Criteria*, New York: Cornell University Housing Research Center, 1960, p. 55.

is a general attitude, which may be characterized by the formula:
"Intimacy—but at a distance."[32]

Recently M. Blenkner has aptly formulated this idea:

> Most older persons under 75 are quite capable of taking care of
> themselves and their affairs. They neither want nor need to be "de-
> pendent", but they do want and need someone to depend on, should
> illness or other crisis arise.[33]

Demographic data[34] show that the post-parental phase of the
married couple in length approximately equals the phase from
the beginning of marriage to the marriage of the last child, after
which the "post-parental phase" starts; both phases tend toward
a span from 25 to 30 years. Consequently, results of sociocultural
change in the realm of the family have a wide field of application.
They affect a long period in the individual life span.

From the point of view of the theoretical position elaborated
in the study "Environment and Family Relations of the Elderly"
(*Umwelt und Familie alter Menschen*)[35] and in "Propositions for a
Sociological Theory of Ageing and the Family"[36] the notion of the

---

[32] Elderly people living with their children have better sanitary and other
equipment but less space for themselves. Leopold Rosenmayr and Eva Köckeis,
Housing conditions and family relations of the elderly; report on an evaluative
study in the city of Vienna, Austria, in *Patterns of Living and Housing of Middle-
Aged and Older People*, Proceedings of Research Conference on Patterns of Living
and Housing of the Middle-Aged and Older People, March 21–23, 1965,
Washington, D.C.: U.S. Department of Health, Education and Welfare,
Public Health Service Publication No. 1496, pp. 33–34. Cf. Eva Köckeis,
review of Rudolf Tartler's book *Das Alter im der modernen Gesellschaft, Kölner Zeit-
schrift für Soziologie und Sozialpsychologie*, **14** (4), (1962), 794.
[33] Blenkner, *op. cit.*, p. 55.
[34] Paul C. Glick, The life cycle of the family, in *Selected Studies in Marriage
and the Family*, edited by Robert F. Winch, R. McGinnis and H. R. Barringer,
New York, 2nd edn., 1962, p. 61. See also Leopold Rosenmayr, Eva Köckeis,
and Albert Kaufmann, Intergenerational Relations and Living Arrangements
in the Course of the Life-Cycle, paper prepared for the Sixth International
Congress of Gerontology, Copenhagen, August, 1963 (mimeographed).
[35] Rosenmayr and Köckeis, *Umwelt und Familie alter Menschen, op. cit.*, see
particularly pp. 89–100 and 116–22.
[36] Rosenmayr and Köckeis, Propositions for a sociological theory of ageing
and the family, *op. cit.*

"modified extended family"[37] seems to be acceptable. Further analysis is needed to state clearly what "modified" means, as different from the "traditional" extended family with its subtypes in primitive culture on the one hand and pre-industrial society on the other.

It remains to be stated clearly where the major modifications of the various types of the traditional extended family lie and how they affect intergenerational relations. The following considerations will not undertake such a definition but are meant to furnish some material to contribute to it.

TOWARD A
REDEFINITION OF FAMILY RELATIONS

Several data have shown that the degree of help desired by the elderly equaled the amount the young generation was willing to give and actually gave. Whereas this result fits into the picture which all the other data on intergenerational relations present, it may very well be that experience with reality has shaped the wish structure of the aged and reduced or limited their expectations. Furthermore, a certain hesitance to put demands on the younger generation, particularly in financial matters—but possibly also in matters of nursing and care—may very well contribute to a picture that looks more harmonious and integrated than it really is. Leonard Caine has observed that the postponement of entry into the labor force for educational reasons, combined with trends towards earlier marriage, provides an open invitation for older parents (at the peak of their earning power) to subsidize their married children. This, of course, may mean psychological dependency and conflict.

[37] Eugene Litwak, Kin relations in an industrial society, in Shanas and Streib (Eds.), *op. cit.*, p. 291. There are some reasons to believe that researchers are still suffering from a retrospective misunderstanding of this pre-industrial family, as they probably overestimate the *emotional* reasons for intergenerational joint living. See Otto Brunner, Das ganze Haus und die alteuropäische Ökonomik, in O. Brunner, *Neue Wege der Sozialgeschichte*, Göttingen: Vandenhoeck and Ruprecht, 1956, p. 40.

This brings the author to the point where, on the basis of these ideas, he would like to suggest a decisive extension of research on family relations. Most studies have taken help patterns as the core of data for the statement of established positive interaction patterns between the generations. Although help certainly is a very important criterion, it may not and cannot generally exclude conflict. Even the attitudes that accompany help may be of a kind to invite conflict, and help may cause conflict.

A recent study of Gordon Streib has made an attempt to go beyond the analysis of help patterns. It is interesting to note that he reports a relatively high self-evaluation of "family cohesion" (74 per cent of the parents and 60 per cent of the adult children say that they form a "close family group"), yet only 40 per cent of the parents and 24 per cent of the children want a good deal more interaction with each other.[38] Both the relationship of those two statements to each other and their independent value seem to be indicative of what the author has just tried to expose: the declaration of family cohesion (in questionnaire replies) seems to correspond to a certain expected standard. It may—particularly on the part of the grown-up children—flow from ethical standards individuals accept for themselves rather than from a self-observed continuity of behavior and powerful sets of attitudes. Future research on family relations should therefore try to study the communicative content of the interaction between the generations—patterns of information, influence, and sentiment. To put it in simple terms: what, e.g., is the degree of interest that adult children have in talking to their parents? What are topics of common interest in various educational and occupational groups? How strong is the influence of overt value positions of the parents on their adult children, and in what areas of decision-making?

[38] Gordon F. Streib, Intergenerational relations: perspectives of the two generations of the older parent, *Journal of Marriage and the Family* **27** (4), (November 1965), 471. Ursula Lehr and Hans Thomae, *Die Stellung des alteren Menschen in der Familie, Beitrage zum Sozialisationsproblem*, contribution to a discussion of the German Sociological Society, Frankfurt, 1 April 1966, p. 24 (mimeographed). Reinhold Bergler, *Psychologie Streotyper Systeme—ein Beitrag zur Sozial- und Entwicklungspsychologie*, Bern and Stuttgart, Huber, 1966.

Family sociology has set the pattern for fruitful studies by falsifying prematurely developed "general theories" like the one of the isolated nuclear family and the isolated elderly. Research into the many dimensions that make up the bundle called "family relations" still lies ahead. It will eventually lead to a definition of the various types and qualities of these relations and possibly to an evaluation of their weight in the wider interaction systems—their consequences for loyalties, orientations, and dependencies of young, middle-aged, and aged personalities. Cohesion and closeness may turn out to be too simple and too crude concepts.

In the future the relationship between the generations in the family will be still more complex through the appearance of a second generation in the age group of the elderly. Not the grandparents but the great-grandparents will be the oldest alive,[39] and both grown-up children and grown-up grandchildren of a similar age status may contribute to support them.

Recent research from Eastern Europe seems to indicate that patterns of interaction and help between the elderly and their adult children in socialist countries are similar to those in Western countries. It is unclear, however, whether this is due to a survival of values and norms internalized by the two generations concerned before the political changes in postwar Eastern Europe, or whether even communist emphasis on loyalties outside the family (from the kindergarten through youth organizations to identifications with the party) now and in the future will not basically affect the dynamics of parent–child relations which up to now guarantees such a significant extent of help for the elderly when they need it.

Further research is also required on the importance of the social class variable in its effect on intergenerational relations in the family. The present emphasis is rather on similarities between classes with the qualification that joint living is more common in the lower classes (even outside agriculture). Reasons for this fact

[39] Peter Townsend, The emergence of the four generation family in industrial society, *New Society* (July, 1966).

lie in the lesser chances of the urban working class obtaining separate apartments or houses for both generations and in the higher degree of female labor which calls for the assistance or even central function of the grandmother in the household. Patterns of exchange and help are not less developed in the middle and upper classes, yet the style includes more ecological[40] and social distance and more freely chosen and granted interaction.

Recent German research has also underlined that important changes take place during the aging process of the elderly. Elisabeth Pfeil[41] has shown that the younger grandmothers are more willing and able to take a lead in the extended family not only because of their better health during the first phase of senescence but also because the grandchildren are more attractive to them and more easily to be handled before their teens.

A not-yet-explored area is the effect on intergenerational relations of the relations between the marriage partners. Equally important seems to be an analysis of family power structure in view of intergenerational relations.[42]

Also, it is difficult to understand that satire and irony through the ages and across nations have exploited the "mother-in-law complex"; yet no data of frictions or tensions with the mother-in-law shed any light on this question, so that one is left with interesting and plausible yet only general hypotheses from the body of Freudian theory.

Although several avenues of refinement are still open, the general picture of intergenerational exchange and interaction within the "modified extended family" seems to be outlined. It is not necessary to discard the idea of intimization of the family[43]

[40] P. A. Braam, The situation of the aged: some sociological aspects, *Sociologia Neerlandica* **3** (2), (Summer, 1966), 69–70; Shanas, Townsend, *et al.*, *op. cit.*

[41] Pfeil, *op. cit.*

[42] Robert O. Blood, Jr., Reuben Hill, Andrée Michel, and Constantina Safilios-Rothschild, Comparative Analysis of Family Power Structure: Problems of Measurement and Interpretation, ISFR/Paper III-1, 9th International Seminar on Family Research, Tokyo, Japan, September 14–20, 1965.

[43] See C. A. Kooy's term of psychic climate: Gerrit A. Kooy, Urbanization and nuclear family individualization; a causal connection? Reprinted above, pp. 297–317.

in industrial and urban environments[44] and under conditions of its reduced functions as a unit of consumption, education, and—to a certain extent—also of leisure activities. This intimization was coupled with processes of dissolution of the traditional extended family with its clearly described internal status structure and socioeconomic functionalism in view of production. Nuclearization was probably never and nowhere as generally and as deeply achieved as some theoreticians supposed, and where it occurred it did not necessarily prevent the reopening of relations to extra-nuclear family members on the basis of the newly established conditions of more equality, less formality of status, and mutual emotional support or even economic exchange, however more on the basis of conscious and rational regulation than according to strictly described or ritualized systems of allocation.

Kooy was undoubtedly right when he said that nuclear family individualization is not identical with nuclear family isolation. His idea of a general need for a closed set of nuclear family relations in order to achieve this individualization is less generally applicable. It may be true for the first phase of the young marriage and perhaps of the family cycle, not for the relations between grown-up children and their parents, however.

Therefore also family exchange and support in the modified extended family have greater chances to be accepted by the elderly without hesitance and the feeling of self-diminution. All public action to give support to the aged classifies them—as Townsend argues[45]—as old. It is the dialectics of generally organized help to a certain group that this group becomes conscious of a certain bereavement; whereas individual and informal help and assistance based on intimacy may avoid this type of conse-

[44] Kooy also reports a levelling of differences between the urban and the rural family in respect to intergenerational relations: Gerrit A. Kooy, Rural Nuclear Family Life in Contemporary Western Society (a policy-oriented cross-national study on social change). ISFR/Paper 11–6, 9th International Seminar of Family Research, Tokyo, Japan, 14–20 September 1965.

[45] Shanas, Townsend, et. al., op. cit.

quence: this is another reason for viewing family support as an important channel of social policy.

FAMILY RELATIONS—
A PRODUCT OF LONG-TERM PROCESSES

Future critical efforts will have to seek refinement also through a new emphasis on the developmental aspects and ought to lead to a sociology of the life cycle and of the family cycle. To study one phase, knowledge about the foregoing phases has to be obtained, as U. Lehr and H. Thomae, R. Bergler,[46] A. I. Goldfarb, and E. Shanas have demonstrated by their own research. Earlier adjustments or conflicts determine later ones. This finding falls in line with A. I. Goldfarb's statement[47] that behavior in old age, to a considerable degree, is related to early education and previous socioeconomic status. E. Shanas is right to refer the various types of alienation from the family back to earlier roots in the life histories of the elderly.[48]

Finally, limitations of the age variable should be emphasized. For some problems and attitudes the age variable is of crucial importance; for others it is less so. Quantities of activities, which are more easily measurable, may vary according to age. Attitudes towards symbols, areas of knowledge, and education and value orientations may be relatively stable over time.

Moreover, as has already been studied in other age groups, namely, adolescents,[49] social conditions of environment—"contextual variables"—direct the process of aging, the "resultant" then being what one may term "maturation". In a sophisticated environment age may lead to more attention to certain symbolic

[46] Lehr and Thomae, *op. cit.*; Bergler, *op. cit.*

[47] Alvin I. Goldfarb, Psychodynamics and the three-generation family, in Shanas and Streib (Eds.), *op. cit.*, p. 35.

[48] Ethel Shanas, The Unmarried Old Person in the United States, paper prepared for the International Social Science Seminar in Gerontology, Markaryd, Sweden, August, 1963.

[49] Leopold Rosenmayr, Eva Köckeis, and Henrik Kreutz, *Kulturelle Interessen von Jugendliche*, München: Juventa/Wien: Hollinek, 1966.

values like music or literature. However, in a culturally impoverished environment, age may lead to a decline in the same area of activities.[50]

Family relations will have to be studied increasingly as one area of symbolic behavior, and they will have to be studied over long periods of the life span of the generations and individuals involved. Sociology will profit—one expects—from a developmental study of interpersonal and intergenerational attitudes and relations. The sociology of the aged (or social gerontology) should be integrated (or may one even say "dissolved"?) into such a wider perspective. Research on the elderly will benefit, one hopes, from such an opening.

[50] Paul F. Lazarsfeld, The general idea of multivariable analysis, interpretation of statistical relations as a research operation, in *The Language of Social Research*, edited by Paul F. Lazarsfeld and Morris Rosenberg, Glencoe, Illinois, The Free Press, 1955, p. 117.

Biographical Notes

BELL, COLIN, Lecturer in Sociology at the University of Essex.
Major publications include: *Middle Class Families* (1968), and various articles on the family and kinship.

CAMPBELL, J. K., Fellow of St. Antony's College, Oxford, and Faculty Lecturer in Modern Balkan History.
Major publications include: *Honour, Family and Patronage* (1964); The Greeks and the West, *The Glass Curtain* (1965); Two case studies of marketing and patronage in Greece, *Acts of the Mediterranean Sociological Conference* (1965); Honour and the Devil, *Honour and Shame* (1966); *Modern Greece* (with Philip Sherrard) (1968); in preparation and *Society and Politics in Greece, 1833–62.*

FRIEDL, ERNESTINE, Professor and Executive Officer of the Ph.D. Progam in Anthropology, Queens College of the City University of New York.
Major publications include: The position of women: appearance and reality (*Anthropological Quarterly*).

HARRIS, C. C., Lecturer in Sociology in the Faculty of Economic and Social Studies, University College of Swansea. Associate Editor, Overseas Section, *Journal of Marriage and the Family*; Area Editor, Great Britain, *International Bibliography of the Family*.
Major publications include: *The Family and Social Change* (with Colin Rosser) Routledge, 1965; Relationships through marriage in a Welsh urban area (with Colin Rosser) *Sociological Review*, 1961; Church, chapels and the Welsh, *New Society*, 1963; The people in between, *New Society*, 1962; *The Family*, Allen & Unwin, 1969; Reform in a normative organisation, *Sociological Review*, 1969.

HOFSTEE, E. W., Professor and Head of the Department of Rural Sociology at the Agricultural University, Wageningen.

KOOY, Gerrit Andries; Professor of Family Sociology at Wageningen (Agricultural University). Sometime International Editor of the *Journal of Marriage and the Family* and a member of the International Sociological Association Committee on Family Research.
Major publications in English include: *The Traditional Household in a Modernized Society; The Changing Countryside, a Sociological Approach;* (with H. Kötter) *Some Problems Encountered in an Investigation Concerning the European Rural Family; Social System and Problem of Aging; Rural Nuclear Family Life in Contemporary Western Society.*

LEYTON, E. H., Acting Director of Sociological Research, Memorial University of Newfoundland, where he was previously Professor of Anthropology.

Major publications include: Conscious models and dispute regulation in an Ulster village, *Man*, 1966; The typical lecturer, *New Society*, 1966. Has published papers on such subjects as fatality rates in the trawler industry, the notion of community, spheres of inheritance and the methodological problems of working with fishermen.

LISON, TOLOSANA, C., Lecturer in Social Anthropology at the University of Madrid.

Major publications include: Una gran encuesta de 1901–1902: Notas para la Historia de la Anthropologia Social en España; Limites simbólicos: Apuntes sobre la parroquia rural en Galicia (both in *Revista Española de la Opinión Pública*).

LOUDON, J. B., Senior Lecturer in Social Anthropology, University College of Swansea; Co-Director, Ministry of Health Research Programme; Member of S.S.R.C. Social Anthropology Committee.

Major publications include: *Psychogenic Disorder and Social Conflict among the Zulu*, 1958; *Attitude of General Practitioners to Psychiatry* (with K. Rawnsley), 1962; *Religious Order and Mental Disorder: a study in a South Wales rural community*, 1965; *Social Aspects of Ideas about Treatment*, 1965; *Social Structure and Health Concepts among the Zulu*, 1957; *Attitudes and Practice of Mental Health Welfare Officers* (with K. Rawnsley), 1961; *Attitudes of Relatives to Patients in Mental Hospitals* (with K. Rawnsley), 1962; *Factors Affecting the Referral of Patients to Psychiatrists by General Practitioners* 1962; *Epidemiology of Mental Disorder in a Closed Community*, 1964; *Private Stress and Public Ritual*, 1966; *Teasing and Socialization in Tristan da Cunha*, due for publication 1970); *Kinship and Marriage on Tristan da Cunha; Tristan in Exile.*

MICHEL, ANDRÉE (née VIELLE), Professor of Sociology at the Faculty of Social Science of the University of Ottawa (Canada) and a staff member of the *Centre National de la Recherche Scientifique* (France). She is a member of the Steering Committee of Family Research of the International Sociological Association.

Major publications include: Les travailleurs algériens en France (Paris, Centre National de la Recherche Scientifique, 1957, Collection: Centre d'Etudes Sociologiques); *Famille, Industrialisation, Logement* (Paris, Centre National de la Recherche Scientifique, 1959, Collection: Centre d'Etudes Sociologique); *La Condition de la Française d'aujourd'hui* (2 volumes in collaboration with Geneviève Texier, Paris, Gonthier, 1964); (in preparation) *La Sociologie de la Famille* and *New Findings and Perspectives in Family Life.*

PIDDINGTON, RALPH, Professor of Anthropology in the University of Auckland, Previously Reader in Social Anthropology at the University of Edinburgh.

Major publications include: *The Psychology of Laughter; Religion and Social Organization in Central Polynesia* and *Essays on Polynesian Ethnology* (both in co-operation with Williamson); *The Kinship Network among French Canadians* (a study of kinship in St. Boniface, Manitoba).

PONSIOEN, JAN, Professor of Sociology at the Institute of Social Studies at the Hague and former President of the Dutch Sociological Association.

Major publications in English include: *The Analysis of Social Change Reconsidered; National Development, a Sociological Contribution*; editor of *Social Welfare Policy*: I—*Contributions to Theory* and II—*Contributions to Methodology*.

ROSENMAYR, LEOPOLD, Director of the Social Science Research Centre and Chairman of the Department of Sociology at the University of Vienna.
Major publications include: *Intergenerational Relations and Living Arrangements in the Course of the Life Cycle* (Sixth International Congress of Gerontology).

STEHOUWER, JAN, Head of Department of Sociology at the Institute of Political Science, University of Aarhus, Denmark.
Major publications include: *Old People in Three Industrial Societies* (co-autho with Shanas *et al.*), Atherton Press and Routledge and Kegan Paul, 1968; *Party Strength and Social Structure* (Aarhus 1968, Sociologi, Copenhagen); author of several national reports from a national study on the aged in Denmark, carried out by the Danish National Institute of Social Research (Household and Housing, Mobility and Capacity for Self-Care, Family Relationships).
†We learned with regret that Dr. Jan Stehouwer died during the publication of this volume.

TAIETZ, PHILIP, Professor of Rural Sociology at Cornell University, with special research interests in social gerontology and community structure. A previous managing editor of *Rural Sociology*. Fellow of the American Sociological Association and the Gerentological Society, member of the Rural Sociological Society.
Major publications include: *Social Participation and Old Age* (with Olaf Larson); *The Rural Aged* (with Jerome Kaplan); *Conflicting Group Norms and the "Third" Person in the Interview*; *Academic Integrity and Social Structure, A Study of Cheating Among College Students* (with John Harp); *Organizational Structure and Disengagement, the Emeritus Professor* (with Paul Roman).

TURNER, CHRISTOPHER, Lecturer in Sociology at the University of East Anglia currently spending an academic year at Boston University on a Fellowship awarded by the American Council of Learned Societies.
Major publications include: *A Conceptual Scheme for Organization Analysis* (with D. S. Pugh, *et al.*), 1963; *An Approach to the Study of Bureaucracy* (with C. R. Hinings, *et al.*), 1967; *Dimensions of Organisation Structure* (with D. S. Pugh, *et al.*), 1968; *Family and Kinship in Modern Britain* (Routledge) 1969; *The Context of Organization Structures* (with D. S. Pugh, *et al.*), 1969.
It is regretted that it has not been possible to obtain biographical notes for E. Lupri and the late G. Baumert.

Author Index

(Figures in italics denote pages where author's name appears in References)

391

Subject Index